Interactive Information Seeking, Behaviour and Retrieval

Interactive Information Seeking, Behaviour and Retrieval

Editor

Fernand Qunicy

scitus academics

Interactive Information Seeking, Behaviour and Retrieval
Edited by **Fernand Qunicy**

ISBN: 978-1-68117-559-1
Library of Congress Control Number: 2016942973

SCITUS Academics LLC,
www.scitusacademics.com
Box No. 4766, 616 Corporate Way,
Suite 2, Valley Cottage,
NY 10989

Notice

Printed in United States of America on Acid Free Paper

Preface

The concepts of information searching, information retrieval (IR) and information behavior are the objects of information science research. The behavior seeking information refers to the way in which people search and use information. Information seeking is connected to, but totally different from, retrieval of information. Recovery of information is a complex human activity supported by advanced systems. Info science has made a significant contribution to the design and analysis of earlier generations of IR system development as well as to our general understanding of how such systems should be created, but due to the growing diversity and success of IR systems, many recent textbooks focus on information retrieval systems themselves and ignore the human side of information research. Information Seeking, Behaviour and Retrieval is intended for students attending all information and library courses and practicing LIS professionals who need to better understand how IR systems are designed, implemented and evaluated. The behavior seeking information is the micro level of behavior used by the search engine to interact with information systems of all kinds, whether between the system and the search engine or perhaps the pure approach to creating and monitoring a search. The digital world is changing the process and the behavior of human information. This book is focused almost exclusively on the use and search for information, the receipt of information, a central method of the procedure is often overlooked. As the search for information continues to migrate to the Internet and artificial intelligence continues to advance the analysis of user behavior through a variety of user interactions, information receiving moves to the center of the process as systems "learn" what users like, want and need in addition to their search habits.

Table of Contents

1

CHAPTER

Balancing Exploration and Exploitation in Listwise and Pairwise Online Learning to Rank for Information Retrieval

Katja Hofmann, Shimon Whiteson, Maarten de Rijke

ISLA, University of Amsterdam, Amsterdam, The Netherlands

ABSTRACT

As retrieval systems become more complex, *learning to rank* approaches are being developed to automatically tune their parameters. Using *online* learning to rank, retrieval systems can learn directly from implicit feedback inferred from user interactions. In such an online setting, algorithms must obtain feedback for effective learning while simultaneously utilizing what has already been learned to produce high quality results. We formulate this challenge as an *exploration–exploitation dilemma* and propose two methods for addressing it. By adding mechanisms for balancing exploration and exploitation during learning, each method extends a state-of-the-art learning to rank method, one based on *listwise* learning and the other on *pairwise* learning. Using a recently developed simulation framework that allows assessment of online performance, we empirically evaluate both methods. Our results show that balancing exploration and exploitation can substantially and significantly improve the online retrieval performance of both listwise and pairwise approaches. In addition, the results demonstrate that such a balance affects the two approaches in different ways, especially when user feedback is noisy, yielding new insights relevant to making online learning to rank effective in practice.

Keywords: Information retrieval; Learning to rank; Implicit feedback

1 INTRODUCTION

Information retrieval (IR) systems are becoming increasingly complex. For example, web search engines may combine hundreds of ranking features that each capture a particular aspect of a query, candidate documents, and the match between the two. 1 In heavily used search engines, these combinations are carefully tuned to fit users' needs. However, on smaller-scale systems, such careful manual tuning is often infeasible.

For automatically tuning the parameters of such a system, machine learning algorithms are invaluable (Liu 2009). Most methods employ supervised learning, i.e., algorithms are trained on examples of relevant and non-relevant documents for particular queries. While large amounts of data are available for training in some applications, such as web search, there are also many situations in which such data cannot be obtained. For example, when deploying a search engine for a company's intranet (enterprise search) or a personal computer (desktop search, personalization), collecting the large amounts of training data required for supervised learning is usually not feasible (Sanderson 2010). Even in environments where training data is available, it may not capture typical information needs and user preferences perfectly (Radlinski and Craswell 2010) and cannot anticipate future changes in user needs.

A promising direction for addressing a lack of resources for manual or supervised training are online approaches for learning to rank (Joachims 2002; Yue and Joachims 2009; Yue et al. 2009). These methods work in settings where no training data is available before deployment. They learn directly from implicit feedback inferred from user interactions, such as clicks, making it possible to adapt to users throughout the lifetime of the system. 2

In an online setting, it is crucial to consider the impact of such learning on the users. In contrast to offline approaches, where the goal is to learn as effectively as possible from the available training data, online learning affects, and is affected by, how user feedback is collected. Ideally, the learning algorithm should not interfere with the user experience, observing user behavior and learning in the background, so as to present search results that meet the user's information needs as well as possible at all times. This would imply passively observing, e.g., clicks on result documents. However, passively observed feedback can be biased towards the top results displayed to the user (Silverstein et al. 1999). Learning from this biased feedback may be suboptimal, thereby reducing the system's performance later on. Consequently, an online learning to rank approach should take into account both the quality of current search results, and the potential to improve that quality in the future, if feedback suitable for learning can be observed.

In this article, we frame this fundamental trade-off as an *exploration–exploitation dilemma*. If the system presents only document lists that it expects will satisfy the user, it cannot obtain feedback on other, potentially better, solutions. However, if it presents document lists from which it can gain a lot of new information, it risks presenting bad results to the user during learning. Therefore, to perform optimally, the system must *explore* new solutions, while also maintaining satisfactory performance by *exploiting* existing solutions. Making online learning to rank for IR work in realistic settings requires effective ways to balance exploration and exploitation.

We investigate mechanisms for achieving a balance between exploration and exploitation when using listwise and pairwise methods, the two most successful approaches for learning to rank in IR (Liu 2009). The pairwise approach takes as input pairs of documents with labels identifying which is preferred and learns a classifier that predicts these labels. In principle, pairwise approaches can be directly applied online, as preference relations can be inferred from clicks (Joachims 2002). However, as we demonstrate in this article, balancing exploration and exploitation is crucial to achieving good performance. In contrast, listwise approaches aim to directly optimize an evaluation measure, such as NDCG, that concerns the entire document list. Since such evaluation measures cannot be computed online, new approaches that work with implicit feedback have been developed (Yue and Joachims 2009). These online approaches rely on interleaving techniques, where preference relations between two ranking functions can be inferred from aggregated clicks (Joachims et al. 2007).

In this article, we present the first two algorithms that can balance exploration and exploitation in settings where only implicit feedback is available. First, we start from a recently developed listwise algorithm that is initially purely exploratory (Yue and Joachims 2009). Second, we develop a similar mechanism for a pairwise approach that is initially purely exploitative.

We assess the resulting algorithms using an evaluation framework that leverages standard learning to rank datasets and models of users' click behavior. Our main result is that finding a proper balance between exploration and exploitation can substantially and significantly improve the online retrieval performance of both listwise and pairwise approaches.

In addition, our results are the first to shed light on the strengths and weaknesses of using pairwise and listwise approaches online, as they have previously only been compared offline. We find that the pairwise approach can learn effectively when feedback is reliable. However, when feedback is noisy, a high amount of exploration is required to obtain reasonable performance. The listwise approach learns more slowly when provided with perfect feedback, but is much more robust to noise than the pairwise approach. We discuss in detail the effects on each approach of balancing exploration and exploitation, the amount of noise in user feedback, and characteristics of the datasets. Finally, we describe the implications of our results for making these approaches work effectively in practice.

The remainder of this paper is organized as follows. We present related work in Sect. 2 and our methods for balancing exploration and exploitation in Sect. 3. Experiments are described in Sect. 4, followed by results and analysis in Sect. 5. We conclude in Sect. 6.

2 RELATED WORK

While our methods are the first to balance exploration and exploitation in a setting where only implicit relative feedback is available, a large body of research addresses related problems. The question of how to explore is addressed by active learning approaches for supervised learning to rank, and in online learning to rank for IR approaches. A large body of work in reinforcement learning (RL), a branch of machine learning where an algorithm learns from interactions with an environment (Sutton and Barto 1998), addresses the problem of balancing exploration and exploitation when explicit feedback can be observed. Below, we first summarize related work in learning to rank for IR and then turn to relevant results from RL.

As an alternative to manual tuning of IR systems, supervised learning to rank has become very popular in recent years (Liu 2009). Various approaches have been developed, the most successful of which are pairwise [e.g., RankSVM (Herbrich et al. 1999; Joachims 2002)] and listwise [e.g., SoftRank (Taylor et al. 2008)] learning to rank. As in other supervised learning settings, supervised learning to rank methods typically assume that a representative set of training data (including judgments) is available at training time, so that characteristics of the data can be estimated from this set.

In contrast to offline supervised learning, we address learning to rank in an online setting, where a system learns directly from interactions with the user. In this setting, labeled training data is not provided but needs to be collected through interaction with the user. A first evaluation of RankSVM in an online setting demonstrated that learning from implicit feedback is possible in principle (Joachims2002). How to best collect feedback for effective learning from implicit feedback has so far not been examined further, but we hypothesize that online approaches need to explore to learn effectively.

Many researchers have considered how best to explore efficiently in information retrieval, without addressing the question of how to balance that exploratory behavior with exploitation. The most common approach is based on active learning, where the focus is on reducing manual labeling. Xu et al. (2007) present an algorithm that learns a linear combination of features based on relevance, document density, and diversity, which is then used to select documents for which to obtain relevance feedback. Similarly, Xu and Akella (2008) follow a probabilistic approach that selects documents expected to minimize model variance. Donmez and Carbonell (2009) apply active learning to two state-of-the-art learning to rank algorithms, RankSVM and RankBoost. Their approach selects the training instances expected to have the largest effect on the current model.

Two recently developed approaches have addressed the problem of exploration in online learning to rank. These stochastic methods infer feedback using interleaved comparison methods (Hofmann et al. 2011b; Radlinski and Craswell 2010). Using such techniques, the algorithms infer relative preferences between an exploratory and an exploitative ranking function (Yue and Joachims 2009; Yue et al. 2009). One algorithm compares a fixed set of ranking functions and selects the best one (Yue et al. 2009). The other algorithm, on which our approach is based, uses relative feedback about two ranking functions for stochastic gradient descent (Yue and Joachims 2009).

In RL, balancing exploration and exploitation is considered important for optimizing performance while learning, and we hypothesize that similar benefits can be achieved in information retrieval. The distinguishing characteristic of RL problems is that an agent interacts with an environment by trying out actions and receiving rewards (Kaelbling et al. 1996). In this setting, the agent can only observe the rewards for the actions it selected, meaning that it is never shown any examples of the optimal action for any situation, as is the case in e.g., supervised learning. For this reason, balancing exploration and exploration is crucial. The agent needs to try out new solutions to be able to learn from the observed feedback, and it needs to exploit what it has already learned to ensure high reward. 3

Particularly relevant to this article are methods for tackling contextual bandit problems, 4 a well-studied type of RL problem (Auer 2003; Barto et al. 1981; Langford and Zhang 2008; Strehl et al. 2006), as they have been successfully applied to problems similar to learning to rank for IR. For example, Langford et al. (2008) consider the ad placement application. Given a website, their algorithm learns the value of placing each of a set of candidate ads on the website. Similarly, Radlinski et al. (2008a) consider how to learn diverse document lists such that different information needs are satisfied; they present an algorithm for doing so that balances exploration and exploitation. Another widely-studied application area of related approaches is news recommendation, where news stories are selected for a user population or for individual users. Work in this area has focused on learning approaches (Agarwal et al. 2008; Li et al. 2010), and methods for offline evaluation (Li et al. 2011). Finally, an application to adaptive filtering is presented in (Zhang et al. 2003). However, like other RL algorithms, these methods all assume access to explicit feedback. For example, in ad placement, clicks provide explicit feedback because they are directly correlated with the value of the ad-website pair (assuming a pay-per-click model). Since explicit feedback is not typically available in online IR settings, these methods are not directly applicable. Note that, while in related areas implicit feedback can often be interpreted as absolute (possibly noisy) reward, this is not possible in our setting.

Within IR, using implicit feedback to improve search results has long been the goal of relevance feedback approaches. Exploration in the relevance feedback setting has, e.g., been formulated in terms of diversifying the list of initial documents that is shown to the user to elicit relevance feedback (Karimzadehgan and Zhai 2010). These methods typically assume explicit feedback (which can be noisy) and do not generalize over queries.

3 APPROACH

In this section, we first formalize the problem of online learning to rank for IR. Then we describe our approaches, starting with the baseline learning algorithms, and extend them to balance exploration and exploitation.

3.1 Problem formulation

Our formulation of learning to rank for IR differs from most other work in learning to rank in that we consider the interactions between users and the search engine as a continuous cycle. A natural fit for this problem are formalizations from RL, in which an algorithm learns by trying out actions (e.g., document lists) that generate rewards (e.g., an evaluation measure such as AP or NDCG) from its environment (e.g., users) (Sutton and Barto 1998). Using this formalization allows us to describe this problem in a principled way and to apply concepts and solutions from this well-studied area.

Figure 1 shows the interaction cycle. A user submits a query to a retrieval system, which generates a document list and presents it to the user. The user interacts with the list, e.g., by clicking on links, from which the retrieval system infers feedback about the quality of the presented document list. This problem formulation directly translates to an RL problem (cf., Figure 1, terminology in italics) in which the retrieval system tries, based only on implicit feedback, to maximize a hidden reward signal that corresponds to some evaluation measure. We make the simplifying assumption that queries are independent, i.e., queries are submitted by different users and there are no sessions. This renders the problem a *contextual bandit problem* (Barto et al. 1981; Langford and Zhang 2008).

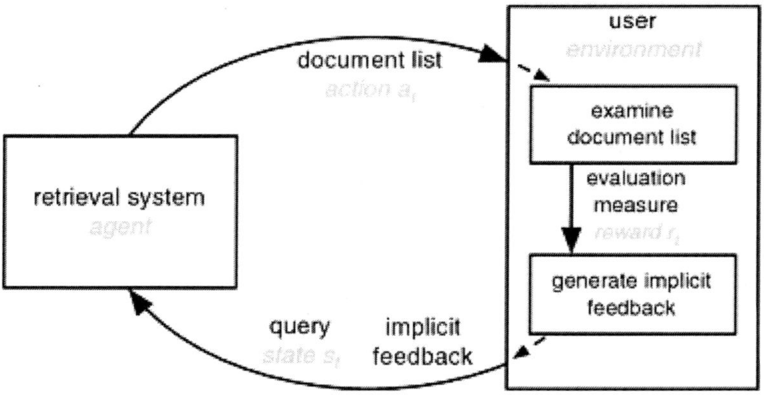

Figure 1. The IR problem modeled as a contextual bandit problem, with IR terminology in *black* and corresponding RL terminology in *green* and *italics*

Since our hypothesis is that balancing exploration and exploitation improves retrieval performance *while learning*, we need to measure this aspect of performance. Previous work in learning to rank for IR has considered only final performance, i.e., performance on unseen data after training is completed (Liu 2009), and, in the case of active learning, learning speed in terms of the number of required training samples (Xu et al. 2010).

As is common in RL, we measure *cumulative reward*, i.e., the sum of rewards over all queries addressed during learning (Sutton and Barto 1998). Many definitions of cumulative reward are possible, depending on the modeling assumptions. We assume an *infinite horizon problem*, a model that is appropriate for IR learning to rank problems that run indefinitely. Such problems include a *discount factor* $\gamma \in [0,1)$ that weights immediate rewards higher than future rewards. One way to interpret the discount factor is to suppose that there is a $1-\gamma$ probability that the task will terminate at each timestep (e.g., users may abandon the retrieval system). Rewards are thus weighted according to the probability that the task will last long enough for them to occur. Then, cumulative reward is defined as the discounted infinite sum of rewards $r_i : C = \sum_{i=1}^{\infty} \gamma^{i-1} r_i$.

To summarize, we model online learning to rank for IR as an interaction cycle between the user and the retrieval system. We assume an infinite horizon setting and use discounting to emphasize immediate reward. The resulting problem formulation differs from those traditionally used in IR because performance depends on cumulative reward during the entire learning process, rather than just the quality of the final retrieval system produced by learning. It also differs from typical contextual bandit problems, which assume that the agent has access to the true immediate reward resulting from its actions. Typical IR evaluation measures require explicit feedback, which is not available in most realistic use cases for online learning to rank. Thus, this contextual bandit problem is distinct in that it requires the learner to cope with implicit feedback such as click behavior.

3.2 Balancing exploration and exploitation in pairwise learning to rank

Our first approach builds off a pairwise formulation of learning to rank, and a stochastic gradient descent learner. Pairwise approaches model the pairwise relations between documents for a given query. Our formulation of the learning to rank problem from implicit feedback follows (Joachims 2002). The learning algorithm is a stochastic gradient descent algorithm, following (Sculley 2009; Zhang 2004).

3.2.1 Baseline learning approach

Pairwise learning to rank approaches for IR construct training data from observed queries and preference relations between pairs of documents. Given an appropriate method of obtaining such pairwise labeled training data, learning in this setting can be reduced to binary classification (Sculley 2009). Our baseline algorithm obtains pairwise labels by observing clicks on an exploitative result list and learns a weight vector w for ranking documents using the learning algorithm from (Sculley 2009; Zhang 2004).

Our pairwise approach infers labels from clicks, following the method developed by (Joachims 2002). This method is based on the observation that clicks on results are too unreliable to allow conclusions about absolute relevance of clicked documents, but that clicked documents that were displayed at lower ranks than a non-clicked document can be assumed to be preferred over the non-clicked document. For example, assume a query q, in response to which the system returns documents (d_1, d_2, d_3), in this order. If the user clicks on documents d_2 and d_3, but not on d_1, we can infer that $d2 \succ d1$ and $d3 \succ d1$. From these observations, labeled data could be extracted as $(d_1, d_2, -1)$ and $(d_1, d_3, -1)$.

Given a set of labeled document pairs, we apply the stochastic gradient descent (SGD) algorithm defined by Zhang (2004, Algorithm 2.1). This algorithm finds a weight vector w^ that minimizes the empirical loss $L(\mathbf{w}, \mathbf{x}, y)$ given a set P of labeled training samples each consisting of a feature vector $\mathbf{x}$ and a label y:

$$\hat{\mathbf{w}} = \arg\min_{\mathbf{w}} \left[\frac{1}{P} \sum_{i=0}^{P} L(\mathbf{w}, \mathbf{x}_i, y_i) + \frac{\lambda}{2} ||\mathbf{w}||_2^2 \right], \quad (1)$$

where the last term is a regularization term. Using the hinge loss, i.e.,$L(\mathbf{w}, \mathbf{x}, y) = \max(0, 1 - y\,\mathbf{w}^T\mathbf{x})$, the algorithm optimizes the same quantity as RankSVM (Joachims 2002). It was shown to perform competitively on standard learning to rank datasets in terms of ranking performance with only a fraction of the training time (Sculley 2009). Here, we follow the implementation provided in sofia-ml,5 and apply it to pairwise learning by setting $x = (x_a - x_b)$, where x_a and x_b are the feature vectors of a document pair.

Combining the above method of inferring pairwise feedback and the pairwise learning method, we obtain our pairwise baseline algorithm (Algorithm 1). It receives as input a document set D, learning rate η, regularizer weight λ, and an initial weight vector $\mathbf{w}_0$. For each observed query q_t, a set of feature vectors $\phi(d_i|q)$ is extracted that characterize the relationship between the query and each candidate document $di \in D$. The document feature vectors are then scored using the weight vector learned so far ($\mathbf{w}_{t\text{-}1}$), and sorted by this score to obtain an exploitative result list (the best ranking given what has been learned so far).

Algorithm 1 Baseline algorithm for the pairwise setting, based on (Joachims 2002; Sculley 2009; Zhang 2004).

Input: $D, \eta, \lambda, \mathbf{w}_0$
for query q_t $(t = 1..T)$ **do**
  $\mathbf{X} = \phi(D|q_t)$ *// extract features*
  // construct exploitative result list
  $S = \mathbf{w}_{t\text{-}1}^T \mathbf{X}$
  $L = \text{sortDescendingByScore}(D, S)$
  $I = L\,[1{:}10]$
  Display I and observe clicked elements C.
  Construct all labeled pairs $P = (\mathbf{x}_a, \mathbf{x}_b, y)$ from I and C.
  for i in $(1\,..\,P)$ **do**
    if $y_i\, \mathbf{w}_{t\text{-}1}^T (\mathbf{x}_{a\_i} - \mathbf{x}_{b\_i}) < 1.0$ and $y_i \neq 0.0$ **then**
      Update w_t as: $\mathbf{w}_t = \mathbf{w}_{t\text{-}1} + \eta y_i (\mathbf{x}_{a\_i} - \mathbf{x}_{b\_i}) - \eta\lambda\, \mathbf{w}_{t\text{-}1}$
return $\mathbf{w}_t$

The constructed exploitative result list is shown to the user, and clicks on any of the result documents are observed. From the observed clicks C, all possible labeled document pairs P are inferred using the pairwise labeling method described above (Joachims 2002).

The labeled samples in P are then used to update the weight vector $\mathbf{w}$. For each pair, the loss is obtained by comparing the current solution to the observed label (line 10, cf. the definition of the hinge loss above). If the labels do not match, or the prediction margin is too small, the weight vector is updated using the update rule $\mathbf{w}_t = \mathbf{w}_{t-1} + \eta y_i (\mathbf{x}_{a\_i} - \mathbf{x}_{b\_i}) - \eta\lambda \mathbf{w}_{t-1}$. Here, we use the unregularized version of this update rule (by setting $\lambda = 0$) and use a small constant η. This formulation was found to show good convergence properties (Zhang 2004) and resulted in good performance in preliminary experiments.

3.2.2 Balancing exploration and exploitation

In previous applications of pairwise learning to implicit feedback scenarios, learning was performed in a batch setting. First, implicit feedback was collected given an initial ranking function. Then, the algorithm was trained on all collected implicit feedback. Finally, this trained system was deployed and evaluated (Joachims2002). In this setting, data collection is naturally exploitative. Users are shown results that are most likely to be relevant according to a current best ranking function. In the online setting, such an exploitative strategy is expected to result in the highest possible short-term performance. However, it is also expected to introduce bias, as some documents may never be shown to the user, which may result in sub-optimal learning and lower long-term performance. This is confirmed in our experiments, as we will see below.

In supervised applications of pairwise learning to rank methods, the learning algorithm is typically trained on the complete dataset. Sculley (2009) developed a sampling scheme that allows training of a stochastic gradient descent learner on a random subset of the data without noticeable loss in performance of the trained algorithm. In this setting, document pairs were sampled randomly such that at each learning step one relevant and one non-relevant document were selected to form a training pair. We expect this strategy, which is fully exploratory, to result in minimal training bias.

In the online setting where we learn from implicit feedback, we cannot directly determine for which document pairs we obtain feedback from the user. Any document list that is presented in response to a query may result in zero or more clicks on documents, such that zero or more pairwise constraints can be extracted. Due to position bias (Silverstein et al. 1999), the higher a document is ranked in the result list presented to the user, the more likely it is to be inspected and clicked.

Here, we ignore explicit dependencies between displayed documents, and define two document lists, one exploratory and one exploitative, that are then combined to balance exploration and exploitation. The exploitative list is generated by applying the learned weights to compute document scores and then sorting by score, as in the baseline algorithm. The exploratory list is generated by uniform random sampling of the documents associated with a query.6

We employ a method for balancing exploration and exploitation that is inspired by ε-*greedy*, a commonly used exploration strategy in RL (Watkins 1989). In ε-greedy exploration, the agent selects an exploratory action with probability ε at each timestep. With probability 1 – ε, it selects the greedy action, i.e., the action with the highest currently estimated value.7

The difference between our approach and ε-greedy is that we do not pick a single action at each timestep, but that we can select a number of actions that are presented simultaneously. This results in Algorithm 2 that differs from our baseline algorithm in how the result list is constructed (line 6).

Algorithm 2 Balancing exploration and exploitation in the pairwise setting.

1: **Input**: $D, \eta, \lambda, \mathbf{w}_0, \epsilon$
2: **for** query q_t $(t = 1..T)$ **do**
3: $\mathbf{X} = \phi(D|q_t)$ *// extract features*
// construct exploitative result list
4: $S = \mathbf{w}_{t-1}^T \mathbf{X}$
5: L = sortDescendingByScore(D, S)
6: $I[r] \leftarrow$ first element of $L \notin I$ with probability ε; element randomly sampled without replacement from $L \setminus I$ with probability $1 - \varepsilon$
7: Display I and observe clicked elements C.
8: Construct all labeled pairs $P = (\mathbf{x}_a, \mathbf{x}_b, y)$ from I and C.
9: **for** i in $(1 .. P)$ **do**
10: **if** $y_i\,(\mathbf{x}_{a\_i} - \mathbf{x}_{b\_i})\,\mathbf{w}_{t-1}^T < 1.0$ and $y_i \neq 0.0$ **then**
11: Update w_t as: $\mathbf{w}_t = \mathbf{w}_{t-1} + \eta y_i\,(\mathbf{x}_{a\_i} - \mathbf{x}_{b\_i}) - \eta\lambda\,\mathbf{w}_{t-1}$
12: **return** $\mathbf{w}_t$

Therefore, we vary the relative number of documents from the exploratory and exploitative lists as determined by $\varepsilon \in [0, 1]$. For each rank, an exploitative action (a document from the exploitative list) is selected with probability $1 - \varepsilon$. A document from the exploratory list is selected with probability ε. Thus, values of ε close to 0 mean that little exploration is taking place, making the algorithm collect feedback in an exploitative way ($\varepsilon = 0$ corresponds to the purely exploitative baseline setting). Values close to 1 mean more exploration.

3.3 Balancing exploration and exploitation in listwise learning to rank

Our second online learning to rank approach builds off a gradient-based policy search algorithm called Dueling Bandit Gradient Descent (DBGD) (Yue and Joachims 2009). This algorithm has been specifically developed for learning to rank in an online setting, and it requires only relative evaluations of the quality of two document lists, and infers such comparisons from implicit feedback (Radlinski et al.2008b).

3.3.1 Baseline learning approach

Similar to the pairwise learning to rank approach discussed in the previous section, DBGD learns a ranking function consisting of a weight vector **w** for a linear weighted combination of feature vectors. Thus, to rank a set of documents D given a query q, feature vectors X={x1,x2,...,xD} that describe the relation between D and q are produced. Next, scores S for each document are produced using $\mathbf{S} = \mathbf{w}\,\mathbf{X}$. Finally, documents are ranked by their scores to generate a ranked document list l.

Algorithm 3 summarizes this approach. It takes as input a comparison method $f(l_1, l_2)$, that compares two document lists, and three parameters, the step sizes α8and δ, and an initial weight vector $\mathbf{w}_0$. At each timestep t, the algorithm observes a query q_t from which two document lists are produced: one exploitative, one exploratory. The exploitative list is produced from the current exploitative weight vector $\mathbf{w}_t$, found to perform best up to the current timestep t. The exploratory list is produced from an exploratory weight vector w′t,wt′, which is generated by moving $\mathbf{w}_t$ in a random direction $\mathbf{u}_t$ by a step of size δ. The exploitative and exploratory lists are then compared using a function $f(l_1, l_2)$. If the exploratory weight vector w'_t is judged to have produced the better document ranking, the current exploitative weight vector $\mathbf{w}_t$ is updated by moving it towards w'_t by a step size α.

Algorithm 3 Baseline Algorithm for the listwise setting.

```
Input: f(l1, l2), α, δ, w0
for query q_t (t = 1..T) do
    Sample unit vector u_t uniformly.
    w'_t ← w_t + δu_t        // generate exploratory w
    if f(l(w_t), l(w'_t)) then
        w_{t+1} ← w_t + αu_t      // update exploitative w
    else
        w_{t+1} ← w_t
return w_{t+1}
```

For the comparison method $f(l_1, l_2)$, several implementations have been suggested (He et al. 2009; Radlinski et al. 2008b). We chose a variant of the*balanced interleave method* as it is efficient, easy to implement, and was found to be more reliable than the similar *team-draft method* both in (He et al. 2009) and in our own preliminary experiments. This method takes as input two document lists and constructs an interleaved result list by randomly selecting a starting list and then interleaving the two lists so that presentation bias between the two lists is minimized. After observing user clicks on the result list, a preference between the lists is inferred as follows. The rank of the lowest clicked document *N* is identified. Then, for each list the number of clicked documents within the top *N* is counted. The list that received more clicks in its top *N* is preferred. Ties are ignored.

3.3.2 Balancing exploration and exploitation

Given an appropriate function for comparing document lists, the baseline algorithm described above learns effectively from implicit feedback. However, the algorithm always explores, i.e., it constructs the result list in a way that minimizes bias between the exploratory and exploitative document lists, which is assumed to produce the best feedback for learning. We now present a comparison function $f(l_1, l_2)$ that does allow balancing exploration and exploitation.

In contrast to previous work, we alter the balanced interleave function to interleave documents probabilistically. Instead of randomizing only the starting position and then interleaving documents deterministically, we randomly select the list to contribute the document at each rank of the result list. In expectation, each list contributes documents to each rank equally often.

Constructing result lists by probabilistic interleaving, allows us to apply a method similar to ε-greedy. Our probabilistic interleave algorithm, which supplies the comparison method that is required by DBGD, is shown in Algorithm 4. The algorithm takes as input two document lists l_1 and l_2, and an exploration rate k. For each rank of the result list to be filled, the algorithm randomly picks one of the two result lists (biased by the exploration rate k). From the selected list, the highest-ranked document that is not yet in the combined result list, is added at this rank. The result list is displayed to the user and clicks C are observed. Then, for each clicked document, a click is attributed to list l_i $(i = 1,\ 2)$ if the document is in the top N of l_i, where N is the lowest-ranked click.

Algorithm 4 $f(l_1, l_2)$ – k-greedy comparison of document lists.

```
Input: l1, l2, k
initialize empty result list I
  // construct result list
for rank r in (1 .. 10) do
    L ← l1 with probability k, l2 with probability 1 − k
    I[r] ← first element of L ∉ I
display I and observe clicked elements C
N = length(C); c1 = c2 = 0
for i in (1 .. N) do
    if C[i] ∈ l1[1:N] then
        c1 = c1 + 1      // count clicks on l1
    if C[i] ∈ l2[1:N] then
        c2 = c2 + 1      // count clicks on l2
  // compensate for bias (Eq. 2)
n1 = | l1[1:N] ∩ I[1:N] |
n2 = | l2[1:N] ∩ I[1:N] |
c2 = n1/n2 * c2
return c1 < c2
```

The exploration rate $k \in [0.0, 0.5]$ controls the relative amount of exploration and exploitation, similar to ε. It determines the probability with which a list is selected to contribute a document to the interleaved result list at each rank. When $k = 0.5$, an equal number of documents are presented to the user in expectation.[9] As $k$decreases, more documents are contributed by the exploitative list, which is expected to improve the quality of the result list but produce noisier feedback.

As k decreases, more documents from the exploitative list are presented, which introduces bias for inferring feedback. The bias linearly increases the expected number of clicks on the exploitative list and reduces the expected number of clicks on the exploratory list. We can partially compensate for this bias since

$$E[c_2] = \frac{n_1}{n_2} * E[c_1], \tag{2}$$

where $E[c_i]$ is the expected number of clicks within the top N of list l_i, and n_i is the number of documents from l_i that were displayed in the top N of the interleaved result list. This compensates for the expected number of clicks, but some bias remains because the observed clicks are converted to binary preference decisions before they are aggregated over queries. While perfectly compensating for bias is possible, it would require making probabilistic updates based on the observed result. This would introduce additional noise, creating a bias/variance trade-off. Preliminary experiments show that the learning algorithm is less susceptible to increased bias than to increased noise. Therefore we use this relatively simple, robust bias correction.

4 EXPERIMENTS

In this section, we describe the experiments that evaluate the algorithms presented in Sect. 3. We first give an overview of the general evaluation setup, before giving further details on specific aspects such as the datasets and runs.

4.1 Evaluation setup

Evaluating the ability of an algorithm to maximize cumulative performance in an online IR setting poses unique experimental challenges. The most realistic experimental setup—in a live setting with actual users—is risky because users may get frustrated with bad search results. The typical TREC-like setup used in supervised learning to rank for IR is not sufficient because information on user behavior is missing. Also, live experiments cannot evaluate and compare many different settings like simulated experiments can.

To address these challenges, we propose an evaluation setup that simulates user interactions. This setup combines datasets with explicit relevance judgments that are typically used for supervised learning to rank with recently developed click models. Given a dataset with queries and explicit relevance judgments, interactions between the retrieval system and the user are simulated (c.f., the box labeled "user/environment" in Figure 1). Submitting a query is simulated by random sampling from the set of queries. After the system has generated a result list for the query, feedback is generated using a click model and the relevance judgments provided with the dataset. Note that the explicit judgments from the dataset are not directly shown to the retrieval system but used to simulate the user feedback and measure cumulative performance.

Using simulated evaluations naturally has limitations. Here, we can show how learning methods behave under different assumptions about user behavior, but to what degree these assumptions apply in specific practical settings needs to be studied in more detail.

4.2 Click model

Our click model is based on the Dependent Click Model (DCM) (Guo et al. 2009a,b), a generalization of the cascade model (Craswell et al. 2008). The model posits that users traverse result lists from top to bottom, examining each document as it is encountered. Based on this examination, the user decides whether to click on the document or skip it. After each clicked document, the user decides whether or not to continue examining the document list. Since the DCM has been shown to effectively predict users' click behavior (Guo et al. 2009b), we believe it is a good model for generating implicit feedback.

When a user examines a document in the result list, he or she does not know the true relevance label of the document. However, aspects of the document's representation in the result list (e.g., its title) make it more likely that a document is clicked if it is relevant. Using this assumption, the ground truth relevance judgments provided in explicitly annotated learning to rank datasets, and the process put forward by the DCM, we define the following model parameters. Relevant documents are clicked with a probability $p(c|R)$, the probability of a click given that a document is relevant. Non-relevant documents can attract (noisy) clicks, with probability $p(c|N\,R)$. After clicking a document, the user may be satisfied with the results and stop examination with probability $p(s|R)$, the probability of stopping examination after clicking on a relevant document. The probability of stopping after visiting a non-relevant document is denoted by $p(s|NR)$.

To instantiate this click model we need to define click and stop probabilities. When the DCM is trained on large click logs, probabilities are estimated for individual query-document pairs, while marginalizing over the position at which documents were presented in the training data. In our setting, learning these probabilities directly is not possible, because no click log data is available. Therefore we instantiate the model heuristically, making choices that allow us to study the behavior of our approach in various settings. Setting these probabilities heuristically is reasonable because learning outcomes for the gradient algorithms used in this paper are influenced mainly by how much more likely users are to click on relevant and non-relevant documents. Thus, this ratio is more important than the actual numbers used to instantiate the model.

Table 1 gives an overview of the click models used in our experiments. First, to obtain an upper bound on the performance that could be obtained if feedback was deterministic, we define a *perfect* model, where all relevant documents are clicked and no non-relevant documents are clicked. We further implement two realistic models, the *navigational* and *informational* models. These two models are based on typical user behavior in web search (Broder 2002; Guo et al. 2009a), because 8 of the 9 datasets we use implement web search tasks (see below). In a navigational task, users look for a specific document they know to exist in a collection, e.g., a company's homepage. Typically, it is easy to distinguish relevant and non-relevant documents and the probability of stopping examination after a relevant hit is high. Therefore, our navigational model is relatively reliable, with a big difference between $p(c|R)$ and $p(c|N R)$. In an informational task, users look for information about a topic, which can be distributed over several pages. Here, users generally know less about what page(s) they are looking for and clicks tend to be noisier.

Table 1. Overview of the click models used

Model	$p(c\|R)$	$p(c\|NR)$	$p(s\|R)$	$p(s\|NR)$
Perfect	1.0	0.0	0.0	0.0
Navigational	0.95	0.05	0.9	0.2
Informational	0.9	0.4	0.5	0.1

4.3 Data

We conducted our experiments using two standard collections for learning to rank: LETOR 3.0 and LETOR 4.0 (Liu et al. 2007). In total, these two collections comprise 9 datasets. Each consists of queries for which features were extracted from a document collection, together with relevance judgements for the considered query-document pairs.

The datasets were compiled from different sources: the 106 queries in OHSUMED are based on a log of a search engine for scientific abstracts drawn from the MedLine database. The remaining datasets are based on Web Track collections run between 2003 and 2008 at TREC. HP2003, HP2004, NP2003, NP2004, TD2003 and TD2004 implement homepage finding, named-page finding, and topic distillation tasks, using a crawl of web pages within the .gov domain. These datasets contain between 50 and 150 queries each, with about 1,000 judged documents per query. MQ2007 and MQ2008 are based on the 2007 and 2008 Million Query track at TREC and use the .GOV2 collection. These two datasets contain substantially more queries, 1,700 and 800 respectively, but far fewer judged documents per query.

The datasets based on the TREC Web track use binary relevance judgments, while OHSUMED, MQ2007 and MQ2008 are judged on a 3-point scale from 0 (non-relevant) to 2 (highly relevant). In all experiments we use binary relevance judgments. For the three datasets that originally contain graded judgments, we treat all judgments greater than zero as relevant. In preliminary experiments with graded relevance, we obtained results nearly identical to those with the simpler binary judgments.10

Each dataset comes split up for machine learning experiments using fivefold cross-validation. We use the training sets for training during the learning cycle and for calculating cumulative performance, and the test sets for measuring final performance.

4.4 Runs

4.4.1 Pairwise approach

In all pairwise experiments, we initialize the starting weight vector $\mathbf{w}_0$ to zero. In preliminary experiments we evaluated offline performance for $\eta \in \{0.0001, 0.001, 0.01, 0.1\}$, and selected the setting that performed best overall data sets ($\eta = 0.001$). Our *baseline* is the pairwise formulation of learning to rank with stochastic gradient descent as described in Sect. 3.2, in the fully exploitative setting ($r = 0$). Against this baseline we compare increasingly exploratory versions of the algorithm ($r \in \{0.2, 0.4, 0.6, 0.8, 1.0\}$). All experiments are run for 1000 iterations.

4.4.2 Listwise approach

In all listwise experiments, we initialize the starting weight vector $\mathbf{w}_0$ to a random point on a unit sphere around the origin, and use the best performing parameter settings from (Yue and Joachims 2009): $\delta = 1$ and $\alpha = 0.01$ (these settings resulted in good performance over all datasets in our preliminary experiments). Our*baseline* is Algorithm 3, based on (Yue and Joachims 2009), which corresponds to a purely exploratory setting of $k = 0.5$ in our extended method.11 Against this baseline we compare *exploit* runs that balance exploration and exploration by varying the exploration rate k between 0.4 and 0.1 as shown in Algorithm 4. Again, we run all experiments for 1000 iterations.

4.5 Discounting

Because our problem formulation assumes an infinite horizon, cumulative performance is defined as an infinite sum of discounted rewards (cf. Sect. 3). Since experiments are necessarily finite, we cannot compute this infinite sum exactly. However, because the sum is discounted, rewards in the far future have little impact and cumulative performance can be approximated with a sufficiently long finite experiment.

In our experiments, we set the discount factor $\gamma = 0.995$. This choice can be justified in two ways. First, it is typical of discount factors used when evaluating RL methods (Sutton and Barto 1998). Choosing a value close to 1 ensures that future rewards have significant weight and thus the system must explore in order to perform well. Second, at this value of γ, cumulative performance can be accurately estimated with the number of queries in our datasets. Since rewards after 1000 iterations have a weight of 1 % or less, our finite runs are good approximations of true cumulative performance.

4.6 Evaluation measures

We use cumulative NDCG on the result list presented to the user to measure cumulative performance of the system. We define cumulative reward as the discounted sum of NDCG that the retrieval system accrues throughout the length of the experiment. Final performance is reported in terms of NDCG on the test set.

For each dataset we repeat all runs 25 times and report results averaged over folds and repetitions. We test for significant differences with the baseline runs (purely exploitative for the pairwise approach ($k = 0.0$), purely exploratory for the listwise approach ($k = 0.5$)) using a two-sided student's *t* test. Runs that significantly outperform the exploratory baseline are marked with △ ($p < 0.05$) or ▲ ($p < 0.01$).

5 RESULTS AND DISCUSSION

The primary goal of this paper is to show that balancing exploration and exploitation in online learning to rank for IR can improve cumulative performance. As there is currently little known about the performance of pairwise and listwise learning to rank approaches in an online setting, we first report on the performance of each baseline algorithm, before turning to our main results. Finally, we compare the performance of the two approaches under the novel perspective of balancing exploration and exploitation.

5.1 Pairwise learning

As a first sanity check, we calculate standard evaluation measures that are typically used to evaluate supervised learning to rank methods for the baseline approach (purely exploitative, i.e., $r = 0.0$). Results in terms of NDCG at 10 (*NDCG@10*), Precision at 10 (*P@10*), and Mean Average Precision (MAP) (Liu 2009) for the*perfect* click model are shown in Table 2. These are computed after 1000 iterations (consisting of 1 query, result list, and learning step each), which means that learning may not have converged and higher results are possible. These results should therefore be interpreted as a rough indication of what performance can typically be achieved by this approach in an implicit feedback setting.

Table 2. NDCG@10, P@10, and MAP for the pairwise baseline algorithm (*perfect* click model)

	NDCG@10	P@10	MAP
HP2003	0.820	0.106	0.753
HP2004	0.803	0.099	0.705
NP2003	0.794	0.093	0.676
NP2004	0.796	0.095	0.672
TD2003	0.271	0.153	0.208
TD2004	0.279	0.217	0.183
OHSUMED	0.321	0.392	0.371
MQ2007	0.377	0.343	0.412
MQ2008	0.490	0.239	0.452

Based on the performance of the pairwise approach relative to state-of-the-art supervised approaches (Liu 2009), we can divide the datasets used in our experiments in two groups. For the first group, which includes the datasets *HP2003, HP2004, NP2003*, and *NP2004*, performance is quite high. In particular, for the datasets *HP2003* (*NDCG@10*=0.820) and *HP2004* (*NDCG @10*=0.803), the pairwise exploitative learner is among the top 3 approaches and even beats the supervised version of Rank SVM (with an *NDCG@10* of 0.807 and 0.768, respectively). For the second group, which includes the remaining datasets, performance is lower both in absolute terms and relative to state-of-the-art supervised learning approaches. Here, performance is comparable to the mid-range of the approaches compared in (Liu 2009).

To analyze the performance differences between datasets, we study the learning curves of two representative datasets, *MQ2007* and *NP2003*, at different levels of exploration. Figure 2 shows the final performance in terms of NDCG (on the whole result list) plotted over time (up to 1,000 iterations). For the dataset *MQ2007* we see that best learning is achieved at high exploration rates (the dark, dashed lines; the difference between settings $r = 0.8$ and $r = 1.0$ is negligible). As expected, when implicit feedback is collected on fully exploratory result lists, it is unbiased and thus results in the best learning. However, we see the opposite for the dataset*NP2003*, where performance further improves when implicit feedback is collected on exploitative result lists ($r = 0$, light and solid lines). Most likely, this increase in performance results from an effect similar to that observed in active learning. Because the current top results are shown, feedback is focused on the part of the document space that is most informative for learning. All datasets for which this effect is observed have few relevant documents, so that focusing feedback on a promising region can have a substantial benefit. For the remaining datasets, there are more relevant documents per query. Thus, feedback that is focused on one part of the solution space (in the exploitative setting) does not improve performance.

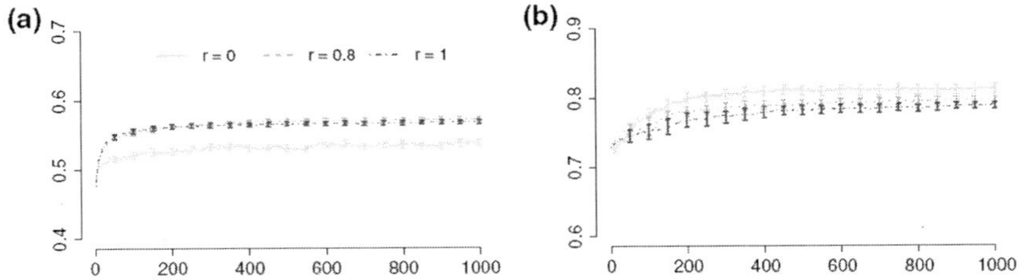

Figure 2. Final performance for the pairwise approach (with 5 % confidence intervals) over time for the datasets (**a**) *MQ2007* and (**b**) *NP2003*, under the *perfect* click model and $r \in \{0.0, 0.8, 1.0\}$.

For all datasets, the absolute difference in final performance at varying exploration rates is relatively small (similar to the two datasets analyzed above) under the *perfect* click model. Much higher variance is observed when we simulate noisy feedback. Figure 3 shows learning curves for the dataset *NP2003* at different settings of *r* for the *navigational* and *informational* click models. For the *navigational* click model (a) final performance improves over time for all *r*, although differences in performance for different *r* are higher than with perfect click feedback. Final performance is lowest for $r = 1.0$ (0.714), and increases for $r = 0.0$ (0.720) and $r = 0.8$ (0.778). For the *informational* click model, final performance degrades dramatically in the purely exploitative baseline settings ($r = 0$, 0.102). In this setting, performance decreases over time. The purely exploratory setting ($r = 1.0$) leads to reasonable final performance, while the best performance is achieved with high exploration but some exploitation ($r = 0.8$, 0.724).

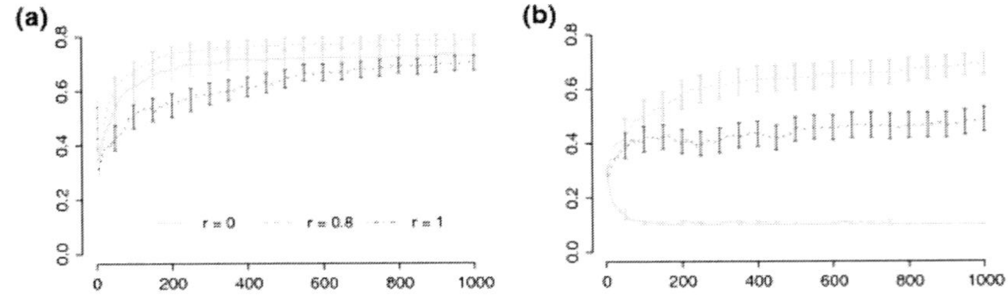

Figure 3. Final performance for the pairwise approach (with 5 % confidence intervals) over time for the dataset *NP2003* for **a** *navigational*, and **b** *informational* click models and $r \in \{0.0, 0.8, 1.0\}$

Our analysis of final performance results in a number of observations. We hypothesized that the best learning would occur with perfect feedback and pure exploration because this setting minimizes variance and bias in user feedback. As expected, learning outcomes were best for perfect feedback and degraded with noisier feedback. However, the effect of the exploration rate changed with the amount of noise in user feedback and characteristics of the dataset. For perfect feedback, little to no exploration sometimes produced the best learning outcomes because exploitative result lists focused feedback on more informative parts of the solution space. Under noisy feedback, higher exploration rates generally improved learning, though the best performance occurred with moderate amounts of exploitation.

5.1.1 Balancing exploration and exploitation

We now turn to our main results for the pairwise approach: the influence of balancing exploration and exploitation on online performance. Above, we saw that the effect of this balance on offline performance is complex and that more exploration does not necessarily imply better learning. When optimizing online performance, a system should generally try to exploit as much as possible. However, if increasing exploration results in sufficiently high learning gains, the short-term cost of this exploration may be outweighed by long-term benefits, as it would increase the quality of exploitative result lists later on.

Table 3 shows our results for comparing runs with varying amounts of exploration ($r \in [0.2, 1.0]$) to the purely exploitative baseline ($r = 0.0$). The best runs per row are highlighted in bold and significant differences are marked as described above. For the *perfect* click model, the best performance is achieved in the baseline settings for 7 out of 9 datasets, ranging from 103.05 (*TD2003*) to 124.75 (*HP2003*). For these datasets, the best learning is achieved at low exploration rates, so that increasing exploration cannot lead to long-term benefits. The modest improvement in offline performance at slightly higher exploration rates (e.g., as for datasets*TD2003* and *TD2004* at $r = 0.2$) is not large enough to outweigh the cost of the increased exploration.

Table 3. Results for the pairwise approach. Online performance (in terms of cumulative NDCG) over 1000 iterations

r	0.0	0.2	0.4	0.6	0.8	1.0
click model: perfect						
HP2003	**124.75**	122.32	109.82 ▼	89.50 ▼	61.12 ▼	1.35 ▼
HP2004	**115.08**	102.15 ▼	87.14 ▼	72.64 ▼	48.79 ▼	1.14 ▼
NP2003	**115.75**	110.72	96.21 ▼	87.43 ▼	54.94 ▼	1.84 ▼
NP2004	**111.26**	104.43	94.37 ▼	76.60 ▼	52.44 ▼	1.17 ▼
TD2003	**103.05**	98.88	85.37 ▼	69.65 ▼	43.63 ▼	8.23 ▼
TD2004	**106.77**	103.93	83.06 ▼	65.56 ▼	44.50 ▼	14.62 ▼
OHSUMED	119.13	**134.53** ▲	127.31 ▲	119.68	111.42 ▼	100.44 ▼
MQ2007	104.12	**107.06** ▲	105.50 ▲	101.53 ▼	95.96 ▼	90.13 ▼
MQ2008	**104.01**	103.38	98.96 ▼	93.70 ▼	87.58 ▼	80.60 ▼
click model: navigational						
HP2003	104.99	**111.01**	108.15	102.48	69.91 ▼	1.39 ▼
HP2004	91.69	**110.26** △	107.83 △	82.70	57.20 ▼	1.27 ▼
NP2003	**115.85**	110.40	106.50	91.94 ▼	61.19 ▼	1.88 ▼
NP2004	93.79	**116.11** ▲	106.39	89.67	64.20 ▼	1.07 ▼
TD2003	64.43	**85.20** ▲	77.85 ▲	66.59	42.80 ▼	8.08 ▼
TD2004	87.59	**97.90** ▲	82.91	66.31 ▼	45.46 ▼	14.30 ▼
OHSUMED	127.05	**129.73**	123.39 ▼	117.64 ▼	110.04 ▼	100.81 ▼
MQ2007	101.68	**102.88** △	101.99	99.13 ▼	95.08 ▼	90.05 ▼
MQ2008	100.16	**100.41**	97.18 ▼	93.06 ▼	87.31 ▼	81.23 ▼
click model: informational						
HP2003	7.21	40.39 ▲	**72.60** ▲	66.52 ▲	55.31 ▲	1.37 ▼
HP2004	6.39	29.81 ▲	51.81 ▲	**67.20** ▲	46.30 ▲	1.11 ▼
NP2003	5.75	24.39 ▲	55.16 ▲	**60.57** ▲	45.04 ▲	1.90 ▼
NP2004	5.64	23.95 ▲	**69.22** ▲	65.58 ▲	52.01 ▲	1.21 ▼
TD2003	7.47	23.64 ▲	43.92 ▲	**43.96** ▲	36.25 ▲	7.85
TD2004	17.31	50.10 ▲	**60.12** ▲	54.58 ▲	38.44 ▲	14.48 ▽
OHSUMED	102.60	121.48 ▲	**122.06** ▲	116.55 ▲	109.53 ▲	101.12
MQ2007	92.76	96.58 ▲	**98.19** ▲	96.66 ▲	95.43 ▲	90.00 ▼
MQ2008	90.00	91.14	**92.45** ▲	91.12	86.88 ▼	81.69 ▼

Best runs per row are highlighted in bold

Exceptions are the datasets *OHSUMED* and *MQ2007*. For both datasets, online performance improves significantly when the exploration rate is increased to $r = 0.2$, with a relative increase of 12.9 % for *OHSUMED* and 2.8 % for *MQ2007*. As discussed above, these datasets have more relevant documents per query. Consequently, the expected utility is high, even when result lists are randomized (this can also be observed when comparing online performance at the purely exploratory setting $r = 1.0$). As a result, the cost of exploration is relatively low and easily outweighed by the long-term learning gains.

In the relatively reliable *navigational* click model, optimal online performance is achieved at the slightly higher exploration rate of $r = 0.2$ for all but one dataset. For 5 of these datasets, this improvement is significant when compared to the baseline setting. Compared to the *perfect* click model, online performance with the noisier *navigational* model is typically lower, as expected. The performance loss due to noise is between 3.5 % (*MQ2008*) and 11.0 % (*HP2003*). One exception is the dataset *NP2003*, for which learning is not strongly affected by the small increase in noise and where performance is close to identical to the *perfect* click model. The second exception is the dataset *NP2004*, for which online performance for the *navigational* click model at the best settings ($r = 0.2$) is 4.4 % higher than for the best setting and the *perfect* click model. Interestingly, this result demonstrates that a small amount of noise and mild exploration can lead to a better exploration of the solution space and an improvement in online performance.

As in earlier results, we see a difference between datasets with high and low ratios of relevant documents. For datasets with a relatively low ratio of relevant documents (*HP**, *NP**, and *TD**) the relative improvement in online performance at this higher exploration rate is typically big (up to 32.2 % for the dataset *TD2003*). Although the short-term cost of exploration for these datasets is high, this high cost is outweighed by even higher long-term benefits (being able to rank the few relevant documents well). For datasets with a high ratio of relevant documents, both the cost of exploration, and its long-term benefits are small. This leads to relative improvements of between 0.3 % (*MQ2008*) and 2.1 % (*OHSUMED*). For dataset *NP2003*, increased exploration does not lead to better online performance.

In the noisier *informational* click model, the trends observed for the *navigational* click model continue. Performance in the purely exploitative setting is substantially lower than for the other click models, as the increase in noise results in lower learning gains and therefore lower online performance. In this setting, the cost of exploration decreases relative to its benefit, so optimal performance is seen at higher exploration rates. For 6 datasets, the best online performance is achieved at $r = 0.4$; for the remaining 3 datasets the best setting is $r = 0.6$. All improvements are statistically significant when compared to the purely exploitative baseline. For the datasets with a low ratio of relevant documents, online performance improves by as much as an order of magnitude. For datasets with a high ratio of relevant documents, improvements range from 2.7 % (*MQ2008*) to 19.0 % (*OHSUMED*). Compared to the *navigational* click model, online performance drops for all datasets, as expected. The increase in noise leads to a drop in online performance of between 4.6 % (*MQ2007*) and 48.4 % (*TD2003*).

Overall, for the pairwise approach the effect of balancing exploration and exploitation depends both on noise in user feedback and characteristics of the datasets. When feedback is reliable, online performance is best in the purely exploitative (baseline) setting. However, the pairwise baseline approach does not learn well when feedback is noisy. Increasing the exploration rate can partially compensate for this. As a result, the best online performance under noisy feedback is achieved at $r = 0.4$ and $r = 0.6$, for which result lists contain about one half exploratory and one half exploitative documents. These findings confirm our hypothesis that balancing exploration and exploitation in the pairwise approach improves online performance.

5.2 Listwise learning

As with the pairwise approach, we start by evaluating the final performance of the listwise baseline approach ($k = 0.5$) in terms of standard evaluation measures. Results for the *perfect* click model after 1000 iterations are listed in Table 4. In this setting, performance is slightly lower than for the pairwise approach for 6 of the 9 datasets used (except for *TD2003, TD2004*, and *OHSUMED*). Despite the limited information available to the algorithm (relative quality of the result list instead of explicit relevance judgment per document), performance is competitive with current supervised learning to rank algorithms (Liu 2009).

Table 4. NDCG@10, P@10, and MAP for the listwise baseline algorithm (*perfect* click model)

	NDCG@10	P@10	MAP
HP2003	0.792	0.102	0.721
HP2004	0.770	0.096	0.676
NP2003	0.761	0.090	0.649
NP2004	0.787	0.093	0.659
TD2003	0.296	0.152	0.231
TD2004	0.298	0.236	0.206
OHSUMED	0.422	0.488	0.437
MQ2007	0.375	0.335	0.410
MQ2008	0.488	0.238	0.447

Figure 4 shows the learning curves for the datasets *MQ2007* and *NP2003* at different settings of *k* and the *perfect* click model. In contrast to the pairwise approach, there is no significant difference in performance after 1000 iterations for either dataset. For *NP2003*, learning in the fully exploratory setting ($k = 0.5$) is slightly faster than in other settings. This is expected, as the best feedback is available at maximal exploration. However, learning at lower exploration rates quickly catches up. Thus, for the listwise approach the exploration rate does not appear to have a significant effect on offline performance when feedback is perfect.

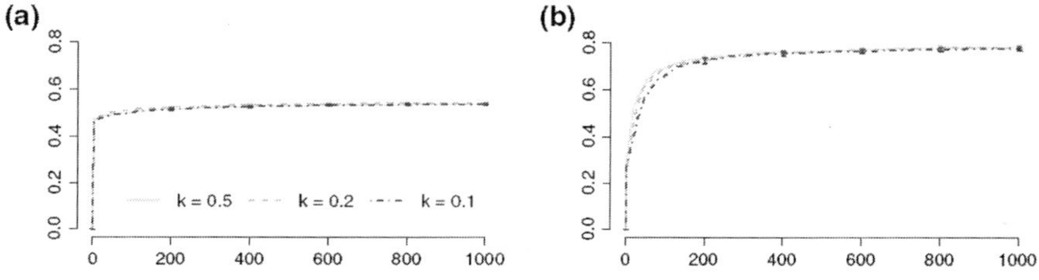

Figure 4. Final performance (with 5 % confidence intervals) over time for the datasets **a** *MQ2007* and **b** *NP2003*for the *perfect* click model and $k \in \{0.1,0.2,0.5\}$

Learning curves for the *navigational* and *informational* click models are shown in Figure 5. As expected, learning is faster when feedback is more reliable. For the idealized *perfect* click model, final performance after 1000 iterations ranges between 0.777 and 0.785 for different settings of *k*. For the noisy *informational* click model, final performance is between 0.412 and 0.546. Although final performance drops substantially as implicit feedback becomes extremely noisy, performance improves over time for all datasets as there is still a signal, i.e., relevant documents are more likely to be clicked than non-relevant ones.

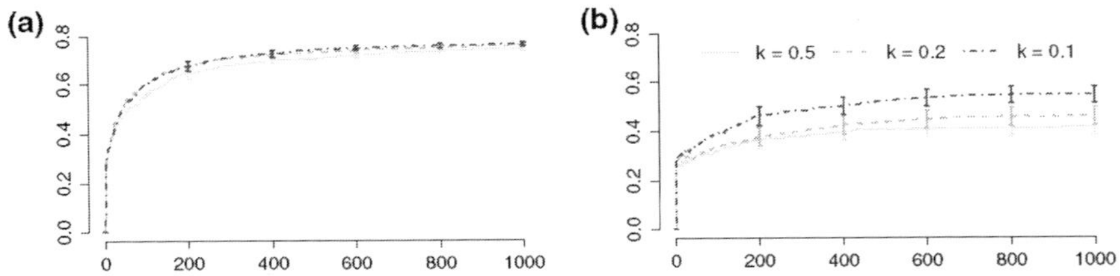

Figure 5. Final performance (with 5 % confidence intervals) over time for the dataset *NP2003* for **a** *navigational*, and **b** *informational* click models and $k \in \{0.1, 0.2, 0.5\}$

Once again there is an interaction effect between click model and exploration rate, although it is different from that of the pairwise approach. Here, there is no significant difference between the final performance at different settings of *k* under the *perfect* click model. Under the *navigational* click model, the effect of noise is small, and results are similar to the *perfect* click model. However, in the *informational* click model, variance increases and there is a large difference between final performance at different settings of *k*. This is a direct and expected consequence of the noise in inferred feedback. More surprising is that final performance improves for smaller *k*, since we expected feedback to be most reliable for the fully exploratory setting $k = 0.5$. Instead, it appears that, since bias is only partially compensated for (cf., Sect. 3), the bias that remains at lower values of *k* smoothes over some of the noise in the click model. At lower exploration rates, fewer results from the exploratory list are presented and it becomes harder for the exploratory list to win the comparison. Thus, instead of noisier updates, the algorithm makes fewer, more reliable updates that on average result in greater performance gains.

5.2.1 Balancing exploration and exploitation for the listwise approach

Our main results for the listwise approach are shown in Table 5. Here, we take the original, purely exploratory, form of the algorithm as the baseline ($k = 0.5$) against which we compare *exploit* runs ($k \in [0.1, 0.4]$). With the *perfect* click model, all lower settings of k outperform the baseline in all datasets. For $k < 0.4$, all improvements over the baseline are statistically significant. The improvements range from 4.1 % (*OHSUMED*) to 12.35 % (*NP2004*).

Table 5. Results for the listwise approach. Cumulative NDCG for *baseline* ($k = 0.5$) and *exploit* ($k \in [0.1, 0.4]$) runs

k	0.5	0.4	0.3	0.2.	0.1
Click model: perfect					
HP2003	119.91	125.71 ▲	129.99 ▲	**130.55** ▲	128.50 ▲
HP2004	109.21	111.57	118.54 ▲	**119.86** ▲	116.46 ▲
NP2003	108.74	113.61 ▲	117.44 ▲	**120.46** ▲	119.06 ▲
NP2004	112.33	119.34 ▲	124.47 ▲	**126.20** ▲	123.70 ▲
TD2003	82.00	84.24	88.20 ▲	**89.36** ▲	86.20 ▲
TD2004	85.67	90.23 ▲	91.00 ▲	**91.71** ▲	88.98 △
OHSUMED	128.12	130.40 ▲	131.16 ▲	**133.37** ▲	131.93 ▲
MQ2007	96.02	97.48	98.54 ▲	**100.28** ▲	98.32 ▲
MQ2008	90.97	92.99 ▲	94.03 ▲	**95.59** ▲	95.14 ▲
Click model: navigational					
HP2003	102.58	109.78 ▲	**118.84** ▲	116.38 ▲	117.52 ▲
HP2004	89.61	97.08 ▲	99.03 ▲	103.36 ▲	**105.69** ▲
NP2003	90.32	100.94 ▲	105.03 ▲	108.15 ▲	**110.12** ▲
NP2004	99.14	104.34 △	110.16 ▲	112.05 ▲	**116.00** ▲
TD2003	70.93	75.20 ▲	**77.64** ▲	77.54 ▲	75.70 △
TD2004	78.83	80.17	82.40 △	**83.54** ▲	80.98

OHSUMED	125.35	126.92 △	127.37 ▲	**127.94** ▲	127.21
MQ2007	95.50	94.99	95.70	**96.02**	94.94
MQ2008	89.39	90.55	91.24 △	**92.36** ▲	92.25 ▲
Click model: informational					
HP2003	59.53	63.91	61.43	70.11 △	**71.19** ▲
HP2004	41.12	52.88 ▲	48.54 △	**55.88** ▲	55.16 ▲
NP2003	53.63	53.64	57.60	58.40	**69.90** ▲
NP2004	60.59	63.38	64.17	63.23	**69.96** △
TD2003	52.78	52.95	51.58	55.76	**57.30**
TD2004	58.49	61.43	59.75	62.88 △	**63.37**
OHSUMED	121.39	123.26	124.01 △	**126.76** ▲	125.40 ▲
MQ2007	91.57	**92.00**	91.66	90.79	90.19
MQ2008	86.06	87.26	85.83	**87.62**	86.29

Best runs per row are highlighted in bold

Results for the *navigational* click model are similar. For all datasets, there are several lower settings of *k* which outperform the baseline. For all but one dataset (*MQ2007*), these improvements are statistically significant. Improvements range from 0.54 % (*MQ2007*) to 21.9 % (*NP2003*).

The trend continues for the *informational* click model. Again, more exploitative settings outperform the purely exploratory baseline in all cases. For 7 out of 9 cases the improvements are statistically significant. The improvement ranges up to 35.9 % for the dataset *HP2004*.

Together, these results demonstrate that, for all click models and all datasets, balancing exploration and exploitation can significantly improve online performance over the purely exploratory baseline. Comparing cumulative performance listed in Table 5 with final performance in Table 4, we find that cumulative performance does not depend only on final performance. For example, NDCG@10 and MAP for*HP2003* are higher than for *OHSUMED*, but cumulative performance is similar (precision scores are low for *HP2003* because there are few relevant documents in general, and are not a good indicator of the relative quality of result rankings). The main factors affecting cumulative performance are the speed of learning and how effectively early learning gains are exploited. Thus, these results underscore the inadequacy of final performance as an evaluation measure for online learning to rank algorithms.

The best setting for exploration rate k is 0.1 or 0.2 in all but two cases. A setting of $k = 0.2$ means that by injecting, on average, only two documents from an exploratory list, the algorithm learns effectively and achieves good online performance for all levels of noise in click feedback. This means that surprisingly little exploration is sufficient for good performance and that the original listwise algorithm explores too much. In contrast, the best setting for the pairwise approach depends on the amount of noise in the click model. When feedback is perfect, little to no exploration is needed. For the *informational* click model, the optimal setting of $r \in \{0.4, 0.6\}$ means that up to 60 % of the result list needs to be exploratory.

While balancing exploration and exploitation improves performance for all datasets, the magnitude of these improvements differs substantially. For example, for the *navigational* click model, the relative improvement between the baseline and best settings for *NP2003* is 21.9 %, while for *MQ2007* the difference is only 0.54 %. Like the differences observed under the pairwise approach, these are a consequence of the differences in the relative number of relevant documents per query. For datasets with few relevant documents, the differences between the exploitative and exploratory document lists are large, leading to a high cost of exploration but also high potential gains if this exploration leads to better learning. For datasets *MQ2007, MQ2008*, and *OHSUMED*, which contain a high ratio of relevant documents, the cost of exploration and the potential long-term gains from improved learning are relatively small. Note that, in realistic settings, it is likely that more candidate documents are considered, so the effect of exploiting more is likely to be stronger.

Cumulative performance is also affected by noise in click feedback, as observed in the results obtained for the different click models. Performance is highest with *perfect* feedback, and decreases as feedback becomes noisier. Performance on some datasets is more strongly affected by noisy feedback. For the *HP, NP*, and *TD* datasets, performance for the *informational* model drops substantially. This may again be related to the large number of non-relevant documents in these datasets. As finding a good ranking is harder, noise has a stronger effect. Despite this drop in performance, balancing exploration and exploitation consistently leads to better cumulative performance than the purely exploratory baseline.

5.3 Comparing the pairwise and listwise approach

For both the pairwise and the listwise approaches, our results confirm our hypothesis that a balance between exploration and exploitation is needed to optimize online performance. The mechanisms of how such a balance affects online performance, however, differ between the two learning approaches. Below, we first discuss how exploration impacts performance for both approaches. Then, we turn to an overall comparison of the online and offline performance of the two approaches, and conclude with implications for putting them in practice.

An unexpected outcome of our analysis is that increasing exploration does not always lead to better learning, i.e., better offline performance. As a result, exploitation can be "free," i.e., the current best solution is also the most useful for collecting feedback for learning. We observed this, e.g., for the pairwise approach under *perfect* click feedback. As click feedback on the exploitative list automatically focuses on an informative part of the document space, increasing exploration does not result in better learning. For the listwise approach, differences in learning for different exploration rates are small under the perfect click model. However, exploration does lead to faster convergence, so exploitation has a small cost.

When click feedback is noisy, the pairwise approach benefits from increased exploration, while the opposite is true for the listwise approach. Exploitation introduces bias in the pairwise approach, which focuses feedback on a relatively narrow part of the solution space that is not informative. Depending on the amount of noise, this effect can result in low final performance. Increasing exploration reduces this bias and improves final performance. As a result, the optimal balance between exploration and exploitation shifts towards increased exploration as feedback becomes noisier. For the listwise approach, an increase in noise also results in some bias. However, in this approach, the bias does not affect the inferred preference judgments (it only increases their variance) but acts as a safeguard against too frequent updates based on noisy data. This leads to less frequent but more reliable updates of the weight vector, thereby improving offline performance. Thus, as noise in click feedback increases, the long-term cost of exploitation increases for the pairwise approach, while it decreases for the listwise approach.

Final performance of the pairwise algorithm with the *perfect* click model is generally high, compared to state-of-the-art supervised learning to rank methods. Final performance also tends to be higher than for the listwise approach (winning on 6 out of the 9 datasets studied), although these results should be considered preliminary as we did not tune the approaches to the characteristics of the datasets and higher performance may be possible.

In terms of online performance, however, the two approaches perform similarly, with the listwise approach beating the pairwise approach on 4 datasets. An advantage of the listwise approach is that the cost of exploitation can be small if the exploratory document list is similar to the exploitative one, which is more likely as learning progresses. For the pairwise approach, the cost of exploration is generally high, so the approach has a disadvantage when a similar level of exploration is required for reasonable learning gains. Thus, at similar final performance and exploration rates, the listwise approach tends to achieve higher online performance than the pairwise approach.

Differences in how implicit feedback is processed by the two approaches lead to pronounced differences in their behavior when feedback is noisy. The performance of the pairwise approach can drop dramatically, especially in the original exploitative setting where often no learning is possible. However, balancing exploration and exploitation allows the algorithm to recover its performance. A relatively high amount of exploration, with about half the result list constructed from exploratory documents, is needed to achieve good learning outcomes and high online performance. The drop in performance due to noise is much less pronounced for the listwise method. Online performance of the algorithm in its original, fully exploratory, version is often an order of magnitude higher than for the original version of the pairwise approach. A possible reason is that, by aggregating feedback over document lists, the algorithm becomes inherently robust to noise. Increasing exploitation can further improve online performance. However, after balancing exploration and exploitation, the two algorithms perform similarly, with the pairwise approach winning on 4 datasets, and the listwise approach winning on 5.

Our analysis suggests that the pairwise and listwise approaches are appropriate for learning from implicit feedback in different settings. If the implicit feedback is known to be reliable, then the pairwise approach should be preferred as it results in good offline performance. Also, in this setting, the pairwise approach requires little to no exploration for substantial learning gains. Thus, it can exploit aggressively, leading to high online performance. However, if feedback is expected to be noisy, the listwise approach should be preferred. In contrast to the pairwise approach, it safeguards against dramatic loss in offline performance, as long as there is some signal in the feedback that prefers truly relevant documents. In addition, under noisy feedback, the listwise approach requires much less exploration than the pairwise approach, and the cost of exploration is lower.

6 CONCLUSION

We demonstrated that balancing exploration and exploitation can substantially and significantly improve online performance in online learning to rank for IR. We introduced two methods for balancing exploration and exploitation in this setting, based on one pairwise and one listwise learning approach. To the best of our knowledge, these are the first algorithms that can achieve such a balance in a setting where only relative feedback is available.

Our experimental results demonstrated that the effect of balancing exploration and exploitation is complex and that there is an interaction effect between the amount of exploitation and the amount of noise in user feedback. When feedback is reliable, both approaches learn well and a high amount of exploitation can be tolerated, which leads to high online performance. As feedback becomes noisier, learning under high exploitation becomes unreliable for the pairwise approach. A higher amount of exploration is required to maintain reasonable performance. For the listwise approach, however, a smoothing effect occurs under high exploitation, so that exploitation is essentially cost-free. This allows the listwise approach to maintain good performance under noisy feedback with a surprisingly small amount of exploration.

Our results also shed new light on the relative performance of online learning to rank methods. The pairwise approach makes very effective use of implicit feedback when there is little noise, leading to final performance comparable to supervised learning to rank approaches. However, it is strongly affected by noise in user feedback. Our results demonstrated that a balance of exploration and exploitation is crucial in such a setting. For the listwise approach, learning can be slower but, due to the aggregation of feedback over multiple result lists, this approach is more robust to noise.

After demonstrating the importance of balancing exploration and exploitation in online learning to rank, a crucial question is how best to explore. This is the direction we are planning to pursue in future work. For the pairwise approach, the cost of random exploration is high. Exploration methods based on active learning approaches (Donmez and Carbonell 2009; Tian and Lease 2011; Xu et al. 2007) are a promising alternative that may reduce its effect on short-term performance, while maintaining or even improving long-term learning. For the listwise approach, the current form of random exploration can lead to inefficient learning. Unlike for the pairwise setting, we are not aware of any active learning methods for the listwise setting that could be used for smarter exploration. Obvious starting points are methods for exploration in policy search reinforcement learning (Kalyanakrishnan and Stone 2010; Whiteson and Stone 2006).

A straightforward way to further improve online performance would be to use annealing schedules that reduce the exploration rate over time, as is common practice in RL. While this technique could improve absolute performance, it is not expected to affect the qualitative outcomes of our analysis. In realistic settings its applicability may be limited as such problems are likely non-stationary, meaning that the exploration rate should never become so small that the retrieval system cannot adapt to changes in user preferences. A more interesting question is whether and how the system could automatically adjust the amount of exploration to a specific setting.

In this paper we focused on evaluating our methods using simulations. This had the advantage that we could conduct experiments for various settings, such as varying the amount of noise in click feedback. Naturally, assumptions underlying these simulations need to be tested before moving these methods to a real setting. Based on our results, we believe that it is particularly important to study the level of noise in user feedback, and collection characteristics such as the typical ratio of relevant and non-relevant documents before applying the methods in a specific environment. Based on such statistics, an informed choice about the appropriate online learning approach and a good balance of exploration and exploitation can be made.

FOOTNOTES

[1]http://www.google.com/corporate/tech.html

[2]This article focuses on learning solutions that generalize to unseen queries. Thus, learning from previous interactions with results for the *same* query is not possible, in contrast to settings assumed by most on-line relevance feedback and re-ranking approaches. These approaches are orthogonal to work in online learning to rank and could, e.g., be used to further improve learned rankings for frequent queries.

[3]Balancing exploration and exploitation also plays an important role in other areas, such as sequential experimental design and in the multi-armed bandit work coming from the applied probability community. Early work includes (Robbins 1952), with an important breakthrough by Gittins (1979). A recent overview can be found in (Mahajan and Teneketzis 2008). Exploration and exploitation have also been extensively studied as fundamental principles of human and animal decision-making behavior (Cohen et al. 2007).

[4]Contextual bandit problems are also known as *bandits with side information*, or *associative RL*.

[5]Provided online at http://code.google.com/p/sofia-ml.

[6]In practice, candidate documents are typically collected based on some feature-based criteria, such as a minimum score. Here, we use the candidate documents provided with the learning to rank data sets used in our experiment, where candidate selection may have

been biased (Minka and Robertson 2008). However, bias in terms of feature values can be neglected here, as the specifics of the learned ranker are not the subject of this study, and all learning methods are affected equally.

[7]More complex schemes of balancing exploration and exploitation are of course possible, but our focus here is on demonstrating the benefit of such a balance over purely exploratory and purely exploitative forms of soliciting feedback. A simple scheme is sufficient for this goal. We also experimented with a more complex softmax-like algorithm and obtained qualitatively similar results. However, such an algorithm is more difficult to tune than the ε-greedy-like algorithm used here (Sutton and Barto 1998; Whiteson and Stone 2006).

[8]In (Yue and Joachims 2009), γ denotes the exploitation step size. We use α to avoid confusion with the discount factor γ.

[9]Note that the setting $k = 0.5$ corresponds to the fully exploratory baseline algorithm. Setting $k > 0.5$ would not increase the amount of information that can be gained from a comparison, but would hurt the expected reward, because fewer exploitative documents would be shown.

[10]The reason appears to be that the learning algorithm works with very coarse feedback, so more finely grained feedback has little influence on the reliability of inferred judgments.

[11]In the listwise approach, the highest level of exploration is reached when the two candidate lists are interleaved in equal parts, i.e., $k = 0.5$.

ACKNOWLEDGEMENTS

This research was partially supported by the European Union's ICT Policy Support Programme as part of the Competitiveness and Innovation Framework Programme, CIP ICT-PSP under grant agreement nr 250430, the European Community's Seventh Framework Programme (FP7/2007-2013) under grant agreements nr 258191 (PROMISE Network of Excellence) and 288024 (LiMoSINe project), the Netherlands Organisation for Scientific Research (NWO) under project nrs 612.061.814, 612.061.815, 640.004.802, 380-70-011, 727.011.005, the Center for Creation, Content and Technology (CCCT), the Hyperlocal Service Platform project funded by the Service Innovation & ICT program, the WAHSP project funded by the CLARIN-nl program, the Dutch national program COMMIT, and by the ESF Research Network Program ELIAS.

REFERENCES

1. Agarwal, D., Chen, B., Elango, P., Motgi, N., Park, S., Ramakrishnan, et al. (2008). Online models for content optimization. In: NIPS'08, pp 17–24.

2. Auer, P. (2003). Using confidence bounds for exploitation-exploration trade-offs. *Journal of Machine Learning Research, 3*, 397–422.

3. Barto, A. G., Sutton, R. S., & Brouwer, P. S. (1981). Associative search network: A reinforcement learning associative memory. *IEEE Transaction on System, Man, and Cybernetics, 40*, 201–211.

4. Broder, A. (2002). A taxonomy of web search. *SIGIR Forum, 36*(2), 3–10.

5. Cohen, J. D., McClure, S. M., & Yu, A. J. (2007). Should I stay or should I go? How the human brain manages the trade-off between exploitation and exploration. *Philosophical Transactions of the Royal Society B: Biological Sciences, 362*(1481), 933–942.

6. Craswell, N., Zoeter, O., Taylor, M., & Ramsey, B. (2008). An experimental comparison of click position-bias models. In: WSDM '08, pp 87–94.

7. Donmez, P., & Carbonell, J. (2009). Active sampling for rank learning via optimizing the area under the ROC curve. In: ECIR'09, pp 78–89.

8. Gittins, J. C. (1979). Bandit processes and dynamic allocation indices. *Journal of the Royal Statistical Society Series B (Methodological) 41*(2), 148–177.

9. Guo, F., Liu, C., & Wang, Y. M. (2009b). Efficient multiple-click models in web search. In: WSDM '09, pp 124–131.

10. Guo, F., Li, L., & Faloutsos, C. (2009a). Tailoring click models to user goals. In: WSCD '09, pp 88–92.

11. He, J., Zhai, C., & Li, X. (2009). Evaluation of methods for relative comparison of retrieval systems based on clickthroughs. In: CIKM '09, pp 2029–2032.

12. Herbrich, R., Graepel, T., & Obermayer, K. (1999). Support vector learning for ordinal regression. In: ICANN '99, vol 1, pp 97–102.

13. Hofmann, K., Whiteson, S., & de Rijke, M. (2011a). Balancing exploration and exploitation in learning to rank online. In: ECIR'11, pp 251–263.

14. Hofmann, K., Whiteson, S., & de Rijke, M. (2011b). A probabilistic method for inferring preferences from clicks. In: CIKM '11, pp 249–258.

15. Joachims, T. (2002). Optimizing search engines using clickthrough data. In: KDD '02, pp 133–142.

16. Joachims, T., Granka, L., Pan, B., Hembrooke, H., Radlinski, F., & Gay, G. (2007). Evaluating the accuracy of implicit feedback from clicks and query reformulations in web search. ACM Transaction of Information and System 25(2):7+.

17. Kaelbling, L. P., Littman, M. L., & Moore, A. W. (1996) Reinforcement learning: A survey. *Journal Artifical Intelligence Research 4*(1), 237–285.

18. Kalyanakrishnan, S., & Stone, P. (2010). Efficient selection of multiple bandit arms: Theory and practice. In: ICML'10, pp 511–518.

19. Karimzadehgan, M., & Zhai, C. (2010). Exploration-exploitation tradeoff in interactive relevance feedback. In: CIKM '10, ACM, New York, NY, USA, pp 1397–1400.

20. Langford, J., & Zhang, T. (2008). The epoch-greedy algorithm for multi-armed bandits with side information. In: NIPS'08, pp 817–824.

21. Langford, J., Strehl, A., & Wortman, J. (2008). Exploration scavenging. In: ICML '08, pp 528–535.

22. Li, L., Chu, W., Langford, J., & Wang, X. (2011). Unbiased offline evaluation of contextual-bandit-based news article recommendation algorithms. In: WSDM '11, pp 297–306.

23. Li, L., Chu, W., Langford, J., & Schapire, R. E. (2010). A contextual-bandit approach to personalized news article recommendation. In: WWW '10, pp 661–670.

24. Liu, T. Y. (2009). Learning to rank for information retrieval. *Foundations and Trends in Information Retrieval, 3*(3), 225–331.

25. Liu, T. Y., Xu, J., Qin, T., Xiong, W., & Li, H. (2007). Letor: Benchmark dataset for research on learning to rank for information retrieval. In: LR4IR '07.

26. Mahajan, A., & Teneketzis, D. (2008). Multi-armed bandit problems. Foundations and Applications of Sensor Management pp 121–151.

27. Minka, T., & Robertson, S. (2008). Selection bias in the LETOR datasets. In: SIGIR Workshop on Learning to Rank for Information Retrieval, pp 48–51.

28. Radlinski, F., & Craswell, N. (2010). Comparing the sensitivity of information retrieval metrics. In: SIGIR '10, pp 667–674.

29. Radlinski, F., Kleinberg, R., & Joachims, T. (2008a). Learning diverse rankings with multi-armed bandits. In: ICML '08, ACM, pp 784–791.

30. Radlinski, F., Kurup, M., & Joachims, T. (2008b). How does clickthrough data reflect retrieval quality? In: CIKM '08, pp 43–52.

31. Robbins, H. (1952). Some aspects of the sequential design of experiments. *Bulletin of the American Mathematical Society 58*, 527–535.

32. Sanderson, M. (2010). Test collection based evaluation of information retrieval systems. *Foundations and Trends in Information Retrieval 4*(4), 247–375.

33. Sculley, D. (2009). Large scale learning to rank. In: NIPS 2009 Workshop on Advances in Ranking.

34. Silverstein, C., Marais, H., Henzinger, M., & Moricz, M. (1999). Analysis of a very large web search engine query log. *SIGIR Forum 33*(1), 6–12.

35. Strehl, A., Mesterharm, C., Littman, M., & Hirsh, H. (2006). Experience-efficient learning in associative bandit problems. In: ICML '06, pp 889–896.

36. Sutton, R. S., & Barto, A. G. (1998). Reinforcement learning: An introduction. MIT Press, Cambridge, MA, USA.

37. Taylor, M., Guiver, J., Robertson, S., & Minka, T. (2008). Softrank: optimizing non-smooth rank metrics. In: WSDM '08, ACM, pp 77–86.

38. Tian, A., & Lease, M. (2011). Active learning to maximize accuracy vs. effort in interactive information retrieval. In: SIGIR '11, pp 145–154.

39. Watkins, C. (1989). Learning from delayed rewards. PhD thesis, Cambridge University.

40. Whiteson, S., & Stone, P. (2006). On-line evolutionary computation for reinforcement learning in stochastic

domains. In: GECCO 2006: Proceedings of the genetic and evolutionary computation conference, pp 1577–1584.

41. Xu, Z., & Akella, R. (2008). A Bayesian logistic regression model for active relevance feedback. In: SIGIR '08, pp 227–234.

42. Xu, Z., Akella, R., & Zhang, Y. (2007). Incorporating diversity and density in active learning for relevance feedback. In: ECIR'07, pp 246–257.

43. Xu, Z., Kersting, K., & Joachims, T. (2010). Fast active exploration for link-based preference learning using gaussian processes. In: ECML PKDD'10, pp 499–514.

44. Yue, Y., & Joachims, T. (2009). Interactively optimizing information retrieval systems as a dueling bandits problem. In: ICML'09, pp 1201–1208.

45. Yue, Y., Broder, J., Kleinberg, R., & Joachims, T. (2009). The k-armed dueling bandits problem. In: COLT'09.

46. Zhang, T. (2004). Solving large scale linear prediction problems using stochastic gradient descent algorithms. In: ICML '04, ACM, pp 116+.

47. Zhang, Y., Xu, W., & Callan, J. (2003). Exploration and exploitation in adaptive filtering based on bayesian active learning. In: ICML '03, pp 896–904

2

CHAPTER

Blog Feed Search with a Post Index

Wouter Weerkamp[1], Krisztian Balog2, Maarten de Rijke[1]

[1]*ISLA, University of Amsterdam, Amsterdam, The Netherlands*

[2]*Department of Computer and Information Science, NTNU, Trondheim, Norway*

ABSTRACT

User generated content forms an important domain for mining knowledge. In this paper, we address the task of blog feed search: to find blogs that are principally devoted to a given topic, as opposed to blogs that merely happen to mention the topic in passing. The large number of blogs makes the blogosphere a challenging domain, both in terms of effectiveness and of storage and retrieval efficiency. We examine the effectiveness of an approach to blog feed search that is based on individual posts as indexing units (instead of full blogs). Working in the setting of a probabilistic language modeling approach to information retrieval, we model the blog feed search task by aggregating over a blogger's posts to collect evidence of relevance to the topic and persistence of interest in the topic. This approach achieves state-of-the-art performance in terms of effectiveness. We then introduce a two-stage model where a pre-selection of candidate blogs is followed by a ranking step. The model integrates aggressive pruning techniques as well as very lean representations of the contents of blog posts, resulting in substantial gains in efficiency while maintaining effectiveness at a very competitive level.

Keywords: Blog feed search; Post-level indexing; Efficiency; Generative language models; Associations

1 INTRODUCTION

We increasingly live our lives online: we keep in touch with friends on Facebook, 1expand our network using LinkedIn, 2 quickly post messages on Twitter, 3 comment on news events on online news paper sites, help others on forums, mailing lists, or community question-answer sites, and report on experiences or give our opinions in blogs. All of these activities involve the creation of content by the end users of these platforms, as opposed to editors or webmasters. This content, i.e., user generated content, is particularly valuable as it offers an insight in what people do, think, need to know, or care about. Organizations look for ways of mining the information that is available in these user generated sources, and to do so, tools and techniques need to be developed that are capable of handling this type of content.

In this paper we focus on *blogs*. A blog is the unedited, unregulated voice of an individual (Mishne 2007), as published on a web page containing time-stamped entries (*blog posts*) in reverse chronological order (i.e., last entry displayed first). In most cases, *bloggers* (the authors of blog entries) offer readers the possibility to reply to entries in the blog (*commenting*), bloggers link to other blogs (*blogroll*), thereby creating a network of blogs, and many blogs are updated regularly. Blogs offer a unique insight in people's minds: whether the blog is about their personal life (which products do people use? what are their needs or wishes?), personal interests (what are their opinions on X?), or a more professional view on topics (can they explain X to me?), getting access to this information is valuable for many others.

Accessing the *blogosphere* (the collection of all blogs) can be done in various ways, but usually revolves around one of two main tasks: (1) identifying relevant blog posts (*blog post retrieval*), and (2) identifying relevant blogs (*blog feed search*). In (1) the goal is to list single blog posts ("utterances") that talk about a given topic; having constructed this list, one can present it to a user or use it in further downstream processing (e.g., sentiment analysis, opinion extraction, mood detection). In (2) the goal is not to return single posts, but to identify blogs that show a *recurring* interest in a given topic. Blogs that only mention the topic sporadically or in passing are considered non-relevant, but a blog (or: the person behind the blog) that talks about this topic regularly would be relevant. Again, one can simply return these blogs to an end user as is, but could also decide to use the results in further processing (e.g., recommending blogs to be followed, identifying networks of expert bloggers, detect topic shifts in blogs). In this paper we specifically look at the second task, identifying relevant blogs given a topic, also known as blog feed search.

The total number of blogs in the world is not known exactly. Technorati, 4 the largest blog directory, was tracking 112 million blogs in 2008, and counted 175,000 new blogs *every day*. These bloggers created about 1.6 million entries per day. Most of these blogs are written in English, but the largest part of the internet users is not English-speaking. The China Internet Network Information Center (CNNIC) 5released a news report in December 2007 stating that about 73 million blogs are being maintained in China, which means that, by now, the number of Chinese blogs is probably close to the number of blogs tracked by Technorati. Although we lack exact numbers on the size of the blogosphere, we can be sure that its size is significant—in terms of blogs, bloggers, and blog posts.

Given the size of the blogosphere and the growing interest in the information available in it, we need effective and efficient ways of accessing it. An important first step concerns indexing. When looking for relevant blog posts, it makes sense to do so on top of an index consisting of individual blog posts: the unit of retrieval is the same as the indexing unit, blog posts. When looking for blogs, however, two options present themselves. We could, again, opt for the "unit of retrieval coincides with the unit of indexing" approach; this would probably entail concatenating a blog's posts into a single pseudo-document and indexing these pseudo-documents. In this paper, we want to pursue an alternative strategy, viz. to drop the assumption that the unit of retrieval and the unit of indexing need to coincide for blog feed search. Instead, we want to use a post-based index (i.e., the indexing unit is a blog post) to support a blog feed search engine (i.e., the unit of retrieval is a blog). This approach has a number of advantages. First, it allows us to support a blog post search engine and a blog feed search engine with a single index. Second, result presentation is easier using blog posts as they represent the natural utterances produced by a blogger. Third, a post index allows for simple incremental indexing and does not require frequent re-computations of pseudo-documents that are meant to represent an entire blog.

We introduce two models, the Blogger model and the Posting model, that are able to rank blogs for a given query based on a post index. Both models use associations between posts and blogs to indicate to which blog their relevance score should contribute. Both models achieve highly competitive retrieval performance (on community-based benchmarks), although the Blogger model consistently outperforms the Posting model in terms of retrieval effectiveness while the Posting model needs to compute substantially fewer associations between posts and blogs and, hence, is more efficient. To improve the efficiency of the Blogger model we integrate our Blogger and Posting models in a single two-stage model which we subject to additional pruning techniques while we maintain (and even increase) effectiveness at a competitive level.

1.1 Research questions and contributions

Our main research question is whether we can *effectively and efficiently* use a blog post index for the task of blog feed search. The Blogger and Posting models that we introduce are tested on effectiveness using standard IR methodologies. To examine their efficiency, we identify core operations that need to be executed to perform blog feed search using either of those two models.

A second set of research questions is centered around a two-stage model that we introduce to combine the strengths of the Blogger and Posting models. Specifically, we introduce a number of pruning techniques aimed at improving efficiency while maintaining (or even improving) effectiveness. We study the impact of these techniques on retrieval effectiveness as well as the impact of integrating alternative blog post representations (title-only vs. full content) into our two-stage model.

Our main contribution is twofold. First, we show that blog feed search can be supported using a post-based index. Second, we propose an effective two-stage blog feed search model together with several techniques aimed at improving its efficiency.

The remainder of this paper is organized as follows. In Sect. 2 we discuss related work on blog feed search and language modeling. The retrieval models that we use in the paper are discussed in Sect. 3. Our experimental setup is detailed in Sect. 4 and our baseline results are established in Sect. 5. Results on our two-stage model and its refinements are presented in Sect. 6. A discussion (Sect. 7) and conclusion (Sect. 8) complete the paper.

2 RELATED WORK

In this paper related work comes in three flavors. We introduce previous research in information access in the blogosphere, we take a look at what has been done more specifically on blog feed search, and we briefly introduce language modeling for information retrieval, as this is the approach underlying our models.

2.1 Information access in the blogosphere

With the growth of the blogosphere comes the need to provide effective access to the knowledge and experience contained in the many tens of millions of blogs out there. Information needs in the blogosphere come in many flavors, addressing many aspects of blogs and thereby extending the notion of relevance, from "being about the same topic" to, for instance, "expressesing opinions about the topic" or "sharing an experience around the topic." In (Mishne and de Rijke 2006), both *ad hoc* and *filtering* queries are considered in the context of a blog search engine; the authors argue that blog searches have different intents than typical web searches, suggesting that the primary targets of blog searchers are tracking references to named entities, identifying posts that express a view on a certain concept and searching blogs that show evidence of a long-term interest in a concept.

In 2006, a blog track (Ounis et al. 2007) was launched by TREC, the Text REtrieval Conference, aimed at evaluating information access tasks in the context of the blogosphere. The first edition of the track focused mainly on finding relevant blog*posts*, i.e., on blog post retrieval, with a special interest in their opinionatedness. The 2007 and 2008 editions of the track featured a *blog distillation* or *blog feed search* task. It addresses a search scenario where the user aims to find a blog to follow or read in their RSS reader. This blog should be principally devoted to a given topic over a significant part of the timespan of the feed. Unlike blog post search tasks, the blog feed search task aims to rank blogs (i.e., aggregates of blog posts by the same blogger) instead of permalink documents.

2.2 Blog feed search

Some commercial blog search facilities provide an integrated blog search tool to allow users to easily find new blogs of interest. In (Fujimura et al. 2006), a multi-faceted blog search engine was proposed that allows users to search for blogs and posts. One of the options was to use a blogger filter: the search results (blog posts) are clustered by blog and the user is presented with a list of blogs that contain one or more relevant posts. Ranking of the blogs is done based on the EigenRumor algorithm (Fujimura et al. 2005); in contrast to the methods that we consider below, this algorithm is query-independent.

An important theme to emerge from the work on systems participating in the TREC 2007 blog feed search tasks is the indexing unit used (Macdonald et al. 2008). While the unit of retrieval is fixed for blog feed search—systems have to return blogs in response to a query—it is up to the individual systems to decide whether to produce a ranking based on a blog index or on a post index. The former views blogs as a single document, disregarding the fact that a blog is constructed from multiple posts. The latter takes samples of posts from blogs and combines the relevance scores of these posts into a single blog score. The most effective approaches to feed distillation at TREC 2007 were based on using the (aggregated) text of entire blogs as indexing units. E.g., Elsas et al. (2008a, b) experiment with a "large document model" in which entire blogs are the indexing units and a"small document model" in which evidence of relevance of a blog is harvested from individual blog posts. They also experiment with combining the two models, obtaining best performance in terms of MAP (Arguello et al. 2008).

Participants in TREC 2007 and 2008 (Macdonald et al. 2009) explored various techniques for improving effectiveness on the blog feed search task: Query expansion using Wikipedia (Elsas et al. 2008), topic maps (Lee et al. 2008), and a particularly interesting approach—one that tries to capture the recurrence patterns of a blog—using the notion of time and relevance (Seki et al. 2007). Although some of the techniques used proved to be useful in both years (e.g., query expansion), most approaches did not lead to significant improvements over a baseline, or even led to a decrease in performance.

In the setting of blog feed search, authors have considered various ways of improving effectiveness: (1) index pruning techniques, (2) modeling topical noise in blogs to measure recurring interest, (3) using blog characteristics such as the number of comments, post length, or the posting time, and (4) mixing different document representations. We briefly sample from publications on each of these four themes.

Starting with index pruning, a pre-processing step in (Seo and Croft 2008b) consists of removing all blogs that consist of only one post, since retrieving these blogs would come down to retrieving posts and would ignore the requirement of retrieving blogs with a recurring interest. We use various types of index pruning in Sects. 5 and 6, including removing non-English blogs and blogs that consist of a single post.

As to capturing the central interest of a blog, several authors attempt to capture the central interest of a blogger by exploiting information about topical patterns in blogs. The voting-model-based approach of Macdonald and Ounis (2008) is competitive with the TREC 2007 blog feed search results reported in (Macdonald et al. 2008) and formulates three possible topical patterns along with models that encode each into the blog retrieval model. In (He et al. 2009) the need to target individual topical patterns and to tune multiple topical-pattern-based scores is eliminated; their proposed use of a coherence score to encode the topical structure of blogs allows them to simultaneously capture the topical focus at the blog level and the tightness of the relatedness of sub-topics within the blog. A different approach is proposed in (Seo and Croft 2008a), where the authors use diversity penalties: blogs with a diverse set of posts receive a penalty. This penalty is integrated in various resource selection models, where a blog is seen as a resource (collection of posts), and given a query, the goal is to determine the best resource. Below, we capture the central interest of a blogger using the KL-divergence between a post and the blog to which it belongs.

The usage of blog-specific features like comments and recency has been shown to be beneficial in blog post retrieval (Mishne 2007, Weerkamp and de Rijke 2008). In blog feed search these features can be applied in the post retrieval stage of the Posting model, but they can also be used to estimate the importance of a post for its parent blog (Weerkamp et al. 2008); we use some of these features in Sects. 5and 6 below.

Finally, blog posts can be represented in different ways. On several occasions people have experimented with using syndicated content (i.e., RSS or ATOM feeds) instead of permalinks (HTML content) (Elsas et al. 2008a, b, Mishne 2007); results of which representation works better are mixed. Other ways of representing documents are, for example, a title-only representation, or an (incoming) anchor text representation; combinations of various representations show increased effectiveness in other web retrieval tasks (e.g., ad hoc retrieval (Eiron and McCurley 2003, Jin et al. 2002)). We increase the efficiency of our most effective model by considering multiple content representations in Sect. 6.

2.3 Language modeling for information retrieval

At the TREC 2007 and 2008 blog tracks, participants used various retrieval plaforms, with a range of underlying document ranking models (Macdonald et al.2008, 2009). We base our ranking methods on probabilistic, generative language models. Here, documents are ranked by the probability of the query being observed during randomly sampling words from the document. Since their introduction to the area of information retrieval, language modeling techniques have attracted a lot of attention (Hiemstra 2001, Miller et al. 1999, Ponte and Croft1998). They are attractive because of their foundations in statistical theory, the great deal of complementary work on language modeling in speech recognition and natural language processing, and the fact that very simple language modeling retrieval methods have performed quite well empirically.

Work on blog feed search shows great resemblance to expert finding: given a topic, identify people that are experts on the topic. Our approach to the blog feed search task is modeled after two well-known language modeling-based models from the expert finding literature. In particular, our Blogger model corresponds to Model 1 in (Balog et al. 2006, 2009), while our Posting model corresponds to their Model 2. These connections were first detailed in (Balog et al. 2008, Weerkamp et al. 2008) and are examined and compared in great detail in this paper.

3 PROBABILISTIC MODELS FOR BLOG FEED SEARCH

In this section we introduce two models for blog feed search, i.e., for the following task: given a topic, identify blogs (that is, feeds) about the topic. The blogs that we are aiming to identify should not just mention the topic in passing but display a recurring central interest in the topic so that readers interested in the topic would add the feed to their feed reader.

To tackle the task of identifying such key blogs given a query, we take a probabilistic approach and formulate the task as follows: *what is the probability of a blog (feed) being a key source given the query topic q?* That is, we determine (*blog*|*q*) and rank blogs according to this probability. Since the query is likely to consist of very few terms to describe the underlying information need, a more accurate estimate can be obtained by applying Bayes' Theorem, and estimating:

$$P(blog|q) = \frac{P(q|blog) \cdot P(blog)}{P(q)}, \tag{1}$$

where $P(blog)$ is the probability of a blog and $P(q)$ is the probability of a query. Since $P(q)$ is constant (for a given query), it can be ignored for the purpose of ranking. Thus, the probability of a blog being a key source given the query q is proportional to the probability of a query given the blog $P(q|blog)$, weighted by the*a priori* belief that a blog is a key source, $P(blog)$:

$$P(blog|q) \propto P(q|blog) \cdot P(blog). \tag{2}$$

Since we focus on a post-based approach to blog distillation, we assume the prior probability of a blog $P(blog)$ to be uniform. The distillation task then boils down to estimating $P(q|blog)$, the likelihood of a blog generating query q.

In order to estimate the probability $P(q|blog)$, we adapt generative probabilistic language models used in Information Retrieval in two different ways. In our first model, the Blogger model (Sect. 3.1), we build a textual representation of a blog, based on posts that belong to the blog. From this representation we estimate the probability of the query topic given the blog's model. Our second model, the Posting model (Sect. 3.2), first retrieves individual blog posts that are relevant to the query, and then considers the blogs from which these posts originate.

The Blogger model and Posting model originate from the field of expert finding and correspond to Model 1 and Model 2 (Balog et al. 2006, 2009). We opt for translating these models to the new setting of blog feed search, and focus on using blog specific associations, combining the models, and improving efficiency. In the remainder of this paper we use the open source implementation of both the Blogger and Posting model, called EARS: 6 Entity and Association Retrieval System.

3.1 Blogger model

The Blogger model estimates the probability of a query given a blog by representing the blog as a multinomial probability distribution over the vocabulary of terms. Therefore, a blog model $\theta_{blogger}(blog)$ is inferred for each blog, such that the probability of a term given the blog model is $P(t|\theta_{blogger}(blog))$. The model is then used to predict how likely a blog would produce a query q. Each query term is assumed to be sampled identically and independently. Thus, the query likelihood is obtained by taking the product across all terms in the query:

$$P(q|\theta_{blogger}(blog)) = \prod_{t \in q} P(t|\theta_{blogger}(blog))^{n(t,q)}, \quad (3)$$

where $n(t, q)$ denotes the number of times term t is present in query q.

To ensure that there are no zero probabilities due to data sparseness, it is standard to employ smoothing. That is, we first obtain an empirical estimate of the probability of a term given a blog $P(t|blog)$, which is then smoothed with the background collection probabilities $P(t)$:

$$P(t|\theta_{blogger}(blog)) = (1 - \lambda_{blog}) \cdot P(t|blog) + \lambda_{blog} \cdot P(t). \quad (4)$$

In Eq. 4, $P(t)$ is the probability of a term in the document repository. In this context, smoothing adds probability mass to the blog model according to how likely it is to be generated (i.e., published) by any blog.

To approximate $P(t|blog)$ we use the blog's posts as a proxy to connect the term $t$and the blog in the following way:

$$P(t|blog) = \sum_{post \in blog} P(t|post, blog) \cdot P(post|blog). \quad (5)$$

We assume that terms are conditionally independent from the blog (given a post), thus $P(t|post, blog) = P(t|post)$. We approximate $P(t|post)$ with the standard maximum likelihood estimate, i.e., the relative frequency of the term in the post. Our first approach to setting the conditional probability $P(post|blog)$ is to allocate the probability mass uniformly across posts, i.e., assuming that all posts of the blog are equally important. In Sect. 6 we explore other ways of estimating this probability.

We set the smoothing parameter as follows: $\lambda_{blog} = \beta/(|blog| + \beta)$ and $(1 - \lambda_{blog}) = |blog|/(|blog| + \beta)$, where $|blog|$ is the size of the blog model, i.e.:

$$|blog| = \sum_{post \in blog} |post| \cdot P(post|blog), \quad (6)$$

where $|post|$ denotes the length of the post. This way, the amount of smoothing is proportional to the information contained in the blog; blogs with fewer posts will rely more on the background probabilities. This method resembles Bayes smoothing with a Dirichlet prior (Mackay and Peto 1994). We set β to be the average blog length in the collection; see Table 4 for the actual values used in our experiments.

3.2 Posting model

Our second model assumes a different perspective on the process of finding blog feeds. Instead of directly modeling the blog, individual posts are modeled and queried (hence the name, Posting model); after that, blogs associated with these posts are considered. Specifically, for each blog we sum up the relevance scores of individual posts ($P(q|\theta_{posting}(post))$), weighted by their relative importance given the blog ($P(post|blog)$). Formally, this can be expressed as:

$$P(q|blog) = \sum_{post \in blog} P(q|\theta_{posting}(post)) \cdot P(post|blog). \qquad (7)$$

Assuming that query terms are sampled independently and identically, the probability of a query given an individual post is:

$$P(q|\theta_{posting}(post)) = \prod_{t \in q} P(t|\theta_{posting}(post))^{n(t,q)}. \qquad (8)$$

The probability of a term t given the post is estimated by inferring a post model$P(t|\theta_{posting}(post))$ for each post following a standard language modeling approach:

$$P(t|\theta_{posting}(post)) = (1 - \lambda_{post}) \cdot P(t|post) + \lambda_{post} \cdot P(t), \qquad (9)$$

where λ_{post} is set proportional to the length of the post, $|post|$, such that $\lambda_{post} = \beta/(|post| + \beta)$ and $(1 - \lambda_{post}) = |post|/(|post| + \beta)$. In this way, short posts receive more smoothing than long ones. We set the value of β to be equal to the average post length in the collection; again, see Table 4 for the actual numbers used in our experiments.

3.3 A two-stage model

We also consider a two-stage model, that integrates the Posting model, which is the more efficient of the two, as we will see, and the Blogger model, which has a better representation of the blogger's interests, into a single model. To achieve this goal, we use two separate stages:

Stage 1:

Use Eq. 8 to retrieve blog posts that match a given query and construct a truncated list *B* of blogs these posts belong to. We do not need to "store" the ranking of this stage.

Stage 2:

Given the list of blogs *B*, we use Eq. 3 to rank just the blogs that are present in this list.

By limiting the list of blogs *B*, in stage 1, that need to be ranked in stage 2, this two-stage approach aims at improving efficiency, while it maintains the ability to construct a ranking based on the complete profile of a blogger.

More precisely, let *N*, *M* be two natural numbers. Let *f* be a ranking function on blog posts: given a set of posts it returns a ranking of those posts; *f* could be recency, length, or it could be a topic dependent function, in which case the query *q* needs to be specified. We write (f↾N)(blog) for the list consisting of the first *N* posts ranked using *f*; if *q* is a query, we write f_q for the post ranking function defined by Eq. 8. Then,

$$P(q|\theta_{two}(blog)) = \begin{cases} 0, & \text{if } (f_q \upharpoonright N)(blog) = \emptyset \\ \prod_{t \in q} P(t|\theta_{two}(blog))^{n(t,q)}, & \text{otherwise,} \end{cases} \quad (10)$$

where (fq↾N)(blog) denotes the set of top *N* relevant posts given the query and $\theta_{two}(blog)$ is defined as a mixture, just like Eq. 4:

$$P(t|\theta_{two}(blog)) = (1 - \lambda_{blog}) \cdot P_{two}(t|blog) + \lambda_{blog} \cdot P(t), \quad (11)$$

in which the key ingredient $P_{two}(t|blog)$ is defined as a variation on Eq. 5, restricted to the top *M* posts of the blog:

$$P_{two}(t|blog) = \sum_{post \in (f \lceil M)(blog)} P(t|post) \cdot P(post|blog). \tag{12}$$

Before examining the impact of the parameters N and M in Eqs. 10 and 12, and more generally, before comparing the models just introduced in terms of their effectiveness and efficiency on the blog feed search task, we detail the experimental setup used to answer our research questions.

4 EXPERIMENTAL SETUP

We use the test sets made available by the TREC 2007 and 2008 blog tracks for the blog feed search task. Those collections consist of (1) a task definition, (2) a document collection, (3) a set of test topics, (4) relevance judgments ("ground truth"), and (5) evaluation metrics. Below, we detail those as well as statistics on our indexes and smoothing parameter β.

4.1 Document collection

The experiments presented in this paper use the TREC Blog06 collection (Macdonald and Ounis 2006). Table 1 lists the original collection statistics. The collection comes with three document types: (1) feeds, (2) permalinks, and (3) homepages. For our experiments, we only use the permalinks, that is, the HTML version of a blog post. During preprocessing, we removed the HTML code, and kept only the page title, and block level elements longer than 15 words, as detailed in (Hofmann and Weerkamp 2008).

Table 1. Statistics of the TRECBlog06 collection

Number of blogs	100,649
Number of posts	3,215,171
Uncompressed post size	88.8 GB
Crawl period	06/12/2005–21/02/2006

4.2 Topic sets

We use two predefined sets of test topics, which have been created during TREC 2007 and TREC 2008. The test topics follow the standard TREC format, consisting of a title (a few keywords), a description (a few sentences on what the topic is), and a narrative (a short story on which documents should be considered relevant and which ones should not). For our experiments, we are only interested in the title of a topic, which is comparable to a query submitted to a search engine by an end user. For each topic, relevance assessments are available: we know which blogs are relevant to the topic and which are not. If a blog has not been assessed for a given topic, the blog is considered to be non-relevant.

Looking at the relevance assessments for the 2007 and 2008 topics, we notice a few differences. Table 2 lists the statistics of the topics and relevance assessments for both years, while Figure 1a shows the number of topics that have a certain number of relevant blogs. To construct this plot, we made bins of 10 relevant blogs, i.e., the first point is a count of topics that have 10 or less relevant blogs in the assessments.

Table 2. Statistics of the 2007 and 2008 topic sets

	2007	2008
Number of topics	45	50
Relevant results	2,221	1,943
Relevant blogs per topic (avg.)	49	39
Topics with ...		
<5 Relevant blogs	0	5
<10 Relevant blogs	5	11
<20 Relevant blogs	12	20
>100 Relevant blogs	6	3

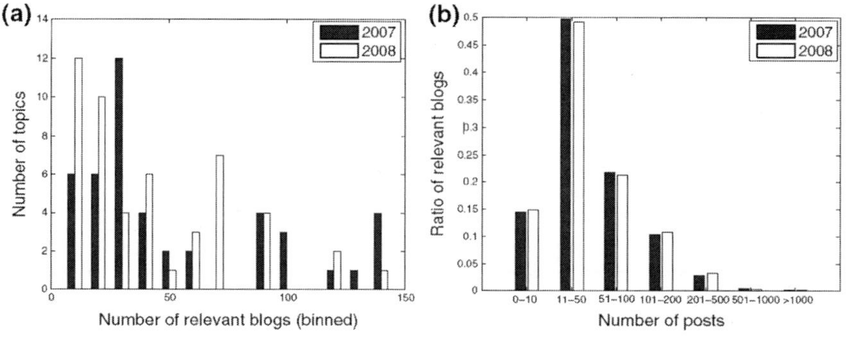

Figure 1. (**a**) Number of relevant blogs (binned, *x* axis) vs number of topics with that number of relevant blogs (*y* axis). (**b**) Ratio of relevant blogs (*y* axis) with a certain size, in number of posts (*x* axis) for both 2007 and 2008 topics

We see that the 2008 topics have fewer relevant blogs per topic than the 2007 topics. Besides, looking at Figure 1a and the last four lines in Table 2, we notice that the 2008 topics are concentrated at the beginning (with a small number of relevant blogs per topic), while the 2007 topics have a later peak, and again a peak at the end of the plot (>130 relevant blogs). These differences seem to be an artifact of the topic development guidelines7,8 used in both years. In 2008, an additional line of instruction was added, stating that "[y]our topic area should be specific enough that there are not likely to be hundreds or thousands of relevant feeds (so 'cars' is probably too vague a topic)." This, it seems, resulted in fewer relevant blogs per topic.

We also look at the size of relevant blogs, in terms of the number of posts in a blog. In Figure 1b we plot how many of the relevant blogs have a certain size; unlike the number of relevant blogs, we do not observe notable differences between the two topic sets. For 2007 the average relevant blog size is 58 posts, and this is 59 posts for the 2008 topics.

4.3 Inverted indexes

We index the collection using the open source software package Lemur9 (version 4.10), no stemming is applied, but we do remove stopwords. Indexing is not just done for the full (permalink) content, as described above, but we also create an index containing title-only representations of the blog posts. Here, documents are constructed using just the blog post title, creating a very lean index of the collection. Index statistics are listed in Table 3.

Table 3. Statistics of the full content and title-only indexes

	Full content	Title-only
Number of posts	3,213,362	3,215,171
Number of blogs	83,320	83,320
Total terms	1,767,023,720	47,480,876
Unique terms	8,925,940	3,524,453
Avg. post length	550	15
Index size	13.0 GB	1.7 GB

4.4 Smoothing

As explained in Sect. 3, our Blogger and Posting models use smoothing, whose influence is determined using a parameter β. Since smoothing is applied at the post level for both models, we take this parameter to be the average post length (for the Blogger model, see Eq. 6), and we list the values of β actually used in the paper in Table 4. We test the sensitivity of our models to the smoothing parameter β in Sect. 7.3.

Table 4. Value of the smoothing parameter β for various runs of the Blogger and Posting model

Run		β (Blogger)	β (Posting)
All posts	Section 5.3	686	550
English posts	Section 5.3	630	506
English, no 1-post	Section 5.3	573	506
English, no 1-post, titles	Section 6.5	12	15
Comments, 50 posts	Section 6.3	595	–
Centrality, 50 posts	Section 6.3	590	–
Date, 50 posts	Section 6.3	575	–
Length, 50 posts	Section 6.3	615	–
Top 5,000 posts	Section 6.3	–	506

4.5 Evaluation metrics and significance testing

To measure effectiveness, we report on three common IR metrics (Manning et al.2008): a measure to capture precision and recall—mean average precision (MAP)—as well as two precision-oriented measures—precision at rank 5 (P@5), and mean reciprocal rank (MRR).

To test for significant differences between runs, we use a two-tailed paired t-test; ▲and▼ reflect significant changes for $\alpha = .01$ and △ and ▽ do the same for $\alpha = .05$.

5 BASELINE RESULTS

Our aim in this section is to establish and compare our baselines, for the Blogger and Posting models. We also examine the impact of two index pruning techniques. Specifically, we look at language detection on blog posts, excluding non-English blogs, and the removal of blogs with a small number of posts, and end up selecting the indexes to be used for further experiments in the paper.

5.1 Language detection

The blog collection we use is a sample from the web (see Sect. 4.1) and contains not only English blogs, but also blogs written in other languages (e.g., Japanese, Chinese, and Spanish). For the task at hand we are only interested in English blogs and we would therefore like to discard all non-English blogs. To this end we apply language detection using TextCat:10 from 3,215,171 posts we remove 640,815 posts that are labeled as non-English, leaving us with 2,574,356 posts.

5.2 Short blogs

The blog feed search task on which we focus requires the retrieval of blogs that have a *recurring* interest in a topic. Blogs with only one or a few posts simply cannot show a recurring interest in the topic, so ignoring them is a reasonable option and should prevent such blogs from polluting the retrieval results. In practice, we would not remove these short blogs from an index, but merely exclude blogs with fewer than *K* posts from our computations until they receive more posts. Potentially, this is a considerable efficiency-enhancing measure, since we do not have to care about blogs that have just started or blogs that were just "try-outs."

In Figure 2 we examine the distribution of the number of posts per blog in our collection, after removing non-English posts. We see that many blogs contain only a limited number of posts, with the exception for the 10, 20, 30, ..., 100 posts. Why these peaks occur is not clear, but it is probably an artefact of the collection construction (see Sect. 4.1). A considerable number of blogs, 4,595 (~4%), consists of a single post. We do not want to exclude too many blogs, and therefore set $K = 1$, only dropping these 4,595 blogs from the index.

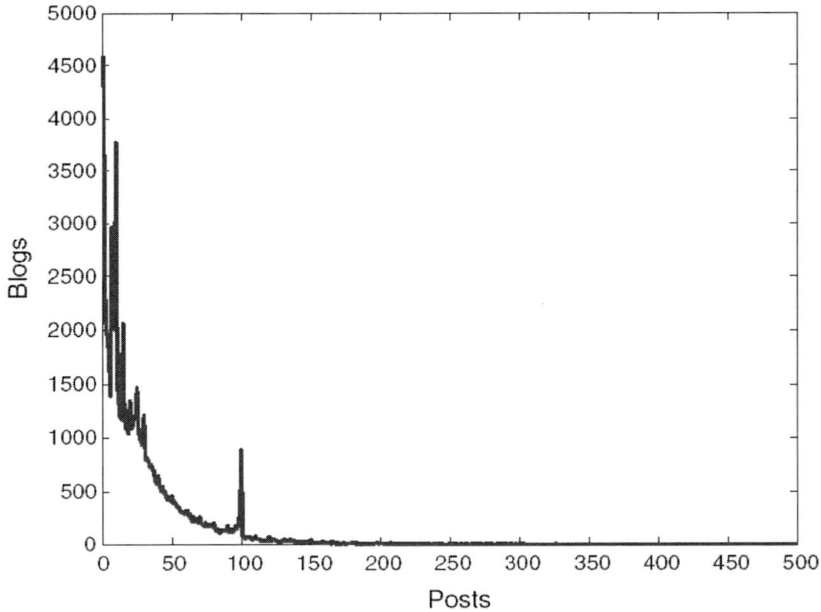

Figure 2. Number of posts per blog

5.3 Baseline results

In Table 5 we list our baseline results on the blog feed search task, using the Blogger and Postings models, on the 2007 and 2008 test topics. We also consider runs that implement the additional index pruning options listed above.

Table 5. Baselines plus results of index pruning

Which posts?	2007			2008		
	MAP	P@5	MRR	MAP	P@5	MRR
Blogger model						
All	0.3183	0.5333	0.7159	0.2482	0.4720	0.7400
English only	0.3165	0.5333	**0.7268**	0.2469	0.4800	0.7209
English only, no short blogs	**0.3260**	**0.5422**	0.7193	**0.2521**	**0.4880**	**0.7447**
Posting model						
All	0.3104	0.5333	0.7028	0.2299$^{\triangledown}$	0.4360	0.7225
English only	0.3002	0.5067	0.6877	0.2226$^{\blacktriangledown}$	0.4160$^{\triangledown}$	0.7021
English only, no short blogs	0.3140	0.5378	0.7055	0.2305$^{\triangledown}$	0.4360	0.7237

Significance tested against Blogger model with all posts (top row)

Let us first consider the 2007 test topics (Table 5, left half). First, the Blogger and Posting models (without index pruning) perform similarly; the difference between the two runs is not significant. When we add the index pruning techniques ("English only" and "no short blogs"), we see slight improvements for the Blogger and Posting models. However, the differences are not significant compared to the Blogger model using all posts. The best performance is achieved by the Blogger model with both index pruning techniques implemented (on MAP as well as P@5).

Turning to the 2008 test topics (Table 5, right half), we see that the Blogger model significantly outperforms the Posting model. Overall best performance (on all metrics) is achieved by the Blogger model with both index pruning options added.

5.4 Analysis

When averaged over the 2007 and 2008 topic sets, the Blogger model has just been found to be more effective than the Posting model. But averages may hide a lot of detail. Our next step, therefore, is to take a look at individual topics and compare the effectiveness of the Blogger model to the Posting model on a per-topic basis. To this end, we plot the difference in average precision between the two models, and use the scores of the Posting model as baseline. We look at both models using the pruned index (after removal of non-English posts and short blogs). Figure 3 shows this plot, for the 2007 and 2008 topics.

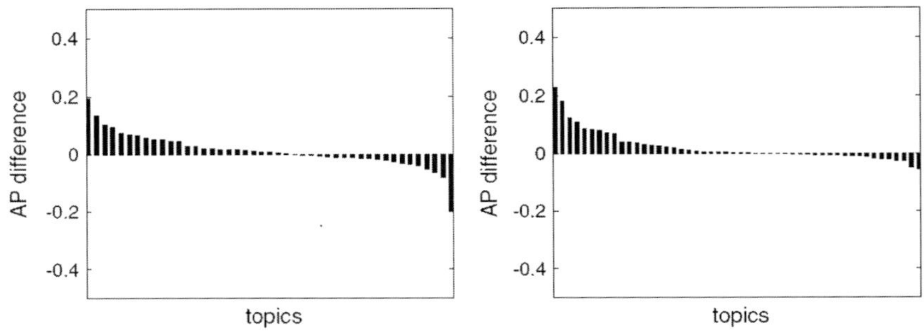

Figure 3. Per-topic comparison on average precision for (*Left*) 2007 and (*Right*) 2008 topics for the Posting model (*baseline*) and the Blogger model

For both years, most topics favor the Blogger model (more topics show an increase in AP over the Posting model when using the Blogger model). Table 6 summarizes the number of topics that prefer the Blogger model and the number of topics that prefer the Posting model.

Table 6. Number of topics that either prefer the Blogger model or the Posting model

Metric	2007		2008	
	Blogger	Posting	Blogger	Posting
AP	26	19	29	19
P@5	11	8	9	3
RR	9	2	8	6

Looking at which topics show very different performance in AP on both models, we find the topics displayed in Table 7. The results in Table 7 suggest that on longer queries the Blogger model may be more effective than the Posting model. To explore this hypothesis in more detail, we group AP differences by query length; see Figure 4. We see that, on average, the Blogger model outperforms the Posting model when the query consists of at least two words. We also see that on single term queries, the Posting model slightly outperforms the Blogger model on average AP.

Table 7. Topics with large difference in AP between Blogger and Posting model

Topic	Increase	Model
Machine learning (982)	0.2000 (25%)	Posting
Photography (983)	0.0635 (44%)	Posting
Dlsr camera review (984)	0.1936 (42%)	Blogger
Buffy the vampire slayer (993)	0.1358 (69%)	Blogger
Organic food and farming (1082)	0.1816 (46%)	Blogger
Veronica mars (1091)	0.2286 (36%)	Blogger

The column labeled "Model" indicates which model performs best. (The number in brackets is the topic ID.)

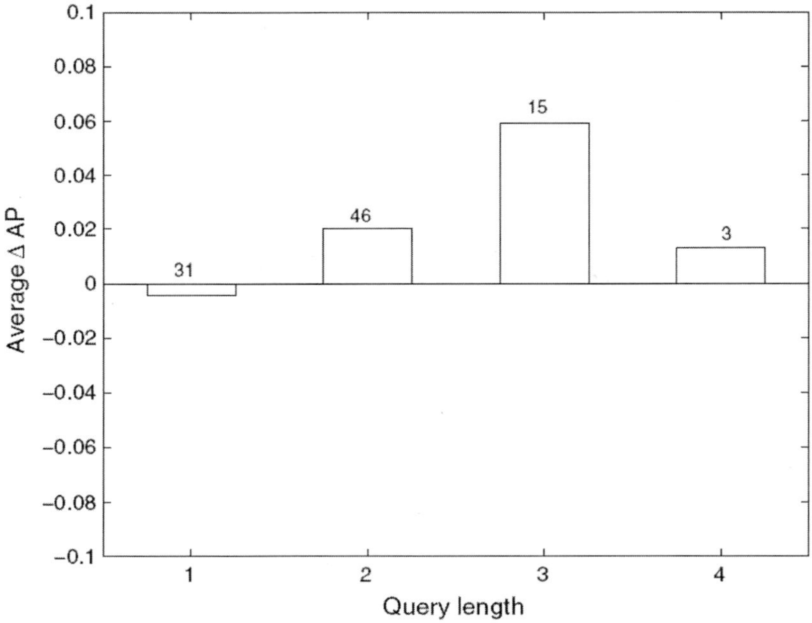

Figure 4. Average improvement in AP for the Blogger model over the Posting model, grouped by query length. The number above the columns indicate the number of topics of that length

In order to quantify to which extent the two models—Blogger and Posting—identify different relevant posts, we count the number of unique retrieved, relevant blogs for each model over the whole set of topics. Table 8 lists the number of relevant blogs retrieved by one model, that are not returned by the other model (in the top 100 results).

Table 8. The number of unique relevant blogs for the Blogger and Posting model in the top 100 results

Model	2007	2008
Blogger	100	96
Posting	76	57

The results indicate that the Blogger model is better at retrieving "new" relevant blogs, but that the Posting model is also capable of retrieving unique relevant blogs. This suggests that a combination of the two models may well outperform both models individually. We explore these uniquely retrieved blogs in more detail and look at the size of the blogs (viz. Sect. 4.2), and list results in Table 9.

Table 9. The average size (in posts) of unique relevant blogs for both models

Model	2007	2008
Blogger	52	56
Posting	37	43

The blogs retrieved only by the Blogger model are comparable in size to the average size of relevant blogs (58 posts); the average size of blogs retrieved only by the Posting model, however, is much smaller. It seems the Blogger model becomes more useful with growing blog sizes, while the Posting model is stronger for smaller blogs.

5.5 Intermediate conclusions

We can achieve good performance on the blog feed search task, using a post index and models based on association finding models originally developed for expert finding. To substantiate this claim we compare the effectiveness of our models to that achieved by TREC participants (Macdonald et al. 2008, 2009). For 2007, both our models would have been ranked second on MAP and around the median for MRR. On the 2008 topics, our models are ranked in the top 5 for both MAP and MRR. Since we are still only looking at baselines of our models, and comparing these to considerably more advanced approaches (that use, e.g., query expansion or link structure), we conclude that our models show good effectiveness on the task of blog feed search.

Comparing the Blogger and Posting model, we see that the Blogger model performs better, with significant differences for the 2008 topics. Finally, combining the two index pruning techniques—removing non-English blogs and blogs consisting of a single post—helps to improve not just the efficiency of our models but also their effectiveness.

Based on these findings, we continue our experiments in the following sections using an index created from English-only posts and without short blogs. The statistics of this index are given in Table 10.

Table 10. Statistics of full content indexes used in the paper

Index	Posts	Blogs	Avg. posts per blog
All posts	3,215,171	83,320	39
All English posts	2,574,356	76,358	34
English, no short blogs	2,569,761	71,763	36

6 A TWO-STAGE MODEL FOR BLOG FEED SEARCH

Given the size of the blogosphere, efficiency is an important concern when addressing tasks such as blog feed search and blog post retrieval. Having introduced models that can use a single index for both tasks is a first step in achieving efficient, yet effective solutions. In Sect. 5 we took a second step and explored ways of index pruning to improve efficiency, while keeping effectiveness at a competitive level.

In this section we continue looking for ways of enhancing efficiency in our models while determining the impact of these enhancements on retrieval effectiveness. We do so by combining the strengths of the Blogger and Posting models into a two-stage model where the Posting model is used to identify a limited set of potentially valuable blog feeds for a given topic and then the Blogger model is used to construct a final ranking of this selection, as specified in Sect. 3.3. In each of the two stages we work with cut-offs on the number of posts or blogs considered.

We start by motivating the two-stage model in more detail. We then consider notions of post importance that can be used for cut-offs. Next, we consider the impact of cut-offs on the effectiveness of the single stage Blogger and Posting models before combining them. We conclude the section with a further enhancement of the two-stage model using a very lean representation of the contents of blogs and their posts.

6.1 **Motivation**

We have seen that the Blogger model is more effective at the task of blog feed search than the Posting model. One clear disadvantage of the Blogger model is that it needs to be computed by considering a large numbers of *associations* $P(post|blog)$ (cf. Eq. 5). What if we could restrict both the blogs and posts that we need to consider without negatively impacting the Blogger model's effectiveness? Our two-stage model uses the Posting model for pre-selecting blogs that are then fed to the Blogger model to produce the final ranking. To increase the efficiency of the Posting model, we restrict the number of blogs that it needs to consider (see Eq. 10) and to further increase the efficiency of the subsequent ranking step by the Blogger model, we restrict the number of posts to consider per blog (see Eq. 12).

To get an idea of the efficiency enhancement that may be obtained by using this two-stage approach, we look at the number of associations that need to be considered. Using the settings employed in our experiments below, after the Posting model stage, we are left with an average of 1,923 blogs per topic. In the second stage, the Blogger model uses *at most* 50 posts per blog. In our experiments below, this leads to a maximum of 96,150 associations that have to be considered for each test topic. Table 11 shows the numbers of associations that need to be looked at by the Blogger model, when it takes all posts into account, only 50 per blog, only 10 per blog, or when it functions as the second stage in the two-stage model with the settings just given. Clearly, then, substantial efficiency improvements can be gained by the two-stage model over the original Blogger model.

Table 11. Number of associations that needs to be considered over all topics; in the two-stage model (bottom row) 1,923 blogs are pre-selected by the Posting model (per test topic, on average) and for each of these, the Blogger model considers at most 50 posts

Setting	Associations	% of All
Blogger, all posts per blog	2,569,761	100
Blogger, 50 posts per blog	1,839,268	72
Blogger, 10 posts per blog	643,252	25
Two-stage model	**96,150**	**4**

6.2 Estimating post importance

Now that we have seen that cut-offs can substantially reduce the number of associations that need to be considered when computing the models, we investigate a number of ways of ranking posts (from a single blog) w.r.t. their importance to their parent blog; cut-offs as implemented in using the restricted summation in Eq. 12 will be based on these importance rankings. Estimating post importance in blogs should ideally make use of blog specific features. In the following paragraphs we introduce three blog-specific features.

6.2.1 Post length

Blog posts are characterized by their relatively small size in terms of number of words. Short blurbs on what a blogger did today, or what she is currently doing make up for many of the blog posts in the blogosphere. We are interested in the posts that contain more information than just these blurbs. We translate this into a preference for longer blog posts and assign higher association strengths to longer posts, viz. Eq. 13:

$$P(post|blog) = \frac{\log(|post|)}{\sum_{post' \in blog} \log(|post'|)} \tag{13}$$

where |*post*| is the length of the post in words.

6.2.2 Centrality

In determining the recurring interest of a blog, we are interested in blog posts that are central to a blog. That is, we want to emphasize posts that differ least from the blog as a whole, and thereby represent the "core" of a blog. We estimate the centrality using the KL-divergence between each post and the blog as a whole (Eq. 14).

$$KL(post||blog) = \sum_{t} P(t|post) \cdot \frac{P(t|post)}{P(t|blog)}. \tag{14}$$

Since a lower KL-divergence indicates a more central blog post, we take the inverse of the KL divergence as the centrality score for a post, and normalize over all posts for a given blog to arrive at the association strength of a post:

$$P(post|blog) = \frac{KL(post||blog)^{-1}}{\sum_{post' \in blog} KL(post'||blog)^{-1}}. \tag{15}$$

6.2.3 Comments

Explicitly marked up social interactions are very characteristic for the blogosphere: bloggers allow readers to comment on what they have written and sometimes get involved in the discussion. We build on the intuition that posts that receive many comments are more likely to be of interest to readers, since many readers before them took the effort of leaving behind a comment. We turn the number of comments received by a post into a reflection of its importance; see Eq. 16:

$$P(post|blog) = \frac{1 + \log(|comm(post)| + 1)}{\sum_{post' \in blog}(1 + \log(|comm(post')| + 1))}, \quad (16)$$

where $|comm(post)|$ is the number of comments received by *post*. To make sure the log is defined, we add one comment before taking the log; we add one comment again after this, to prevent zero probabilities. To estimate the number of comments per post, we build on the observation that comments on blog posts follow a similar pattern across different posts: All comments consist of an author, actual comment content, and a timestamp. We use a part of this pattern, the timestamps, and count the number of occurrences of these in a blog post. Manual assessment of several samples revealed that this is a good indicator of the actual number of comments.

Other social aspects of the blogosphere, the blogroll and permalinks, are not considered here, but could also be of interest: blogs that are mentioned a lot in blogrolls could be of more interest, while a larger number of permalinks to a post could also reflect post importance.

6.3 Pruning the single stage models

With multiple notions of post importance in place, we examine the impact on retrieval effectiveness of pruning the computations to the top *N* posts ordered by importance (according to one of the notions of importance). In this section we do not aim at obtaining the highest scores, but focus on the influence of pruning on retrieval performance for both models.

Both baseline models—Blogger and Posting—offer a natural way of improving efficiency: the Blogger model allows one to limit the number of posts to be taken into account for estimating the model; that is, instead of Eq. 5, we compute

$$P(t|blog) = \sum_{post \in (f \upharpoonright N)(blog)} P(t|post) \cdot P(post|blog),$$

where (f↾N)(blog) is a restricted set of posts. In the Posting model we can similarly limit ourselves to a small number of posts when aggregating scores, using

$$P(q|blog) = \sum_{post \in (f_q \upharpoonright N)(blog)} P(q|\theta_{posting}(blog)) \cdot P(post|blog)$$

instead of Eq. 7. Below, we explore the impact of these efficiency improvements on the retrieval effectiveness; we take the top *N* posts, ranked using the importance factors provided above.

6.3.1 Blogger model

Here, we can vary the number of posts to include when constructing the model of a blog. Besides looking at the obvious recency ordering of posts before pruning (newest to oldest post), we also look at the blog importance features considered above: comments, centrality, and post length. We order the list of posts for each blog based on each of these features and prune the list to at most *N* posts. Figure 5 shows the performance in terms of MAP for the various ways of ordering and for multiple values of *N*.

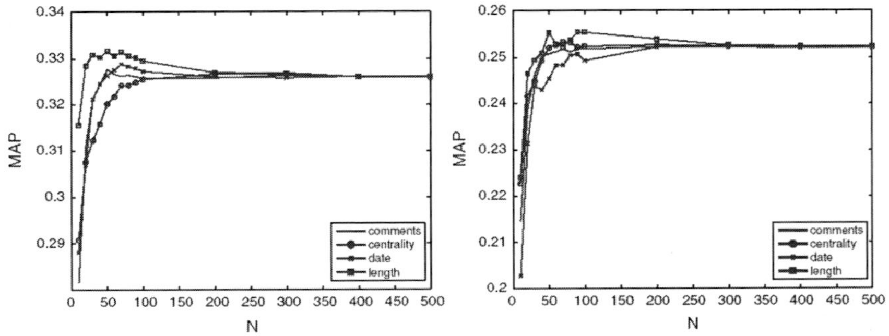

Figure 5. Influence of selecting at most *N* posts on MAP of the Blogger model for (*Left*) 2007 and (*Right*) 2008, where posts are ordered by recency, comments, centrality, or length

The plots show that we can improve effectiveness on MAP by limiting the number of posts we take into account when constructing the Blogger model, an insight that we will use in setting up the two-stage model below. Even more interesting is the fact that the "original" ordering (by recency) is outperformed by other ways of ordering posts, especially ordering by post length. Table 12 displays the number of associations (i.e., $P(post|blog)$ values) that need to be considered for different values of N and shows that by pruning the post list, we substantially reduce this number.

Table 12. Number of associations that need to be considered when up to N posts are used for creating a Blogger model (regardless of ordering)

N	Associations	% of All
all	2,569,761	100
500	2,510,802	98
100	2,281,165	89
50	**1,839,268**	**72**
20	1,095,378	43
10	643,252	25

Table 13 shows the effectiveness of limiting the number of posts used to construct the Blogger model to 50, for various ways of ordering the posts. We observe that all orderings improve effectiveness for at least some of the metrics, but *length*shows best overall improvements.

Table 13. Results on the blog feed search task of the Blogger model built using at most top 50 posts, under various orderings

Ordering	2007			2008		
	MAP	P@5	MRR	MAP	P@5	MRR
– (All posts)	0.3260	0.5422	0.7193	0.2521	0.4880	0.7447
Recency	0.3263	**0.5600**	0.7110	0.2454$^{\triangledown}$	0.4840	0.7423
Centrality	0.3201$^{\triangledown}$	0.5333	0.7081	0.2521	0.4880	0.7632
Comments	0.3276	0.5556	**0.7422**	0.2508	**0.5000**	0.7351
Length	**0.3316**	0.5467	0.7310	**0.2553**	0.4960	**0.7665**

Significance tested against all posts (top row)

6.3.2 Posting model

Next we explore the impact of pruning on the effectiveness of the Posting model. In Figure 6 we plot the number of posts that are taken into account when aggregating post scores into blog scores against the various metrics for both topic sets. From the plots we observe that we do not need to take all posts into account when scoring blogs. Rather, we can do with only a relative small number of posts—again, an insight that we will use in setting up the two-stage model below.

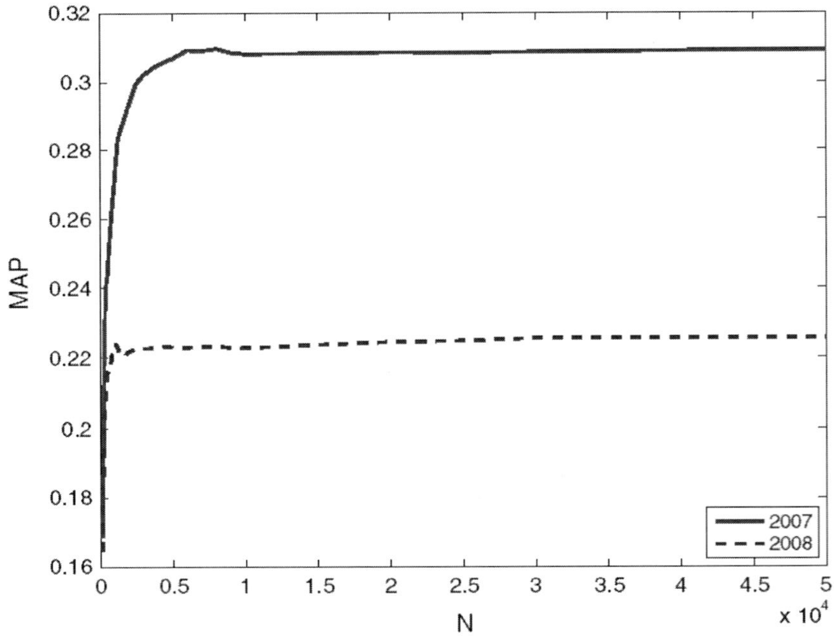

Figure 6. Impact of limiting to the top *N* posts on MAP of the Posting model

Table 14 lists the effectiveness of pruning the post list for the Posting model. Even though the best performance is achieved using all posts, scores after pruning the list to 5,000 posts are promising. Given the efficiency improvement we achieve by going back from over 2.5M posts to only 5,000, we feel that this drop in effectiveness is defendable. As an aside, we explored using the three blog characteristics (comments, centrality, and post length) as estimates of the association strength in the Posting model, and its influence on pruning. Results, however, did not show an improvement over a uniform probability.

Table 14. Results on the blog feed search task of the Posting model, with pruning, selecting only the top *N*posts

N	2007			2008		
	MAP	P@5	MRR	MAP	P@5	MRR
2,569,761 (all)	**0.3140**	**0.5378**	**0.7055**	**0.2305**	0.4360	0.7237
10,000	0.3081$^{\blacktriangledown}$	0.5244	0.6907	0.2228$^{\blacktriangledown}$	0.4360	0.7229
5,000	0.3069$^{\triangledown}$	0.5289	0.6912	0.2230$^{\blacktriangledown}$	0.4320	0.7232
1,000	0.2712$^{\blacktriangledown}$	0.5156	0.6821	0.2232	**0.4440**	**0.7403**
100	0.1688$^{\blacktriangledown}$	0.4489$^{\blacktriangledown}$	0.6729	0.1645$^{\blacktriangledown}$	0.4120	0.6980

Significance tested against the all posts runs (top row)

The values of 50 (for the Blogger model) and 5,000 (for the posting model) were obtained by using 1 year as the training set and the other as the test set and averaging the optimal outcomes.

6.4 Evaluating the two-stage model

We quickly turn to the results achieved by the two-stage model as defined in Sect.3.3. Table 15 lists the results of four settings, three of which we have already discussed: (1) the Blogger model (all posts), (2) the Blogger model with 50 posts (length ordered), (3) the Posting model with 5,000 posts, and (4) the two-stage model using items (2), and (3) as components (that is, with $N = 5{,}000$ and $M = 50$ in Eqs. 10 and 12, respectively).

Table 15. Results on the blog feed search task of the combined approach

Setting	2007			2008		
	MAP	P@5	MRR	MAP	P@5	MRR
Blogger (all)	0.3260	0.5422	0.7193	0.2521	0.4880	0.7447
Blogger (top 50)	0.3316	**0.5467**	0.7310	0.2553	0.4960	**0.7665**
Posting (top 5,000)	0.3069$^{\triangledown}$	0.5289	0.6912	0.2230$^{\blacktriangledown}$	0.4320	0.7232
Two-stage model	**0.3334**	**0.5467**	**0.7321**	**0.2566**	**0.5040**	**0.7665**

Significance tested against the baseline (i.e., top row)

The results show that our two-stage model not only improves efficiency over the Blogger model, but it also leads to an increase in effectiveness. For the both topic sets we achieve the best performance in terms of all metrics using the two-stage model.

6.5 A further reduction

In Sect. 4.3 we introduced two document representations of the blog posts in our collection: A full content representation, *full*, and a title-only representation, *title*. The title-only representation is much smaller in terms of disk space and average document length, and is therefore more efficient to search in than the full content representation. In this section we explore the effects of using various (combinations of) document representations in our two-stage model.

We compare four combinations of the two representations: (1) full content for both stages, (2) title-only for the Posting model (stage 1), full content for the Blogger model (stage 2), (3) full content for the Posting model (stage 1), title-only for the Blogger model (stage 2), and (4) title-only in both stages. The results of these combinations are displayed in Table 16. For the 2007 topics the run using a title-only representation in stage 1, and the full content in stage 2 performs best on MAP, P@5, and MRR; the 2008 topics show a slightly mixed result, with full content representations in both stages performing best on MAP and P@5. What do these results mean? Using a lean title-only document representation in stage 1, the Posting model, is sufficient to select the right blogs. In stage 2 however, we need a full content representation to construct blog models and use these to rank the blogs.

6.6 Per-topic analysis of the two-stage model

To better understand the performance of the two-stage model, we compare the runs using different document representations to a baseline, the Blogger model. We plot the baseline as the "zero" line, and plot for each topic the difference in average precision for two ways of combining the models, full+full and title+full (see Table 16 for the average results). The plots are given in Figure 7.

Table 16. Results on the blog feed search task of different document representations in the two-stage model

Stage 1 (Posting)	Stage 2 (Blogger)	2007			2008		
		MAP	P@5	MRR	MAP	P@5	MRR
Full	Full	0.3334	0.5467	0.7321	**0.2566**	**0.5040**	0.7665
Title	Full	**0.3556**	**0.6533**▲	**0.8574**▲	0.2415	0.4840	**0.7794**
Full	Title	0.2719▼	0.6178	0.7816	0.1995▼	0.4776	0.7125
Title	Title	0.2601▼	0.6133	0.7810	0.1889▼	0.4640	0.6983

Significance tested against the best performing settings using full content for both stages (top row)

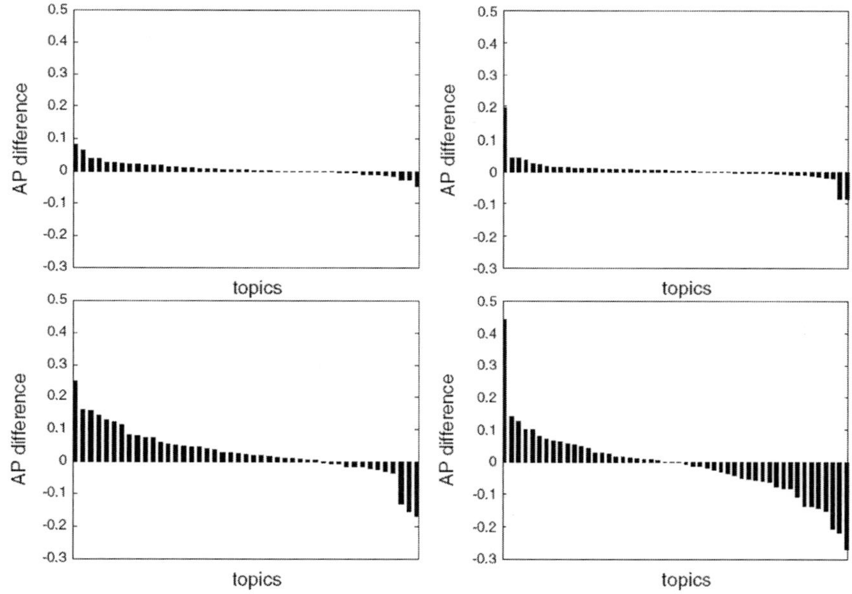

Figure 7. Per-topic comparison for (*Left*) 2007 and (*Right*) 2008 topics on average precision (AP) for the baseline (Blogger model) compared to the two-stage model using (*Top*) full+full and (*Bottom*) title+full.*Positive bars* indicate better performance by the two-stage model, *negative bars* indicate better performance by the Blogger model

We can see that for the full+full document representation, improvements are modest, with slightly more topics improving over the baseline than not. The results for the title+full run are more outspoken: we see a lot of 2007 topics with a steady improvement over the baseline, whereas for the 2008 topics there appears to be a tendency towards a decrease in performance compared to the Blogger model. We provide a different perspective on the matter by listing the number of topics that shows either an increase or decrease in performance over the Blogger model baseline; see Table 17. We see that the combined title+full model increases performance in terms of AP for most 2007 topics, while hurting only a few of them. In terms of reciprocal rank, the title+full run has equal performance to the Blogger baseline for most topics, but also achieves an increase for 15 topics. As to 2008, more topics are hurt than helped according to AP, while the balance is positive for P@5 and RR.

Table 17. Number of topics where performance goes "up" (⇑) or "down" (⇓) compared to the Blogger baseline

Run	2007						2008					
	AP		P@5		RR		AP		P@5		RR	
	⇑	⇓	⇑	⇓	⇑	⇓	⇑	⇓	⇑	⇓	⇑	⇓
Full+full	27	17	4	3	3	3	29	21	6	2	5	4
Title+full	32	13	23	5	15	1	23	25	13	9	13	3
Title+title	13	32	21	12	12	11	15	34	14	13	9	14

Next, we take a closer look at which topics improve most on any of the metrics with respect to the baseline, when we use the two-stage model with the title-only representation in the first stage. Table 18 shows these topics. It is interesting to examine the number of relevant retrieved blogs per topic for the Blogger model and for the two-stage model. From the top improving topics, displayed in Table 18, only topics 968 and 988 have more relevant results retrieved by the two-stage model. The other topics get their improvements from an improved ranking. Topic 993 (*buffy the vampire slayer*) loses 11 relevant blogs in the two-stage model (reflected in a drop in AP), but still improves a lot on precision metrics. Over all topics, the Blogger model finds 179 more relevant blogs than the two-stage model (9%), but the two-stage model is, in general, better at ranking the relevant blogs higher. This is reflected in Figure 8, where we see that (especially for 2008) the Blogger model retrieves more relevant blogs for most topics than the two-stage model.

Table 18. Topics that show an increase in performance on any metric going from the baseline to the two-stage model (title+full)

Topic	ΔAP	ΔP@5	ΔRR
Christmas (968)	0.0378	0.4000	0.6667
Robot companions (988)	0.1599	0.4000	0.2500
Lost tv (990)	0.2496	0.2000	0.5000
Buffy the vampire slayer (993)	−0.0311	0.6000	0.8333
Celebrity babies (1078)	0.4444	0.2000	0.8889
3d Cities globes (1086)	0.0164	0.2000	0.6667

The number in brackets is the topic ID

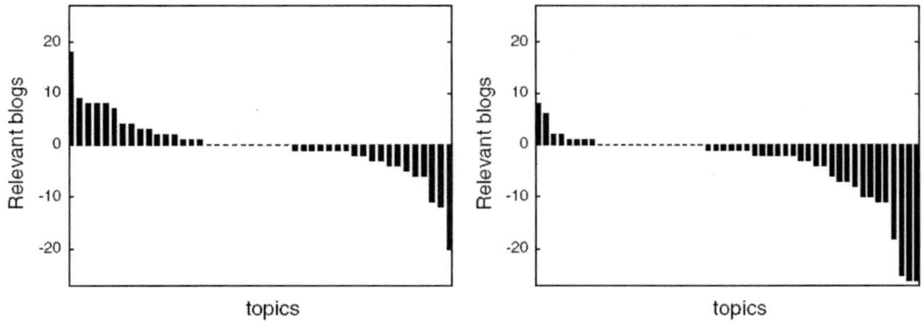

Figure 8. Per-topic comparison for (*Left*) 2007 and (*Right*) 2008 topics on the number of relevant retrieved blogs for the baseline (Blogger model) and the combined model (title+full). *Positive bars* indicate more relevant results are retrieved by the two-stage model, *negative bars* indicate more relevant results are retrieved by the Blogger model

The differences in the number of retrieved relevant blogs are also reflected in the number of unique relevant blogs for the Blogger model and the two-stage model. Table 19 shows that both models are capable of retrieving relevant blogs that are ignored by the other model. Interestingly, the unique blogs retrieved by the two-stage model are much larger (in terms of number of posts) than the unique results of the Blogger model.

Table 19. The average size (in posts) of unique relevant blogs for both models

Model	2007		2008	
	Uniq. blogs	Size	Uniq. blogs	Size
Blogger (baseline)	213	31	311	39
Two-stage (title+full)	209	78	136	86

Finally, we look at the influence of the two-stage model on queries of different length, as we did in Figure 4. In this case, we compare results between the baseline Blogger model, and the two-stage model, and group the difference in AP by query length. The results in Figure 9 show that the two-stage model outperforms the Blogger model on one and two term queries, but shows a (very) slight decrease for longer queries.

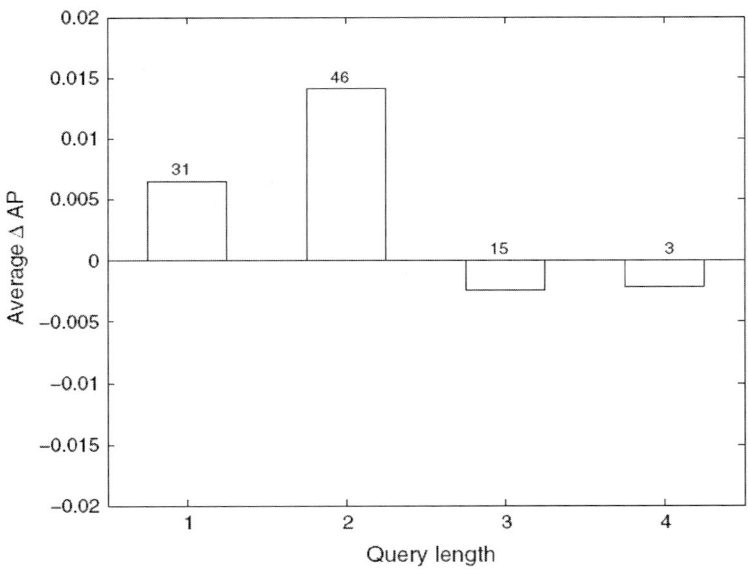

Figure 9. Average improvement in AP for the two-stage model (title+full) over the Blogger model, grouped by query length. The number above the columns indicate the number of topics of that length

6.7 Intermediate conclusions

The aim in this section was to examine our two-stage model, whose motivation lies in combining the Blogger model's effectiveness with the Posting model's potential for efficiency. We improved the efficiency of our models by limiting the number of posts we take into account when ranking blogs. Here, we saw that pruning post lists in the Blogger and Posting models improves efficiency, while increasing effectiveness for the Blogger model, and showing only a slight drop in effectiveness for the Posting model.

Results on our two-stage model showed that effectiveness increases when using a two-stage approach while the number of associations that need to be considered drops to just 4% of the original number of associations.

The use of a lean title-only document representation of a blog post leads to a significant drop in average post length and thus to an improvement in efficiency. Results show that using a title-only representation in stage 1 of our two-stage model (i.e., for the Posting model) is sufficient for collecting the blogs for which we need to construct a blog model in stage 2 (i.e., run the Blogger model). Both efficiency and effectiveness show improvements using the two document representations in different stages of the two-stage model.

Our detailed analysis shows that by using the two-stage model we can correct for the decrease in performance of the Blogger model in comparison with the Posting model on short queries (Figure 4); the two-stage model improves over the Blogger model for short queries, and only loses marginally on longer queries, suggesting that the two-stage model "takes the best of both worlds."

7 DISCUSSION

We reflect on the issue of efficiency vs. effectiveness of the models that we have examined and briefly touch on very high early precision functionality.

7.1 Efficiency vs. effectiveness

In this section we take a closer look at efficiency in comparison to effectiveness on the blog feed search task. Measures for effectiveness were introduced in Sect. 4. For measuring efficiency of our models, we look at the number of blog posts a model needs to take into account when constructing the final ranking of blogs for a given topic. In Table 20 we report on efficiency and effectiveness of our models.

Table 20. Efficiency vs. effectiveness for the Blogger model, Posting model, and the two-stage model

Model	Posts	2007			2008		
		MAP	P@5	MRR	MAP	P@5	MRR
Blogger model							
Baseline	963,995	0.3260	0.5422	0.7193	0.2521	0.4880	0.7447
N=50/blog	598,530	0.3316	0.5467	0.7310	0.2553	0.4960	0.7665
Posting model							
Baseline	90,037	0.3140	0.5378	0.7055	0.2305	0.4360	0.7237
N=5,000/query	90,037	0.3069	0.5289	0.6912	0.2230	0.4320	0.7232
Two-stage model							
Full+full	164,002	0.3334	0.5467	0.7321	0.2566	0.5040	0.7665
Title+full	181,004	0.3556	0.6533	0.8574	0.2415	0.4840	0.7794

From the results we see that pruning for the Posting model does not influence the efficiency in terms of the number of posts that are scored, since we apply pruning only after scoring posts. The efficiency increase here is obtained when aggregating scores over posts: before pruning we aggregate over all 90,037 posts, after pruning we aggregate over 5,000 posts. Pruning the Blogger model shows a definite increase in efficiency, scoring 38% fewer posts after pruning. The efficiency-enhancing effects of pruning on both models directly influences efficiency of the two-stage model.

Looking at the two-stage model, we observe that the number of posts scored is 73% lower than for the Blogger model. This increase in efficiency is by no means accompanied by a decrease in effectiveness: the two-stage model maintains the Blogger model's effectiveness, and even improves it.

7.2 Very high early precision

The well-known "I'm feeling lucky ......" search variant boils down to returning a relevant result at the top of the ranking. Our runs in Sect. 6 show (very) high early precision scores, as witnessed by the mean reciprocal rank scores. How often do they actually return a relevant result at rank 1, and if the first relevant result does not occur at rank 1, where does it occur? We look at the position of the first relevant result per topic for the 2007 and 2008 topic sets; the results are listed in Table 21. For most topics (80% for 2007, 67% for 2008), we do find a relevant result at rank 1. Overall, for only a small number of topics (10), we are not able to return a first relevant result in the top 4.

Table 21. Number of topics grouped by the rank of the first relevant result

First relevant result	Number of topics	
	2007	2008
Position 1	36	34
Position 2	2	7
Position 3	3	2
Position 4	1	0
Position 5–100	3	7

Topics that prove to be particularly hard are topic 969 (*planet*), topic 991 (*U.S. Election 2008*), topic 1068 (*theater*), topic 1077 (*road cycling*), and topic 1092 (*mac os leopard*). We identify three main reasons why these topics fail to produce a relevant result in the top 4, and propose possible solutions that can be used on top of our models. In some cases the keyword descriptions of the topic are simply not specific enough for our models to be able to distinguish relevant from non-relevant blogs. This holds true for *planet, theater,* and *U.S. Elections 2008* (which boils down to "Elections" after query preprocessing). A possible solution to this problem is to use authoritative external sources for query expansion (Weerkamp et al. 2009) (adding related terms to the original query, to create a better representation of the user information need).

A second source of errors appears to be a slight mismatch between the query and the narrative that comes with it. The narrative sometimes imposes a very specific reading of the query that is not apparent from the (keyword) query itself. This is the case for *road cycling*, where many returned results talk about road cycling, but are non-relevant according to the narrative: female road cycling, personal cycling diaries, etc. One solution here would be to add terms from the description that comes with the topic to specify the topic better.

A final source of error are assessment inconsistencies. For some topics (e.g., *mac os leopard*) assessments are inconsistent: certain blogs that discuss mainly Mac OS-related topics are considered relevant (without a specific focus on the "Leopard" version of the operating system), while other blogs that do talk about the Mac OS are judged non-relevant. There is no obvious solution to this problem: it simply reflects the nature of human judgments.

7.3 Smoothing parameter

In Sect. 4.4 we briefly discussed the setting of smoothing parameter β for both models. It is well known that this parameter can have a significant impact on the effectiveness of language modeling-based retrieval methods (Zhai and Lafferty2004). To give an impression of this impact we run a baseline experiment for our two models (comparable to the "All" runs in Sect. 5.3). We compare the automatic setting of β (as detailed in Table 4) to a range of different β values (1, 10, 100, 1,000, 2,000, and 5,000) and list the results in Table 22.

We observe that in some cases the Blogger model favors β values slightly smaller than ours. As to the Posting model, we find that our automatic setting delivers the highest scores on the 2007 topic set for all retrieval metrics. On the 2008 set, a mixed picture emerges: best MAP and P@5 scores are achieved with slightly larger β values, while MRR tops when $\beta = 1$ is used. In sum, we conclude that our method of estimating the value of β based on average representation length delivers good performance across the board.

Table 22. Impact of smoothing parameter β on effectiveness for the Blogger and the Posting model

β	2007			2008		
	MAP	P@5	MRR	MAP	P@5	MRR
Blogger model						
1	0.3038	0.4756	0.5955	0.2303	0.4320	0.7634
10	0.3124	0.4844	0.6374	0.2400	0.4400	0.7665
100	**0.3385**	**0.5378**	0.6850	**0.2585**	0.4600	**0.7823**
686	*0.3183*	*0.5333*	***0.7159***	*0.2482*	***0.4720***	*0.7400*
1,000	0.3086	0.5289	0.7068	0.2414	0.4560	0.7069
2,000	0.2830	0.4978	0.6916	0.2256	0.4320	0.7045
5,000	0.2477	0.4489	0.6390	0.2045	0.4080	0.6590
Posting model						
1	0.2752	0.4400	0.5590	0.1983	0.4000	**0.7552**
10	0.2797	0.4844	0.5574	0.2035	0.4080	0.7491
100	0.3021	0.5200	0.6494	0.2185	0.4160	0.7360
550	***0.3104***	***0.5333***	***0.7028***	*0.2299*	*0.4360*	*0.7225*
1,000	0.3029	0.5244	0.7017	**0.2308**	0.4480	0.7014
2,000	0.2873	0.5022	0.6810	0.2239	**0.4640**	0.6731
5,000	0.2628	0.4756	0.6379	0.2069	0.4480	0.6665

Values corresponding to the automatic setting are typeset in italic

8 CONCLUSIONS

In the paper we addressed the problem of supporting blog feed search and blog post retrieval from a single post-based index. In particular, we examined the balance between effectiveness and efficiency when using a post-based index for blog feed search. A Blogger and Posting model were adapted from the area of expert finding and complemented with a third, two-stage model that integrates the two.

A large part of the paper was devoted to pruning and representation techniques aimed at improving the efficiency of our models, especially that of the two-stage model, while maintaining (or even improving) effectiveness. Evaluations of the effectiveness of our models were performed using community-based benchmarking and complemented with topic-level analyses, as well as an analysis of the efficiency of our models as measured in terms of the number of core operations to be executed.

Our two-stage blog feed search model, complemented with aggressive pruning techniques and lean document representations, was found to be very competitive both in terms of standard retrieval metrics and in terms of the number of core operations required.

As to future work, we are interested in complementing our two-stage model with query modeling techniques as in (Elsas et al. 2008, Weerkamp et al. 2009), in going beyond the default implementations of the models to improve efficiency, in exploiting the ability of the two-stage model in ranking a relevant blog at position one (e.g., in extracting "relevant" characteristics), and in using different blog-specific features for ordering blog posts prior to pruning.

FOOTNOTES

[1]http://www.facebook.com.

[2]http://www.linkedin.com.

[3]http://www.twitter.com.

[4]http://technorati.com/blogging/feature/state-of-the-blogosphere-2008/.

[5]http://www.cnnic.cn.

[6]http://code.google.com/p/ears.

[7]http://ir.dcs.gla.ac.uk/wiki/TREC-BLOG/TREC2007.

[8]http://ir.dcs.gla.ac.uk/wiki/TREC-BLOG/TREC2008.

[9]http://www.lemurproject.com.

[10]http://odur.let.rug.nl/~vannoord/TextCat/.

ACKNOWLEDGMENTS

We are grateful to our reviewers and the editors of the journal for providing valuable comments and feedback. This research was supported by the European Union's ICT Policy Support Programme as part of the Competitiveness and Innovation Framework Programme, CIP ICT-PSP under grant agreement nr 250430 (GALATEAS), the 7th Framework Program of the European Commission, grant agreement no. 258191 (PROMISE), the DuOMAn project carried out within the STEVIN programme which is funded by the Dutch and Flemish Governments under project nr STE-09-12, the Netherlands Organisation for Scientific Research (NWO) under project nrs 612.061.814, 612.061.815, 640.004.802, 380-70-011, the Center for Creation, Content and Technology (CCCT), the Hyperlocal Service Platform project funded by the Service Innovation & ICT program, and the WAHSP project funded by the CLARIN-nl program.

REFERENCES

1. Arguello, J., Elsas, J., Callan, J., & Carbonell, J. (2008). Document representation and query expansion models for blog recommendation. In ICWSM 2008.

2. Balog, K., Azzopardi, L., & de Rijke, M. (2006). Formal models for expert finding in enterprise corpora. In*Proceedings of the 29th annual international ACM SIGIR conference on Research and development in information retrieval (SIGIR 2006)* (pp. 43–50). New York, NY, USA: ACM Press.

3. Balog, K., Azzopardi, L., & de Rijke, M. (2009). A language modeling framework for expert finding. *Information Processing and Management, 45*(1), 1–19.

4. Balog, K., de Rijke, M., & Weerkamp, W. (2008). Bloggers as experts: feed distillation using expert retrieval models. In *Proceedings of the 31st annual international ACM SIGIR conference on Research and development in information retrieval (SIGIR 2008)* (pp. 753–754). New York, NY, USA: ACM.

5. Eiron, N., & McCurley, K. S. (2003) Analysis of anchor text for web search. In *Proceedings of the 26th annual international ACM SIGIR conference on Research and development in informaion retrieval (SIGIR 2003)* (pp. 459–460).

6. Elsas, J., Arguello, J., Callan, J., & Carbonell, J. (2008). Retrieval and feedback models for blog distillation. In *The sixteenth text REtrieval conference proceedings (TREC 2007)*. NIST.

7. Elsas, J. L., Arguello, J., Callan, J., & Carbonell, J.G. (2008). Retrieval and feedback models for blog feed search. In *Proceedings of the 31st annual international ACM SIGIR conference on research and development in information retrieval (SIGIR 2008)* (pp. 347–354). New York, NY, USA: ACM.

8. Fujimura, K., Inoue, T., & Sugisaki, M. (2005). The eigenrumor algorithm for ranking blogs. In *WWW 2005 2nd annual workshop on the weblogging ecosystem: Aggregation, analysis and dynamics*. Chiba, Japan.

9. Fujimura, K., Toda, H., Inoue, T., Hiroshima, N., Kataoka, R., & Sugizaki, M. (2006). Blogranger—a multi-faceted blog search engine. In *Proceedings of the WWW 2006 3nd annual workshop on the weblogging ecosystem: Aggregation, analysis and dynamics*.

10. He, J., Weerkamp, W., Larson, M., & de Rijke, M. (2009). An effective coherence measure to determine topical consistency in user generated content. *International Journal on Document Analysis and Recognition, 12*(3), 185–203.

11. Hiemstra, D. (2001). Using language models for information retrieval. Ph.D. thesis, University of Twente.

12. Hofmann, K., & Weerkamp, W. (2008). Content extraction for information retrieval in blogs and intranets. Tech. rep., University of Amsterdam URL http://ilps.science.uva.nl/biblio/content-extraction-information-retrieval-blogs-and-intranets.

13. Jin, R., Hauptmann, A. G., & Zhai, C. X. (2002). Title language model for information retrieval. In *Proceedings of the 25th*

annual international ACM SIGIR conference on research and development in information retrieval (SIGIR 2002) (pp. 42–48).

14. Lee, W. L., Lommatzsch, A., & Scheel, C. (2008). Feed distillation using adaboost and topic maps. In *The Sixteenth Text REtrieval Conference Proceedings (TREC 2007)*. NIST.

15. Macdonald, C., & Ounis, I. (2006). The TREC Blogs06 collection: Creating and analysing a blog test collection. Tech. Rep. TR-2006-224, Department of Computer Science, University of Glasgow.

16. Macdonald, C., & Ounis, I. (2008). Key blog distillation: ranking aggregates. In *Proceeding of the 17th ACM Conference on Information and Knowledge Management (CIKM 2008)*, (pp. 1043–1052) New York, NY, USA: ACM.

17. Macdonald, C., Ounis, I., & Soboroff, I. (2008). Overview of the TREC 2007 Blog Track. In *The sixteenth text REtrieval conference proceedings (TREC 2007)*. NIST.

18. Macdonald, C., Ounis, I., & Soboroff, I. (2009). Overview of the TREC 2008 blog track. In *The seventeenth text REtrieval conference proceedings (TREC 2008)*. NIST.

19. Mackay, D. J. C., & Peto, L. (1994). A hierarchical dirichlet language model. *Natural Language Engineering, 1*(3), 1–19.

20. Manning, C., Raghavan, P., & Schütze, H. (2008). *Introduction to information retrieval*. Cambridge: Cambridge University Press.

21. Miller, D., Leek, T., Schwartz, R. (1999). A hidden Markov model information retrieval system. In *Proceedings of the 22nd annual international ACM SIGIR conference on research and development in information retrieval (SIGIR 1999)* (pp. 214–221).

22. Mishne, G. (2007) Applied text analytics for blogs. Ph.D. thesis, University of Amsterdam.

23. Mishne, G., & de Rijke, M. (2006). A study of blog search. In M. Lalmas, A. MacFarlane, S. Rüger, A. Tombros, T. Tsikrika, & A. Yavlinsky (Eds) *Advances in information retrieval: Proceedings 28th European conference on IR research (ECIR 2006), LNCS* (Vol. 3936, pp. 289–301). New York: Springer.

24. Ounis, I., Macdonald, C., de Rijke, M., Mishne, G., & Soboroff, I. (2007). Overview of the TREC 2006 Blog Track. In *The fifteenth text retrieval conference (TREC 2006)*. NIST.

25. Ponte, J. M., & Croft, W. B. (1998) A language modeling approach to information retrieval. In *Proceedings of the 21st annual international ACM SIGIR conference on research and development in information retrieval (SIGIR 2008)* (pp. 275–281). New York, NY, USA: ACM Press.

26. Seki, K., Kino, Y., Sato, S., & Uehara, K. (2007). TREC 2007 Blog Track Experiments at Kobe University. In *The sixteenth text REtrieval conference proceedings (TREC 2007)*. NIST.

27. Seo, J., & Croft, W. (2008). Blog site search using resource selection. In *Proceedings of the 17th ACM conference on information and knowledge management (CIKM 2008)* (pp. 1053–1062).

28. Seo, J., & Croft, W. B. (2008). UMass at TREC 2007 Blog distillation task. In *The sixteenth text REtrieval conference proceedings (TREC 2007)*. NIST.

29. Weerkamp, W., Balog, K., & de Rijke, M. (2008). Finding key bloggers, one post at a time. In *18th European conference on articificial intelligence (ECAI 2008)* (pp. 318–322). Patras, Greece.

30. Weerkamp, W., Balog, K., & de Rijke, M. (2009). A generative blog post retrieval model that uses query expansion based on external collections. In *Proceedings of the joint conference of the 47th annual meeting of the ACL and the 4th international joint conference on natural language processing of the AFNLP* (pp. 1057–1065). Association for Computational Linguistics, Singapore.

31. Weerkamp, W., & de Rijke, M. (2008). Credibility improves topical blog post retrieval. In *Proceedings of ACL-08: HLT* (pp. 923–931). Columbus, Ohio: Association for Computational Linguistics.

32. Zhai, C., & Lafferty, J. (2004). A study of smoothing methods for language models applied to information retrieval.*ACM Transactions on Information Systems, 22*(2), 179–214.

3

CHAPTER

Information-Seeking Behaviour of Iranian Extension Managers and Specialists

Gholamreza Pezeshki-Rad and Naser Zamani

Department of Agricultural Extension and Education, Tarbiat Modares University, Tehran, Iran

ABSTRACT

Introduction. We report an investigation designed to explore the information-seeking behaviour of extension managers and specialists in Iran, and to identify the factors that correlate with this behaviour.

Method. A questionnaire was developed to explore information-seeking behaviour of extension managers and specialists. The questionnaire was distributed to thirty-eight public extension managers and 175 public extension specialists who work for Deputy of Extension and Farming System of Iran's Ministry of Agriculture.

Analysis. Data collected were analyzed using the statistical package for the social sciences (SPSS). Appropriate statistical procedures for description (frequencies, percent, means, and standard deviations) were used.

Results. The main motivation for seeking job-related information by both public extension managers and specialists was interest in developing their own job-related information. The top three mostly used information sources by extension managers and specialists were Persian books, Persian scientific magazines, and scientific-technical reports. Concerning communication channels,interpersonal communication with colleagues, in-service training courses and scientific-technical conventions were ranked respectively as the three top communication channels used by respondents. There was a negative correlation between managers' years of extension work and their information-seeking behaviour. For specialists, a significant positive correlation was found between years of education, level of job satisfaction and information-seeking behaviour.

Conclusion. Providing valuable information sources, and removing information seeking barriers, can improve information-seeking behaviour of extension specialists and managers.

INTRODUCTION

Using information is a key issue in the information age. The real challenge of our time is not producing information or storing information, but getting people to use information. Information is a critical resource in the operation and management of organizations. Timely availability of relevant information is vital for effective performance of managerial functions such as planning, organizing, leading, and controlling (Babu, *et al.* 1997). A well-established and well-designed information system to facilitate decision making in various agricultural development projects is critical to the success of any organization. To be successful, any project requires efficient management of human and material resources. This cannot be done unless accurate, timely, and relevant information is available to decision makers (Waheed Khan 1990). In extension organization, like other organizations, information has its own importance to the individuals who are working in managerial or any other positions in the organization to make right decisions. Furthermore, because communicating information and knowledge from information resources or developers to extension clientele is an integral part of the extension process (Blackburn and Flaherty 1994), the flow of information in extension organizations is of more importance than in organizations that are not responsible for providing their clients with useful information. In the information age, extension has a major role in pointing the way to increasing the use of knowledge and information through its people orientation. As Buford (1990) points out, agricultural extension depends to a large extent on information exchange between and among farmers on the one hand, and a broad range of other actors on the other hand. Extension, along with education and research is typically seen as a service, public or private, that responds to the needs of farmers and rural people for knowledge that they can use to improve their productivity, incomes and welfare and to manage the natural resources, on which they depend, in a sustainable way. It brings information and new technologies to farming communities, allowing them to improve their production, incomes and standards of living. Considering this situation, extension has little choice but to become information-based.

Information behaviour is a broad term encompassing the ways individuals articulate their information needs, seek, evaluate, select, and use information. In other words, information-seeking behaviour is purposive in nature and is a consequence of a need to satisfy some goal. In the course of seeking, the individual may interact with people, manual information systems, or with computer-oriented information systems (Wilson 2000). According to Pettigrew (1996), information-seeking behaviour involves personal reasons for seeking information, the kinds of information which are being sought, and the ways and sources with which needed information is being sought. Barriers that prevent individuals from seeking and getting information are also of great importance in understanding the information-seeking behaviour of individuals and organizations.

Information use is a behaviour that leads an individual to the use of information in order to meet his or her information needs. Information use is an indicator of information needs, but they are not identical (Meho and Hass 2001). As Line (1973) points out, individuals do not use all the information they need (partly because they are not always able to obtain what they need, partly because the materials may not be relevant when they obtain them, and partly because individuals sometimes do not know what they need). In addition, sometimes, individuals do not need all the information they intend to use.

Knowledge about the information-seeking behaviour and information use of individuals is crucial for effectively meeting their information needs. This knowledge may also lead to the discovery of novel information behaviour and user profiles that can be used to enhance existing information models or even develop new ones. Moreover, for librarians and other information professionals to be effective information providers, they require a fuller understanding of the information-seeking behaviour, needs, and uses of individuals. Wilson (1981) noted that the study of information-seeking behaviour can stand on its own as an area of applied research where the motive for investing is pragmatically related to system design and development. A different motivation is involved if we wish to understand why the information seeker behaves as he does. This is an area of basic research and, although the resulting knowledge may have practical applications, there is no necessity that it should. Therefore, what, when, and how information is gathered and used by extension managers and specialists is of critical importance to meet their information needs and, consequently, the needs of the clientele they serve (Radhakrishna and Thomson 1996).

It has been often accepted that information needs and information seeking processes depend on worker's tasks (Belkin *et al.* 1982; Ingwersen 1992; Mick *et al.* 1980). A complex task may require several of information seeking processes. If the needs are satisfied, the task (or one step through it) can be completed. If the needs can not be satisfied, the task can not be completed at all or it must be reformulated. If further information is still needed, new seeking actions are initiated. The process may be interrupted at any time if the worker sees no way to proceed (Byström and Järvelin 1995). For example, the work of managers is information-intensive and the environment in which it is done is very information-rich. Although the information-seeking behaviour of managers is in some ways the same as other people working in the organization, studies have shown that managers often prefer oral, face-to-face communication, quick resolution favouring access and speed to accuracy, not necessarily rational decision-making because of the instability, conflict, and uncertainty of situations. However, these situations are constrained and structured by managerial roles and activities, decision-making, and problem dimensions (Katzer and Fletche 1992).

According to Shin and Evans (1991), the main reason for seeking information by Illinois agriculture and horticulture Extension advisors was to answer client inquiries. In their study, they categorized information sources into three types: oral, written and electronic. Written-only sources accounted for the largest single share (45.9%), followed closely by written and oral combination (43%). Less than three percent used electronic information sources. Radhakrishna and Thomson (1996) found that extension agents regularly seek information to carry out their day-to-day work. Extension agents frequently communicate with a variety of information sources. Prominent among these were: clients, another agent in the office, another agent in another county, extension specialists, their immediate supervisor, local news agencies, local business organizations, state, and federal agencies, and local school teachers and administrators. In exploring communication sources used by extension personnel in cotton and wheat technologies, Singh, *et al.* (2003) found that the most important source of acquisition of farm technology was state department of agriculture and the most important communication mode was staff specialists, while the least used mode was personal correspondence with researchers. According to Niedzwiedzka (2003), Polish health care managers obtained job-related information from various intermediaries. Turning to intermediaries (managers of a lower level, information officers, co-workers, etc.) was the most frequent and typical information behaviour of managers, while the personal use of information services (information centres, archives, libraries) or direct interaction with search systems (databases, Internet) was marginal and rare behaviour. An intermediary was the most important element in managers' information activity. Mohammadi (2002) investigated the factors influencing information-seeking behaviour of Extension workers in Zanjan Province, Iran. His research showed that there was a significant relationship between age, level of education, years of experience, and the worker's level of job-related information with information-seeking behaviour. The main reason for seeking information by extension workers was holding training courses, followed by solving daily problems of farmers and up-dating their information, respectively. According to Malek-Mohammadi (2000), Provincial Extension Specialists who were working for the Ministry of Jihad-e Sazandegi reported radio, TV, computer, seminars and training courses as their five most used information sources and channels. They indicated the lack of knowledgeable and skilled information personnel as the main problem of the information system of the Ministry of Jihad-e Sazandegi in Iran.

As Iran's Ministry of Jihad-e Agriculture addresses the goal of establishing an Agricultural Information Systems Network, exploring information-seeking behaviour of individuals who will be involved in this network, including extension managers and specialists, and determining several factors influencing their behaviour are of great importance. This article identifies the reasons why extension managers and specialists seek job-related information, the information sources and communication channels they use to get information and the barriers to seeking information.

PURPOSE AND OBJECTIVES

The major purpose of this study was to explore information-seeking behaviour of extension managers and specialists in Iran. Specific objectives of this study were to:

1. determine extension managers' and specialists' motivations for seeking and using job-related information;
2. identify information sources that extension managers and specialists used to get job-related information; and
3. identify communication channels that extension managers and specialists used to get job-related information;
4. identify organization-related barriers that prevented extension managers and specialists from seeking and using information.

METHODS AND PROCEDURE

The descriptive research methodology was used in this study. The population consisted of thirty-eight public extension managers across the country, and 175 public extension specialists who work for Deputy of Extension and Farming System of Iran's Ministry of Agriculture in Tehran. The frame was obtained from Deputy of

Extension and Farming System, Ministry of Jihad-e Agriculture. A questionnaire was developed to explore information-seeking behaviour of extension managers and specialists. The questionnaire covered four areas: demographic characteristics such as age, sex, marital status, and levels of education; reasons for seeking job-related Information (the extent of importance of six reasons for information seeking were measured on a five-point, Likert scale which ranged from 0 (not important) to 4 (extremely important)); the extent of use of sixteen selected information sources and eleven communication channels was measured on a five-point, Likert scale which ranged from 0 (never) to 4 (most frequently); and organization-related barriers for seeking job-related information (a multi choice question including six organization-related barriers). Face and content validity of the questionnaire was established using a panel of experts consisting of faculty in the Department of Agricultural and Extension Education at Tarbiat Modarres University, faculty in the Department of Information at Tehran University, and extension officers in the Ministry of Jihad-e Agriculture.

The questionnaire was field-tested in two provinces not included in the population. A pilot test was conducted to determine the questionnaire's reliability (Cronbach's alpha=0.83). After the initial mailing and two follow-ups (calling and sending another copy of the instrument), a total of 36 managers and 108 specialists responded, for a return of 95% and 62%, respectively. For specialists, the number of individuals who did not return the questionnaire was rather high and this could affect the results. For this reason, and since, as research has shown, late responders are often similar to non-responders (Miller and Smith 1983), early and late responders were compared on variables identified in the questionnaire as suggested by Lindner and Wingenbach (2002), to handle non-response error that threaten the external validity of the study. No significant differences were found between early and late respondents, and the data were generalized to the population.

Data collected were analyzed using the Statistical Package for the Social Sciences (SPSS). Appropriate statistical procedures for description (frequencies, per cent, means, and standard deviations) were used.

FINDINGS

Personal and socio-economic characteristics of respondents

The age of extension managers ranged from 32 to 47 years, and for extension specialists from 26 to 45 years. Extension managers were, on average, 40.67 years old and extension specialists 34.85 years old. Most of the managers (94.4%), and more than half of the specialists were male. The results showed that the majority of both managers (88.9%) and specialists (78.7%) were married. Only 2.8% of the specialists had high school education, 33.3% of the managers and 53.7% of the specialists had Bachelor of Science degrees, 44.4% of the managers and 20.9% of the specialists had Master's degrees and none of the managers and only one of the specialists had a Ph.D. degree. The number of years managers spent in education was on average 17.25, and for specialists it was 16.58. For both managers and specialists, years of experience in doing extension activities ranged from 1 to 24 years, but managers' experience was much higher (13.61 years) than extension specialists' experience (8.61 years).

Respondents' level of job satisfaction

Job satisfaction is a factor that can influence the information-seeking behaviour of individuals. In this research, managers' and specialists' job satisfaction was measured using a Likert-scale, including ten factors that affect job satisfaction. These factors were derived from several previous studies and were applied after a pilot-test and discussion with information and extension scientists. Table 1 shows the perception of the respondents' level of job satisfaction. As shown in Table 1, managers were very satisfied with the social position of their job, and specialists were very satisfied with their friendly relationship with co-workers. Both groups were rather unsatisfied with the salary paid for the work they did.

Table 1. Respondents' level of job satisfaction.

Factor	Job position							
	Manager				Specialist			
	N	Mean	SD.	Rank	N	Mean	SD.	Rank
Social position of job	34	2.44	0.70	1	100	2.07	0.79	4
Level of job security	34	2.44	0.85	2	101	1.68	1.13	5
Opportunity to applying personal abilities	34	2.38	0.81	3	101	2.16	1.20	2
Friendly relationship among co-workers	34	2.32	1.12	4	101	2.21	1.09	1
Time flexibility for doing tasks	34	2.31	0.64	5	99	2.12	1.16	3
Level of authority for doing tasks	34	2.26	0.79	6	101	1.65	1.18	7
Managerial method in organization	34	2.17	0.79	7	100	1.64	1.02	6
Rate of promotion	34	1.88	1.06	8	101	1.34	1.02	8
Basis for promotion	34	1.47	0.99	9	101	1.26	1.04	9
Salary in terms of work done by personnel	34	1	0.92	10	101	1.08	0.96	10

Note: Scale: 1) None; 2) Little; 3) Somewhat; 4) Much; 5) Very much

Motivations for seeking job-related information

Motivations for seeking job-related information is one of the components of information-seeking behaviour, and influence other concepts of this behaviour. Some motivations, which had been mostly investigated in previous studies, were selected and six were used in the questionnaire. The respondents were asked to indicate the extent of importance that each motivation had to them for seeking job-related information.

Table 2 provides ranking of different information seeking motivations based on their relative importance as perceived by the respondents. *Interest in developing job-related information* was the most important motivation for seeking information by both extension managers and specialists with mean scores of 3.47 and 3.27, respectively. *To update specialized information to improve organizational tasks* was the second most important motivation for seeking information by managers (mean=3.41), and for extension specialists it was *To do job tasks* (mean=2.98). Both groups ranked *competition against co-workers* as the least important motivation for seeking information.

Table 2. Relative importance of different motivations for seeking information

Motivation	Job position							
	Manager				Specialist			
	N	Mean	SD.	Rank	N	Mean	SD.	Rank
Interest in developing job-related information	36	3.47	0.50	1	108	3.27	0.62	1
To update specialized information for doing tasks better	36	3.41	0.73	2	108	2.96	0.87	3
To do job tasks	36	3.02	1.05	3	106	2.98	0.94	2
To publish written materials for increasing job security	36	2.44	0.90	4	105	2.72	1.10	4
To publish written materials for showing off abilities and knowledge	36	2.16	1.02	5	106	2.25	1.00	5
Competition against co-workers	36	1.69	1.03	6	105	1.74	1.15	6

Note: Scale: 1) Not important; 2) Little important; 3) Somewhat important; 4) Very important; 5) Extremely important.

The extent of use of information sources and communication channels

The extent of use of information sources and communication channels are another two components of information-seeking behaviour. Respondents were asked to indicate on a scale of 0 (never) to 4 (most frequently), the extent of use of selected information resources and communication channels. The data presented in Table 3 reveals that the top three information sources for both extension managers and specialists were *Persian books* with mean scores of 3.27 and 2.99, respectively; followed by *Persian scientific magazines*, and *scientific-technical reports* respectively. Both groups used *Non-Persian scientific magazines* least frequently.

Concerning use of communication channels, *interpersonal communication with colleagues*, *in-service training courses*, and *scientific-technical conventions* were ranked respectively as the first, second, and third communication channels mostly used by both extension managers and specialists. Among eleven selected communication channels, internet, as a modern communication channel, was ranked as eighth and sixth important communication channel used by managers and specialists, respectively.

Table 3. The extent of use of information sources and communication channels

Variable	Job position							
	Manager				Specialist			
	N	Mean	SD	Rank	N	Mean	SD	Rank
Information sources								
Persian books	36	3.27	0.65	1	108	2.99	0.95	1
Persian scientific magazines	34	3.05	0.73	2	108	2.78	0.89	2
Scientific-technical reports	36	2.97	0.65	3	107	2.48	0.82	3
Research reports	36	2.69	0.62	4	107	2.13	0.97	7
Reports on agricultural statistics	36	2.50	0.77	5	106	2.01	1.09	8
Video tapes	36	2.44	0.87	6	106	1.23	1.12	14
News papers	36	2.44	1.20	7	106	2.44	1.08	4
Inter-organizational newsletters	36	2.41	0.87	8	107	2.29	1.05	6
Reports on organization performance	36	2.33	0.86	9	107	2.34	0.98	5
Academic theses	36	2.30	0.95	10	108	1.75	1.15	9
Compact discs (CDs)	36	2.11	0.97	11	107	1.61	1.01	10
Floppy discs	36	1.94	0.79	12	106	1.50	1.04	11
Non-Persian books	34	1.38	0.65	13	108	1.46	1.10	12

Slides	36	1.33	0.67	14	106	0.76	0.93	15
Non-Persian scientific magazines	35	1.17	0.85	15	107	1.18	0.98	13
Communication channels								
Personal communication with co-workers	36	2.86	0.86	1	105	2.81	0.88	1
In-service training courses	36	2.75	0.55	2	107	2.40	0.87	2
Scientific-technical conventions	36	2.72	0.56	3	108	2.31	0.92	3
TV	36	2.69	1.30	4	105	2.08	1.20	8
Personal library	36	2.47	0.99	5	108	2.18	1.13	5
Office library	36	2.25	0.73	6	107	2.24	1.04	4
Scientific associations	34	2.17	0.71	7	107	1.78	1.09	9
Internet	36	2.05	0.79	8	104	2.10	1.26	6
Radio	36	1.83	1.10	9	106	1.39	1.05	11
Telephone	36	1.83	1.15	10	105	2.09	1.13	7
Other public libraries	36	1.77	0.63	11	106	1.71	1.10	10

Note: Scale: 1) Never; 2) occasionally; 3) At times; 4) Frequently; 5) Most frequently

Organization-related barriers to seeking job-related information

To obtain additional insight into organizational factors that influence information-seeking behaviour and use, study participants were asked to indicate the most important barrier to their use of job-related information in a multiple choice question including six organizational barriers. It is clear from Table 4 that eight out of sixteen managers, and eighteen out of fifty specialists who answered this question blamed *lack of time flexibility for doing job tasks* as the main barrier that prevented them from seeking and getting information, followed by *job complexity and ambiguity in tasks* which was mentioned as the main barrier by five managers and sixteen specialists.

Table 4. Organizational barriers to seeking job-related information

Organizational factor	Job position					
	Manager			Specialist		
	N	Percent	Rank	N	Percent	Rank
Lack of time flexibility for doing job tasks	8	22.2	1	18	16.7	1
Job complexity and ambiguity in tasks	5	13.9	2	16	14.8	2
Some needed information is classified	2	5.6	3	7	6.5	4
No access to internet at office	1	2.8	4	11	10.2	3
Lack of in-service training courses	-	-	-	4	3.7	5
No access to direct telephone line at office	-	-	-	1	0.9	6

Correlation between selected personal and organizational characteristics and factors making information-seeking behaviour

To change factors making "information seeking behaviour" to score variables, and seek their correlation with selected personal and organizational characteristics, Likert Scale scores of each factor were calculated for every person. The Pearson coefficient of correlation was used to explore the relationships. The correlation between some selected respondents' characteristics with factors encompassing their information-seeking behaviour is shown in Table 5. For both managers and specialists, there was a statistically significant correlation between the extent of use of information sources and motivation to seek information. There was a significant relationship between the extent of use of communication channels and motivation to seek information. For managers, the motivation to seek information was correlated with the extent of using information sources. For specialists, years of education, level of job satisfaction, motivation to seek information and the extent to which communication channels were used were correlated with the information sources use. In both groups, a significant correlation was found between the extent of information seeking motivation with the extent to which communication channels were used. For specialists, there was a significant correlation between the level of job satisfaction and the extent of using information sources with the extent to which communication channels were used.

Table 5. Pearson correlation between some selected variables with factors making information-seeking behavior

Variable	The extent of information seeking motivation (r)		The extent to which information sources are used(r)		The extent to which communication channels are used(r)	
	Manager	Specialist	Manager	Specialist	Manager	Specialist
Age	-0.067	0.014	-0.118	0.058	-0.194	0.086
Years of extension work	-0.237	-0.085	-0.310	0.074	-0.420*	0.077
Years of education	-0.359	0.196	0.25	0.215*	0.318	0.241*
Level of job satisfaction	-0.200	-0.137	-0.135	0.296**	0.078	0.383**
The extent of information seeking motivation	-	-	0.475**	0.420**	0.353**	0.468**
The extent to which information sources are used	0.475**	0.420**	-	-	0.2904	0.693**
The extent to which communication channels are used	0.353**	0.468**	0.290	0.693**	-	-

Note. *: r <0.05; **: r <0.01

Correlation between some personal and organizational characteristics with information-seeking behaviour of respondents

To seek correlation between some selected factors and information-seeking behaviour of respondents, Likert scale scores for three factors which make information seeking behaviour, including (1) the extent to which individuals use information sources, (2) the extent to which individuals use communication channels, and (3) the extent of individuals' information-seeking motivation, were calculated for every person. Finally, to make *information-seeking behaviour* a scored variable, the above score factors were calculated. As shown in Table 6, the Pearson coefficient of correlation was used to explore the correlations between some selected respondents' characteristics with their information-seeking behaviour. According to the correlation analysis, there was a negative correlation between managers' years of extension work and their information-seeking behaviour; in other words, when managers' years of extension work increases, their information-seeking behaviour decreases. This may be the result of pride or too great self-confidence that they hold after some time doing extension activities and feel they are fully aware of everything concerning their job and do not need to seek additional information. For specialists, there was a significant positive correlation between both years of education and level of job satisfaction with their information-seeking behaviour.

Table 6. Pearson correlation between some selected variables with information-seeking behavior

Variable	Information seeking behaviour (r)	
	Manager	Specialist
Age	-0.168	0.67
Years of extension work	-0.423	0.46
Years of education	0.024	0.262*
Level of job satisfaction	-0.109	0.339**

Note. *: r <0.05; **: r <0.01

CONCLUSIONS AND RECOMMENDATIONS

This study has provided insight into the information-seeking behaviour of public extension managers throughout Iran and extension specialists who work for the Extension and Farming Systems Deputy of Iran's Ministry of Agriculture in Tehran, a group that has not received much attention in information-seeking behaviour studies. In particular, the information-seeking behaviour of these individuals was examined in the context of their use and non-use of job-related information. The results show that the main motivation for seeking information by both groups was because they were interested in developing their own job-related information. The top three mostly used information sources by extension managers and specialists were *Persian books*, *Persian scientific magazines*, and *scientific-technical reports*, respectively. Concerning communication channels, *interpersonal communication with colleagues*, *in-service training courses*, and *scientific-technical conventions* were ranked respectively as the three top communication channels which were used by respondents for seeking and getting information. The results also showed that the majority of managers and specialists who believed their organization did not support them in seeking and getting information, reported *lack of time flexibility for doing job tasks* as the main barrier that prevented them from information seeking. There was a significant negative correlation between managers' years of extension work with their information-seeking behaviour. A significant positive correlation was found between specialists' years of education and their level of job satisfaction with their information seeking behaviour. Because of the significant positive correlation between specialists' level of job satisfaction and their information-seeking behaviour, it is recommended that extension organizations try to increase specialists' level of job satisfaction; it may consequently improve the information-seeking behaviour of extension specialists. According to the findings, there was a positive correlation between specialists' level of job satisfaction with the salary they received, it seems that increasing specialists' salary may increase their job satisfaction and consequently improve their information-seeking behaviour. Considering the significant negative correlation between managers' years of extension work and their information-seeking behaviour, managers should be taught about the importance of the flow of information in the organization, and the necessity of having up-to-date and relevant information to make the right decisions. In-service training courses could be useful to teach managers in this regard. In both groups, there was a significant positive correlation between individuals' information seeking motivation and the extent to which they used information sources and communication channels, it seems, therefore, that motivating extension managers and specialists to seek and get information, will increase their use of information sources and communication channels and may consequently improve their information-seeking behaviour. Since knowledge about information seeking behaviour of extension managers and specialists plays a vital role in meeting their information needs effectively, the results of this study can be used to provide valuable information sources for extension personnel and remove information seeking barriers to facilitate the flow of agricultural information around the country and meet information needs of extension personnel and their clients consequently. The findings of this study should be shared with the officials and other individuals who are involved in establishing the Agricultural Information Systems Network so that the right decisions can be made.

REFERENCES

1. Babu, A.R., Singh, Y.P., & Sachdeva, R.K. (1997). Establishing a management information system. In B. E. Swanson, R. P. Bentz, & A. J. Sotranko. (Eds.), *Improving agricultural extension (A reference manual)*. (pp. 161-169). Rome: Food and Agriculture Organization.

2. Belkin, N., Brooks, H.M., & Oddy, R.N. (1982). ASK for information retrieval. *Journal of Documentation,* **38**(2), 61-71.

3. Blackburn, D.J. & Flaherty, J. (1994). Historical roots. In D.J. Blackburn (Ed.) *Extension handbook: process and practices* (pp/ 1-7). Toronto: Thompson Educational Publishing, Inc.

4. Buford, J.A. (1990). Extension management in the information age. *Journal of Extension,* **28**(1). Retrieved 15 February, 2005 from http://www.joe.org/joe/1990spring/fut2.html

5. Bystrom, K. & Jarvelin, K. (1995). Task complexity affects information-seeking and use. *Information Processing and Management: an International Journal,* **31**(2), 191-213.

6. Ingwersen, P. (1992). *Information retrieval interaction.* London: Taylor Graham.

7. Katzer, J. & Fletcher, P. (1992). The Information environment of managers. In M. Williams (Ed.), *Annual review of information science and technology* (pp. 227-263). Medford, NJ: Learned Information.

8. Lindner, J.R. & Wingenbach, G.J. (2002). Communicating the handling of non-response error in *Journal of Extension* research in brief articles. *Journal of Extension,* **40**(6). Retrieved 15 February, 2005 from http://www.joe.org/joe/2002december/rb1.shtml

9. Line, M. B. (1973). Information needs of the social sciences. *INSPEL,* **8**(2), 29-39.

10. Malek-Mohammadi, I. (2000). *An investigation of current information system in the Ministry of Jihad-e Sazandegi.* Tehran, Iran: Ministry of Jihad-e Sazandegi.

11. Meho, L.I. & Hass, S. W. (2001). Information seeking behavior and use of social science faculty studying stateless nations: A case study. *Library and Information Science Research,* **23**, 5-25.

12. Mick, C.K., Lindsey, G.N., & Callahan, D. (1980). Towards usable user studies. *Journal of the American Society for Information Science,* **31**(5), 347-365.

13. Miller, L.E., & Smith, K.L. (1983). Handling non-response issues. *Journal of Extension,* **21**(5). Retrieved 15 February, 2005 from http://www.joe.org/1983september/83-5.a7.pdf

14. Mohammadi, D. (2002). *An Investigation of the factors influencing information-seeking behaviour of extension workers in Zanjan province of Iran.* Unpublished Master's thesis, Tehran University, Tehran, Iran.

15. Niedzwiedzka, B. (2003). A proposed general model of information behaviour. *Information Research,* **9**(1), paper 164. Retrieved 15 February, 2005 from http://InformationR.net/ir/9-1/paper164.html

16. Patton, M. Q. (1985). Extension excellence in the information age. *Journal of Extension,* **23**(2). Retrieved 15 February, 2005 from http://www.joe.org/1985summer/a1.html

17. Pettigrew, K. E. (1996). Modeling the information seeking of professionals. *Library Quarterly*, **66**(2), 161-193.

18. Radhakrishna, R. B., & Thomson, J. S. (1996).Extension agents' use of information sources. *Journal of Extension*, **34**(1). Retrieved 15 February, 2005 from http://www.Joe.org/joe/1996february/rb2.html

19. Shin, W. R. & Evans, J. F. (1991). Where field staff get information. *Journal of Extension*, **29**(3). Retrieved 15 February, 2005 from http://www.Joe.org/joe/1991february/a5.html

20. Singh, B., Narwal, R. S., & Malik, S. J. (2003). Communication sources used by extension personnel and farmers. *Indian Journal of Extension Education*, **39**(1/2), 26-30.

21. Waheed Khan, A. (1990). Rural development through communications. In *Information technology development* (pp. 73-89). Tokyo: Asian Productivity Organization.

22. Wilson, T.D. (1981). On user studies and information needs. *The Journal of Documentation*, **37**(1), 3-15.

23. Wilson, T.D. (2000). Human information behavior. *Informing Sciences*, **3**(2), 49-55.

4

CHAPTER

Credibility-Inspired Ranking For Blog Post Retrieval

Wouter Weerkamp, Maarten de Rijke

ISLA, University of Amsterdam, Amsterdam, The Netherlands

ABSTRACT

Credibility of information refers to its believability or the believability of its sources. We explore the impact of credibility-inspired indicators on the task of blog post retrieval, following the intuition that more credible blog posts are preferred by searchers. Based on a previously introduced credibility framework for blogs, we define several credibility indicators, and divide them into post-level (e.g., spelling, timeliness, document length) and blog-level (e.g., regularity, expertise, comments) indicators. The retrieval task at hand is precision-oriented, and we hypothesize that the use of credibility-inspired indicators will positively impact precision. We propose to use ideas from the credibility framework in a reranking approach to the blog post retrieval problem: We introduce two simple ways of reranking the top *n* of an initial run. The first approach, Credibility-inspired reranking, simply reranks the top *n* of a baseline based on the credibility-inspired score. The second approach, Combined reranking, multiplies the credibility-inspired score of the top *n* results by their retrieval score, and reranks based on this score. Results show that Credibility-inspired reranking leads to larger improvements over the baseline than Combined reranking, but both approaches are capable of improving over an already strong baseline. For Credibility-inspired reranking the best performance is achieved using a combination of all post-level indicators. Combined reranking works best using the post-level indicators combined with comments and pronouns. The blog-level indicators expertise, regularity, and coherence do not contribute positively to the performance, although analysis shows that they can be useful for certain topics. Additional analysis shows that a relative small value of n (15–25) leads to the best results, and that posts that move up the ranking due to the integration of reranking based on credibility-inspired indicators do indeed appear to be more credible than the ones that go down.

Keywords: Credibility Blog post retrieval Reranking

1 INTRODUCTION

In recent years there has been an ever growing usage of social media, web-based platforms that allow the easy creation and exchange of user generated content. Social media can be centered around video (e.g., Youtube, Vimeo), audio (e.g., Last.fm, MySpace), pictures (e.g., Flickr, Picassa), other media types (bookmarks, books, etc.), and people (e.g., Facebook, Friendster). However, one of the most popular media types is still text. Textual social media come in various forms, each with its own characteristics and users: examples are (micro)blogs, forums, mailing lists, reviews, and comments. In this paper we look at one particular type of social media, blogs. Blogging platforms allow people (bloggers) to write diary entries (blog posts) about topics of their choice.

The growing amount of social media content available online creates new challenges for the information retrieval (IR) community, in terms of search and analysis tasks for this type of content (Weerkamp 2011). One of the main challenges lies in the fact that creators of social media content, the bloggers, are given a large degree of freedom: operating without top-down editorial rules and editors, they produce blog posts of hugely varying quality. Some of the posts are edited, news article-like, whereas others are of very low quality. The quality of a blog post may have an impact on its suitability of being returned in response to a query.

Although some approaches to blog post retrieval (finding blog posts that are relevant to a given topic) use indirect quality measures like elaborate spam filtering (Java et al. 2007) or counting inlinks

(Mishne 2007b), few systems turn the*credibility* (Metzger 2007) of blog posts into an aspect that can benefit the retrieval process. Our hypothesis is that we can use credibility-inspired indicators to improve topical blog post retrieval. In this paper we explore the impact of these credibility-inspired indicators on the task of blog post retrieval.

To make matters concrete, consider Figure 1: both (blog) posts are relevant to the query "tennis," but based on obvious surface level features of the posts we quickly determine *Post 2* to be more *credible* than *Post 1*. The most obvious features are spelling errors, the lack of leading capitals, the large number of exclamation marks and personal pronouns, and the fact that the language usage in the second post is more easily associated with credible information about tennis than the language usage in the first post.

Post 1
as for today (monday) we had no school! yaay labor day. but we had tennis from 9-11 at the highschool. after that me suzi melis & ashley had a picnic at cecil park and then played tennis. i just got home right now. it was a very very very fun afternoon. (...) we will have a short week. mine will be even shorter b/c i wont be there all day on friday cuz we have the Big 7 Tournament at like keystone oaks or sumthin. so i will miss school the whole day.

Post 2
Wimbledon champion Venus Williams has pulled out of next week's Kremlin Cup with a knee injury, tournament organisers said on Friday. The American has not played since pulling out injured of last month's China Open. The former world number one has been troubled by various injuries (...) Williams's withdrawal is the latest blow for organisers after Australian Open champion and home favorite Marat Safin withdrew (...).

Figure 1. Two blog posts relevant to the query "tennis"

Another case in which credibility plays an important role is so-called online reputation management (Klewes and Wreschniok 2009): companies monitor online activities, for example on blogs and social networking sites, to find mentions of themselves or of their products and services. The goal here is to identify potentially harmful messages, and try to respond fast and adequately to these. While monitoring a company's reputation, one can come across posts like the ones in Figure 2: The first post is an extensive and well-written description of someone's encounter with company X's help desk. The second is a short, apparently angry shout by a frustrated customer. Company X might decide to act fast after spotting the first post, given that this post sounds reliable, and other people reading it might believe it. The second post is useful for overall statistics on reputation, but is not as important as an individual post.

Post 3
Yesterday I tried to contact company X to ask a question regarding their service Y. After waiting for at least 30 minutes, the woman "helping" me didn't know what I was talking about. (...) I guess I won't be trying to contact them ever again, I should probably switch to company Z instead.

Post 4
Aarrggghhh, u got 2be joking... I HATE X!!!

Figure 2. Two blog posts about "Company X"

Similarly, when looking for information on company X, searchers might be more interested in reading the first post than the second. The first will give them insight in what particular service of this company is not as it should be; the second post does not contain much information besides conveying an opinion.

The idea of considering credibility in the blogosphere is not new: Rubin and Liddy (2006) define a framework for assessing blog credibility, consisting of four main categories: blogger's expertise and offline identity disclosure; blogger's trustworthiness and value system; information quality; and appeals and triggers of a personal nature. Under these four categories the authors list a large number of indicators, some of which can be determined from textual sources (e.g., literary appeal), and some of which typically need non-textual evidence (e.g., curiosity trigger). We discuss the indicators in Sect. 3.

Although the Rubin and Liddy (2006) framework is not the only available credibility framework, it is the only framework specifically designed for the blogosphere. Other credibility assessments in social media, like Weimer et al. (2007)'s assessment of forum posts and Agichtein et al. (2008)'s quality detection in cQA, have the advantage that they already identified measurable indicators and have tested the performance of these indicators, but these "frameworks" are specifically designed for other social media platforms. This results in a large group of indicators that do not necessarily apply to our (blog) setting, like content ratings ("thumbs up"), user ratings, and inclusion of HTML code, signatures, and quotes in posts. The indicators proposed by Rubin and Liddy (2006) are not (yet) instantiated and give us the freedom to find appropriate ways of measuring these indicators.

In this paper, we instantiate Rubin and Liddy (2006)'s indicators in a concrete manner and test their impact on blog post retrieval effectiveness. Specifically, we only consider indicators that are textual in nature, and to ensure reproducibility of our results, we only consider indicators that can be derived from the collection at hand (see Sect. 5) and that do not need additional resources such as bloggers' profiles, that may be hard to obtain for technical or legal reasons. We identify two groups of indicators: (1) blog-level, and (2) post-level indicators. The former group refers to the blog as a whole, that is, to the blogger, and the latter group deals only with characteristics of the post at hand. Blog post retrieval is a precision-oriented task, similar to web search (Manning et al. 2008, Chapter 19). Taking credibility-inspired indicators into account in the retrieval process aims at enhancing precision; there is no obvious reason why these indicators should or could improve recall.

Note that we do not try to explicitly measure the credibility of posts. Although this would be a very interesting and challenging task, we currently have no ways of evaluating the performance on such a task. Rather, we take ideas from the credibility framework and propose a set of credibility-inspired indicators that we put to use on the task of blog post retrieval.

We ask the following research questions:

1. Given the credibility framework developed by Rubin and Liddy (2006), which indicators can we measure from the text of blog posts?

2. Can we incorporate credibility-inspired indicators in the retrieval process, keeping in mind the precision-oriented nature of the task? We try two methods: (i) "Credibility-inspired reranking" based on credibility-inspired scores and (ii) "Combined reranking" based both on credibility-inspired scores and retrieval scores.

3. Can individual credibility-inspired indicators improve precision over a strong baseline?

4. Can we improve performance (further) by combining indicators in blog and post-level groups? And by combining them all?

In our extensive analysis we discuss five issues that were raised during the experiments:

1. What is the performance of our (simple) spam classification system?
2. Given the reranking approaches we take, how do these actually change the rankings of blog posts?
3. Which specific posts are helped or hurt by the credibility-inspired indicators?
4. What is the impact on performance of the number of results we use in reranking?
5. Do we observe differences between topics with regard to the performance of credi-bility-inspired indicators?
6. Which of the credibility-inspired indicators have most influence on retrieval performance and why is this?

Our main findings are that reranking the top results based on credibility-inspired scores is beneficial for precision. Especially indicators on the post level contribute to a great extent to this improvement. We can choose for a more radical reranking approach, leading to high gains and losses, or a smoothed version, leading to more stable results.

In Sect. 2 we discuss related work. We follow in Sect. 3 with the introduction of the credibility framework. We define our credibility-inspired indicators in Sect. 4, and describe the experimental setup for testing their impact on retrieval effectiveness in Sect. 5. We discuss the results of our two methods for incorporating credibility-inspired indicators in Sect. 6 and analyze them in detail in Sect. 7. Finally, we draw conclusions in Sect. 8.

2 RELATED WORK

Related work comes in two kinds. First, we briefly introduce work related to credibility assessment in web settings. Next, we zoom in on social media and credibility. Then, the next section introduces the credibility framework by Rubin and Liddy (2006) that we use as basis for our work.

2.1 Credibility on the web

In a web setting, credibility is often couched in terms of authoritativeness and estimated by exploiting the hyperlink structure. Two well-known examples are the PageRank and HITS algorithms (Liu 2007), that use the link structure in a topic independent or topic dependent way, respectively. The idea behind these algorithms is that more pages linking to a certain document is an indication of this page being more authoritative. In calculating the authoritativeness for a page, the authoritativeness of pages linking to it is taken into account.

The idea of using link structure for improving blog post retrieval has been studied, but results do not show improvements, e.g., Mishne (2007b) finds that retrieval performance decreased, probably because linking in blogs indicates a social relation rather than a vote of authoritativeness. This confirms lessons from the TREC web tracks, where participants found no conclusive benefit from the use of link information for ad hoc retrieval tasks (Hawking and Craswell 2002). And although some work suggests that social links can be useful in quality prediction (Lu et al. 2010), this mostly works in (dense) social networks. The blog data at hand contains too little social linkage to show this.

Mandl (2006) tries to determine the quality of web pages using a machine learning approach and uses this automatic assessment in a web search engine; features are mainly extracted from the HTML code and DOM tree.

2.2 Credibility in social media

Credibility-related work in social media comes in various forms, and is applied to different platforms. Weimer et al. (2007) discuss the automatic assessment of forum post quality; they use surface, lexical, syntactic and forum-specific features to classify forum posts as bad posts or good posts. The use of forum-specific features (such as whether or not the post contains HTML, and the fraction of characters that are inside quotes of other posts), gives the highest benefits to the classification.

Working in the community question/answering domain, Agichtein et al. (2008) use content features, as well non-content information available, such as links between items and explicit quality ratings from members of the community to identify high-quality content. In the same domain, Su et al. (2010) try to detect text trustworthiness by incorporating evidentiality (e.g., "I'm *certain* of this") in their feature set.

To allow for better presentation of online reviews to users, O'Mahony and Smyth (2009) try to determine the helpfulness of reviews. Their features are divided in reputation features, content features, social features, and sentiment features. Follow-up work also includes readability features (O'Mahony and Smyth 2010).

For blogs, most work related to credibility is aimed at trying to identify blogs worth following. Sriphaew et al. (2008) try to identify "cool blogs," i.e., blogs that are worth exploring. Their approach follows a combination of credibility-like features with topic consistency, as used in blog feed search (Macdonald et al. 2008b). Similar work is done by Chen and Ohta (2010), who try to filter blog posts using topic concentration and topic variety. One of our indicators (see Sect. 4) is post length, which was further explored by Hearst and Dumais (2009). They found that there is a correlation between the length of posts in a blog and the popularity of that blog. Mishne and de Rijke (2006)'s observation that bloggers often report on news events is the basis for the credibility assessment in Juffinger et al. (2009). The authors compare blog posts to news articles about the same topic, and assign a credibility level based on the similarity between the two. We use a similar technique, but acknowledge that not all blog posts are about news events, hence the need for other indicators. Spam identification may be part of estimating credibility, not only for blogs (or blog posts), but also for other (web) documents. Spam identification has been successfully applied in the blogosphere to improve retrieval effectiveness, for example by Java et al. (2007) and Mishne (2007a).

Recently, credibility-inspired indicators have been successfully applied to post finding in a specific type of blog environment: microblogs (Massoudi et al. 2011). Besides translating indicators to the new environment, the authors also introduced platform-specific indicators like followers, retweets, and recency. For the task of exploring trending topics on Twitter, Castillo et al. (2011) use a similar set of indicators to assess credibility of tweets, and use human assessments to test their approach.

Research into credibility of content is not restricted to textual content. Tsagkias et al. (2010) try to establish the credibility of a particular type of audio: podcasts. They show that, besides podcast-wide metadata (e.g., podcast logo, description length), episode data also plays an important role in determining credibility. We use a similar notion by combining blog level and post level indicators in our work. Finally, Diakopoulos and Essa (2010) explore credibility in video, mainly through the use of smart interfaces and knowledge sharing.

3 CREDIBILITY FRAMEWORK

In our choice of credibility indicators we use Rubin and Liddy (2006)'s work as a reference point. We recall the main points of their framework and relate our indicators to it. Rubin and Liddy (2006) proposed a four factor analytical framework for blog readers' credibility assessment of blog sites, based in part on evidentiality theory (Chafe 1986), website credibility assessment surveys (Stanford et al. 2002), and Van House (2004)'s observations on blog credibility. The four factors—plus indicators for each of them—are listed below.

1. Blogger's expertise and offline identity disclosure:
    a. name and geographic location
    b. credentials
    c. affiliations
    d. hyperlinks to others
    e. stated competencies
    f. mode of knowing

2. Blogger's trustworthiness and value system:
    a. Biases
    b. Beliefs
    c. Opinions
    d. Honesty
    e. Preferences
    f. Habits
    g. Slogans

3. Information quality:
    a. Completeness
    b. Accuracy
    c. Appropriateness
    d. Timeliness
    e. organization (by categories or chronology
    f. match to prior expectations
    g. match to information need

4. Appeals and triggers of a personal nature:
    a. aesthetic appeal
    b. literary appeal (i.e., writing style)
    c. curiosity trigger
    d. memory trigger
    e. personal connection

In our decision which indicators to include in our experiments, we followed the following steps. For each, we indicate which of the credibility indicators from Rubin and Liddy (2006)'s framework are excluded.

A. We do not use credibility indicators that make use of the searcher's or blogger's identity (excluding 1a, 1c, 1e, 2e);

B. We include indicators that can be estimated automatically from available test collections only so as to facilitate repeatability of our experiments (excluding 3e, 4a, 4c, 4d, 4e);

C. We only select indicators that can be reliably estimated with state-of-the-art language technology (excluding 2b, 2c, 2d, 2g).

D. Finally, given the findings by Mishne (2007b), we ignore the "hyperlinks to others" indicator (1d).

Of the 11 indicators that we do consider—1b, 1f, 2a, 2f, 3a, 3b, 3c, 3d, 3f, 3g, 4b—one is part of the baseline retrieval system (3f), and does not require an indicator. The others are organized in two groups, depending on the information source that we use to estimate them: *post level* and *blog(ger) level*. The former depends solely on information contained in an individual blog post, and ignores the blog it belongs to. The latter aggregates or averages information from posts to the blog level; these indicator values are therefore equal for all posts in the same blog.

In the next section we explore the 10 selected indicators from Rubin and Liddy (2006)'s credibility framework and introduce ways of estimating these indicators so that they can be applied to the task at hand: blog post retrieval.

4 CREDIBILITY-INSPIRED INDICATORS

In this section we introduce our credibility-inspired indicators, explain how they are related to the work by Rubin and Liddy (2006) that was described in the previous section, and offer ways of estimating the indicators. Table 1 summarizes this section, and lists our credibility-inspired indicators and their originating counterpart.

Table 1. Our credibility-inspired indicators and their origins in Rubin and Liddy (2006)

Blog-level indicator	Rubin and Liddy (2006)	Post-level indicator	Rubin and Liddy (2006)
Comments	Credentials	Post length	Completeness
Expertise	Mode of knowing	Semantics	Accuracy/appropriateness
Regularity	Habits	Timeliness	Timeliness
Consistency	Habits	Capitalization	Literary appeal
Spamminess	Information quality	Emoticons	Literary appeal
Pronouns	Biases	Shouting	Literary appeal
		Spelling	Literary appeal
		Punctuation	Literary appeal

Next, we specify how each of the credibility-inspired indicators is estimated, and briefly discuss why and how these indicators address the issue of credibility. We start with the eight post-level indicators (Sect. 4.1) and conclude with the six blog-level indicators (Sect. 4.2).

4.1 Post-level indicators

As mentioned previously, post-level indicators make use of information contained within individual posts. We go through the indicators capitalization, emoticons, shouting, spelling, punctuation, post length, timeliness, and semantics.

4.1.1 Capitalization

We estimate the capitalization score as follows:

$$S_{capitalization}(post) = \frac{n(caps, s_{post})}{|s_{post}|}, \qquad (1)$$

where $n(caps, s_{post})$ is the number of sentences in post *post*starting with a capital and $|s_{post}|$ is the number of sentences in the post; we only consider sentences with five or more words. We consider the use of capitalization to be an indicator of good writing style, which in turn contributes to a sense of credibility.

4.1.2 Emoticons

The emoticons score is estimated as

$$S_{emoticons}(post) = 1 - \left(\frac{n(emo, post)}{|post|}\right), \tag{2}$$

where *n*(*emo, post*) is the number of emoticons in the post and |*post*| is the length of the post in words. We identify Western style emoticons (e.g., :-) and :-D) in blog posts, and assume that excessive use indicates a less credible blog post.

4.1.3 Shouting

We use the following equation to estimate the shouting score:

$$S_{shouting}(post) = 1 - \left(\frac{n(shout, post)}{|post|}\right), \tag{3}$$

where *n*(*shout, post*) is the number of all caps words in blog post *post* and |*post*| is the post length in words. Words written in all caps are considered shouting in a web environment; we consider shouting to be indicative for non-credible posts. Note that nowadays the use of repeated characters could also be considered shouting, but that we did not try to detect this notion of shouting.

4.1.4 Spelling

The spelling score is estimated as

$$S_{spelling}(post) = 1 - \left(\frac{n(error, post)}{|post|}\right), \tag{4}$$

where *n*(*error, post*) is the number of misspelled or unknown words (with more than 4 characters) in post *post* and |*post*| is the post length in words. A credible author should be able to write without (a lot of) spelling errors; the more spelling errors occur in a blog post, the less credible we consider it to be.

4.1.5 Punctuation

The punctuation score is calculated as follows:

$$S_{punctuation}(post) = 1 - \left(\frac{n(punc, post)}{|post|}\right), \tag{5}$$

where $n(punc, post)$ is the number of repetitive occurrences of dots, question marks, or exclamation marks (e.g., "look at this!!!", "wel...", or "can you believe it??") and $|post|$ is the post length in words. If n(punc,post)·|post|−1 is larger than 1, we set $S_{punctuation}(post) = 0$. We assume that excessive use of repeated punctuation marks is an indication of non-credible posts.

4.1.6 Post length

The post length score is estimated using $|post|$, the post length in words:

$$S_{length}(post) = \log(|post|). \tag{6}$$

We assume that credible texts have a reasonable length; the text should supply enough information to convince the reader of the author's credibility, and it is an indication of "completeness."

4.1.7 Timeliness

Assuming that much of what goes on in the blogosphere is inspired by events in the news (Mishne and de Rijke 2006), we believe that, for news related topics, a blog post is more credible if it is published around the time of the triggering news event: it is timely. Bloggers that take (much) longer to respond to news events are considered less timely. To estimate timeliness, we first identify peaks for a topic in a collection of news articles, by summing over the retrieval scores for each date in the the top 500 results, and taking dates with a value higher than twice the standard deviation to be "peak dates". Two example topics and their peaks are given in Figure 3.

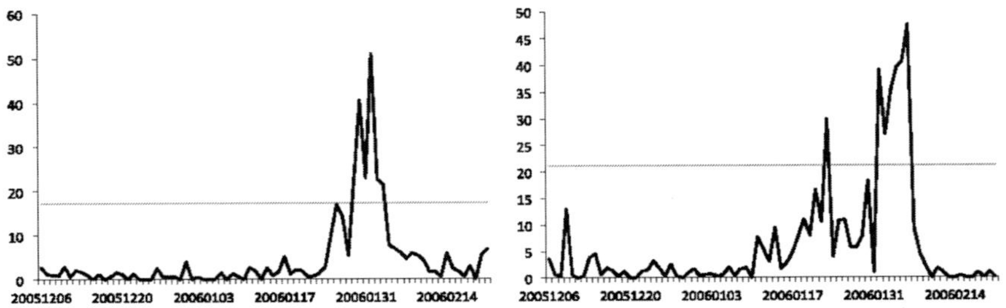

Figure 3. Peaks in news articles for (*Left*) topic 853, *State of the Union*, which was held on January 31, 2006. (*Right*) topic 882, *Seahawks*, an American football team that won the NFC on January 22, 2006, and played the Super Bowl on February 5, 2006

Having identified peaks for certain topics, we take the timeliness to be the difference in days between the peak date and the day of the post. More formally:

$$S_{timeliness}(post, Q) = \begin{cases} e^{-(|\tau_{post} - \tau_{peak_Q}|)} & \text{if } \tau_{post} - \tau_{peak_Q} > -2 \\ 0 & \text{otherwise.} \end{cases} \quad (7)$$

Here, τpeakQτpeakQ is the date of the peak (in case the peak spans several days, it is the date closest to the post date), and τ_{post} is the post date. The difference between the dates is calculated in days.

4.1.8 Semantics

For news-related topics, we are looking for posts that "mimic" the semantics of credible sources, like actual news articles. For this, we use a query expansion approach, based on previous work (Diaz and Metzler 2006; Weerkamp et al. 2009). We query the same news collection as before for the topics, and select the top 10 retrieved articles. From these articles we select the 10 most important terms, using Lavrenko and Croft (2001)'s relevance model 2. The selected terms, $\theta_{semantic,Q}$, represent credible semantics for the given topic, and we use these terms as query to score blog posts on the semantics indicator. Table 2 shows the extracted credible terms for three example topics.

Table 2. Terms indicating credible semantics for three topics: *Macbook Pro* deals with laptops by Apple; *Cheney hunting* discusses a hunting accident involving vice-president Cheney and his friend Whittington; *David Irving* is an Austrian historian on trial for denying the Holocaust

Topic 856: *Macbook Pro*	Topic 867: *Cheney hunting*	Topic 1042: *David Irving*
Macbook	Cheney	Irving
Intel	Whittington	David
Apple	President	Holocaust
Computer	Accidentally	Court
Start	Hunting	British
Pro	Shot	Austian
Chip	Attack	Monday
Shipping	Heart	Urgent
Notebook	Doctors	Historian
Laptop	Minor	Prison

4.1.9 Text quality

To limit the number of experiments to run, we combine the following indicators into one *text quality* indicator: spelling, emoticons, capitalization, shouting, and punctuation. To combine these indicators, we first normalize each individual indicator using min-max normalization (Lee 1995). Then, we take the average value over all these indicators to be the text quality indicator.

4.2 **Blog-level indicators**

Blog-level indicators say something about the blog as a whole, or about the blogger who wrote the posts. Most indicators aggregate information from individual posts to the blog level, and they all lead to posts from the same blog having equal scores. Here, we go through the indicators spamminess, comments, regularity, consistency, pronouns, and expertise.

4.2.1 Spamminess

To estimate the spamminess of a blog, we take a simple approach. First, we observe that blogs are either completely spam ("splogs") or not (i.e., there are no blogs with half of the posts spam and half of them non-spam), and this is why we consider this indicator on the blog level. We train an SVM classifier on a labeled splog blog dataset (Kolari et al. 2006) using the top 1,500 words for both spam and non-spam blogs as features. We then apply the trained classifier to our set of blog posts, and assign a spam or no-spam label to each post. We calculate the ratio of spam posts in each blog, and use this ratio as indication of spamminess for the full blog.

$$S_{spam}(post) = \frac{n(post_{spam}, blog)}{|blog|}, \tag{8}$$

where $n(post_{spam}, blog)$ is the number of spam posts in the blog, and $|blog|$ is the size of the blog in number of posts. Splogs are not considered credible and we want to demote them in or filter them from the search results. Although the list of splogs for our test collection (see Sect. 5.1) is available, we do not use it in any way in this paper, ensuring our results are still comparable to previously published results. Future work could look at the performance of our spam classification.

4.2.2 Comments

We estimate the comment score as

$$S_{comment}(post) = \log\left(\frac{\sum_{post \in blog} n(comment, post)}{|blog|} + 1\right), \tag{9}$$

where $n(comment, post)$ is the number of comments on post *post*, and $|blog|$ is the size of the blog in number of posts. Comments are a notable blog feature: readers of a blog post often have the possibility of leaving a comment for other readers or the author. When people comment on a blog post they apparently find the post worth putting effort in, which can be seen as an indicator of credibility (Mishne and Glance 2006).

4.2.3 Regularity

To estimate the regularity score we use

$$S_{regularity}(post) = \log(\sigma_{interval,blog}), \tag{10}$$

where $\sigma_{interval,blog}$ expresses the standard deviation of the temporal intervals between two successive posts in a blog. Blogs consist of multiple posts in (reverse) chronological order. The temporal aspect of blogs may indicate credibility: we assume that bloggers with an irregular posting behavior are less credible than bloggers who post regularly.

4.2.4 Topical consistency

We take into consideration the topical fluctuation of a blogger's posts. When looking for credible information we would like to retrieve posts from bloggers that have a certain level of (topical) consistency: not the fluctuating behavior of a (personal) blogger, but a solid interest. The coherence score indicator (He et al.2009) is a relatively cheap, topic-independent way of estimating this. Given a set of blog posts from a blog, $blog = \{post_i\}_{i=1}^{M}$, which is drawn from a background collection C, i.e., $blog \subseteq C$ (i.e., the blogosphere), the coherence score is defined as the proportion of "coherent" pairs of blog posts with respect to the total number of post pairs within *blog*. The criterion of being a "coherent" pair is that the similarity between the two posts in the pair should meet or exceed a given threshold. Formally, the coherence (Co) of a blog *blog* is defined as

$$Co(blog) = \frac{\sum_{i \neq j \in \{1,\ldots,M\}} \delta(post_i, post_j)}{\frac{1}{2}M(M-1)}, \tag{11}$$

where $\delta(post_i, post_j)$ is 1 if posts are similar and 0 otherwise. We use cosine similarity to determine the similarity between two blog posts. More details on the coherence score can be found in (He et al. 2008, He et al. 2009).

4.2.5 Pronouns

We estimate the pronouns score as follows

$$S_{pronouns}(post) = 1 - \left(\frac{\sum_{post \in blog} \frac{n(pron,post)}{|post|}}{|blog|} \right), \tag{12}$$

where $n(pron, post)$ is the number of first person pronouns (I, me, mine, we, us, ...) in post *post*, $|post|$ is the size of the post in words, and $|blog|$ is the size of the blog in number of posts. First person pronouns express a bias towards ones own interpretation, and we feel this could harm the credibility of a blog (post). Note that we use simple string matching for this indicator and that this might lead to an overestimation for some pronouns (e.g., "mine" can be used as noun and verb as well). We believe, however, that this is only a marginal issue and should not influence the results of this indicator.

4.2.6 Expertise

To estimate a blogger's expertise for a given topic, we use the approach described in Weerkamp et al. (2011). We look at the posts written by a blogger, and try to estimate to what extent the given topic is central to the blog. Blogs that are most likely to be relevant to this query are retrieved, and we assign posts in those blogs a higher score on the expertise indicator. As an example, consider topic 856, *macbook pro*: the top retrieved blogs are (1) *MacBook Garage*, (2) *Enterprise Mac*, and (3) *tech ronin*. The first two are very Apple/Mac oriented, and the third result is more general technology-oriented, but with an interest in Macs. We consider posts from these blogs, blogs with a *recurring interest* in the topic, to be more credible than posts from blogs mentioning the topic only occasionally.

$$S_{expertise}(post, Q) = P(blog|Q), \tag{13}$$

where $P(blog|Q)$ is the retrieval score for blog *blog* on query Q as given by the Blogger model from Weerkamp et al. (2011).

On top of the individual credibility indicators, we report on the performance of combinations of indicators. We combine indicators into our two levels (post and blog level) and into a full combination, using these steps: (1) normalize indicator scores using min-max normalization (Lee 1995) and (2) average over the indicators belonging to the combination at hand (post level, blog level, or all).

We already introduced the difference between post-level and blog-level indicators, but there is one more dimension on which we can seperate indicators: whether or not the indicator depends on the topic. Most of the indicators get their score independent of the topic (e.g., spelling errors, capitalization), however, three indicators do depend on the topic: semantics, timeliness, and expertise. To summarize this section, Table 3 shows all our indicators and their characteristics.

Table 3. Our credibility-inspired indicators and their characteristics

	Topic independent	Topic dependent
Post level	Post length	
	Spelling	
	Shouting	Semantics
	Emoticons	Timeliness
	Capitalization	
	Punctuation	
Blog level	Regularity	
	Comments	
	Coherence	Expertise
	Spamminess	
	Pronouns	

5 EXPERIMENTAL SETUP

This section describes the task and collection we use to test our credibility-inspired indicators (Sect. 5.1), the general retrieval framework (Sect. 5.2), and the evaluation metrics (Sect. 5.3).

5.1 Task and collection

We apply our credibility-inspired indicators to the task of retrieving topically relevant blog posts. This task ran at the Text REtrieval Conference (TREC), as part of the blog track, in 2006–2008 (Macdonald et al. 2008a; Ounis et al. 2006, 2009). Given a set of blog posts and a query, we are asked to return relevant blog posts for that query. We apply our model and indicators to the TREC Blog06 corpus (Macdonald and Ounis 2006). This corpus has been constructed by monitoring around 100,000 blog feeds for a period of

11 weeks in early 2006, downloading all posts created in this period. For each permalink (HTML page containing one blog post) the feed id is registered. We can use this id to aggregate post level features to the blog level. In our experiments we use only the HTML documents, and ignore syndicated (RSS) data. We perform two preprocessing steps: (1) keep long sentences (Hofmann and Weerkamp 2008), and (2) apply language identification using TextCat,1 to select English posts. The collection statistics are displayed in Table 4.

Table 4. Collection statistics before and after preprocessing

Period	12/06/2005–02/21/2006
Original data	
Number of blog posts	3,215,171
Number of blogs	100,649
- of which splogs	17,969
After preprocessing	
Number of blog posts	2,574,356
Number of blogs	76,358
Average post length	506

The TREC 2006, 2007, and 2008 Blog tracks each offer 50 topics and assessments, offering us 150 topics in total. For topical relevancy, assessment was done using a standard two-level scale: the content of the post was judged to be topically relevant or not. For all our retrieval tasks we only use the title field (T) of the topic statement as query; this boils down to the use of keyword queries. Table 5 lists several statistics of the queries in our test collection. We see that for 2006 more posts were assessed than for 2007 and 2008, which leads to more relevant posts per query. As to the number of terms per query, we see that 2008 queries are, on average, quite a bit longer than the 2006 and 2007 queries.

Table 5. Query statistics for 2006, 2007, and 2008

	2006	2007	2008
Queries	50	50	50
Assessed posts	67,382	54,621	53,815
Relevant posts	19,891	12,187	11,735
Rel. posts/query	397	244	235
Query terms	99	85	128
Terms/query	2.0	1.7	2.6

To estimate the semantics and timeliness credibility indicators, we need a collection of news papers. Here, we use AQUAINT-2, a set of about 907,000 newswire articles (AQUAINT-2. Guidelines 2007) from six different news sources. Of these articles, 135,763 are contemporaneous with the TREC Blog06 collection, and we use only this subset in our experiments. All news articles are written in English.

5.2 Retrieval framework

Our retrieval framework uses a language modeling for IR approach (Croft and Lafferty 2003), where we estimate the probability of a document generating the query. We select this framework because it is theoretically sound and has shown good and robust performance on a broad range of retrieval tasks. We use the implementation as provided by Indri.2

5.3 Evaluation and significance

As explained before, we consider blog post retrieval to be a precision-oriented task, and focus mainly on precision metrics. The evaluation metrics on which we focus are standard precision-oriented IR metrics: mean reciprocal rank (MRR), and precision at ranks 5 and 10 (P5 and P10) (Baeza-Yates and Ribeiro-Neto 2010). For the sake of completeness we also report on the commonly used mean average precision (MAP) metric. In each table the best performing run per metric is bold-faced.

We test for statistical significant differences using a two-tailed paired t-test. Significant improvements over the baseline are marked with △(α=0.05)△ or ▲ ($\alpha = 0.01$), and we use ▽ and ▼ for a drop in performance (for $\alpha = 0.05$ and $\alpha = 0.01$, respectively).

6 RESULTS

We present our results in three sections. First, we show the performance of our baseline, see how it compares to previous approaches at TREC, and we show what the influence of spam filtering is (Sect. 6.1). We continue by applying our credibility-inspired indicators on top of our (spam filtered) baseline. Since we aim at improving precision using credibility, we mainly aim at reranking originally retrieved results, assuming that the baseline has a sufficiently strong recall. We start by reranking the top *n* of the initial run based solely on the credibility-inspired scores (Credibility-inspired reranking) in Sect. 6.2. We then take a step back, and combine retrieval scores and credibility-inspired scores in our Combined reranking approach in Sect. 6.3, and explore reranking the top *n* results using this combined score.

Both our reranking approaches are applied on the top *n* of the baseline ranking after spam filtering. We need to decide on a value for *n* to use, and to make results from the two approaches comparable, we choose the same *n* for both of them. For the result section we take $n = 20$, as this value allows measuring changes in early precision (at ranks 5 and 10), without ignoring the initial ranking too much. In Sect. 7.3 we come back to this issue, and explore the influence of *n* on the performance of our approaches.

6.1 Baseline and spam filtering

We start by establishing our baseline: Table 6 shows the results on the three topic sets. Note that the baseline is strong: Its performance is better than or close to the best performing runs at TREC for all 3 years (our runs would have been at rank 1/15, 4/20, and 8/20). This is impressive knowing that the participating systems incorporate additional techniques like (external) query expansion, especially in 2007 and 2008.

Table 6. Preliminary baseline scores for all three topic sets and their combination (150 topics)

Year	MRR	P5	P10	MAP
2006	0.7339	0.6880	0.6720	0.3365
2007	0.8200	0.7200	0.7240	0.4514
2008	0.7629	0.6760	0.6920	0.3800
All	0.7722	0.6947	0.6960	0.3893

We detailed our spam classification approach in Sect. 4.2, where we assigned a score to each blog based on the ratio of spam posts in that blog. To turn this score into a filter, we need a threshold for this ratio: every blog that has a higher ratio than this threshold is considered a splog and is removed from the results. Given the orientation towards precision we consider blogs that have >25% of their posts classified as spam posts to be splogs. This threshold leads to the removal of 6,412 splogs (198,065 posts).

Table 7 shows the results after filtering out spam. Results show similar performance on the precision metrics and a slight, though significant, drop in terms of MAP. We revisit the results of our spam classifier in Sect. 7.1.

Table 7. Results before and after filtering spam. Significance tested against the baseline

Run	MRR	P5	P10	MAP
Baseline	0.7722	0.6947	0.6960	0.3893
Spam-filtered baseline	**0.7894**	**0.7107**	**0.7087**	0.3774$^{\triangledown}$

In the remainder of the paper we have two notions of a "baseline." First, when it comes to comparing performance of our approaches, we do so against the baseline (row one in Table 7). Second, the ranking that is produced after filtering splogs (spam-filtered baseline; row two in Table 7) serves as the starting on top of which we apply our two reranking approaches: Credibility-inspired reranking and Combined reranking; put differently, in our discussions below reranking always includes spam filtering.

6.2 Credibility-inspired reranking

The first method of reranking we explore is Credibility-inspired reranking. As the name indicates, this approach takes only the credibility-inspired scores into account when reranking the top 20 results of our baseline ranking. That is, we take the ranking produced after filtering spam, ignore retrieval scores for the top 20 results, and assign to each of the top 20 posts the score as assigned by each credibility-inspired indicator (viz. Sect. 4), and construct the new ranking based on these scores. The posts ranked lower than position 20 keep their original retrieval score/ranking.

We present the results of Credibility-inspired reranking in Table 8. The results are divided into four groups: (1) the baseline and the manual upper bound (which reranks the posts based on their relevance assessments), (2) the individual post-level indicators, (3) the individual blog-level indicators, and (iv) the combined indicators on post level, blog level, and both. We first focus on the individual indicators.

Table 8. Results for Credibility-inspired reranking on the top 20 results based on each of the credibility-inspired indicator scores for all 150 topics. Significance tested against the baseline

Run	MRR	P5	P10	MAP
Baseline	0.7722	0.6947	0.6960	**0.3893**
Upperbound	0.9806	0.9507	0.8787	0.3976
Post-level indicators				
Quality	0.8200	0.7040	0.6980	0.3749$^{\blacktriangledown}$
Document length	0.7702	0.6907	0.6840	0.3731$^{\blacktriangledown}$
Timeliness	0.8138$^{\vartriangle}$	0.7213	0.7127	0.3782$^{\triangledown}$
Semantics	0.8144	0.7200	0.7167	0.3751$^{\blacktriangledown}$
Blog-level indicators				
Comments	0.8252$^{\vartriangle}$	0.7187	0.7120	0.3743$^{\blacktriangledown}$
Pronouns	0.7270	0.6173$^{\blacktriangledown}$	0.6620$^{\triangledown}$	0.3716$^{\blacktriangledown}$
Coherence	0.7648	0.6720	0.6707	0.3730$^{\blacktriangledown}$
Regularity	0.7080$^{\triangledown}$	0.6493$^{\triangledown}$	0.6640$^{\triangledown}$	0.3705$^{\blacktriangledown}$
Expertise	0.7595	0.6653	0.6793	0.3766$^{\triangledown}$
Combinations				
Post level	**0.8289**	**0.7347**	**0.7193**	0.3748$^{\blacktriangledown}$
Blog level	0.7659	0.6560	0.6673$^{\triangledown}$	0.3741$^{\blacktriangledown}$
All	0.8163	0.7067	0.6920	0.3755$^{\triangledown}$

The individual indicators show a wide range in performance. All indicators show a drop in MAP compared to the baseline, but this was expected. We focus on the precision metrics and here we observe that almost all post-level indicators seem to improve over the baseline, although only the improvement on MRR by timeliness is significant. Looking at the blog-level indicators, we find that only the comments indicator improves over the baseline, with MRR showing a significant increase. The other blog-level indicators perform worse than or similar to the baseline. The highest scores on the precision metrics, when looking at the individual indicators, are achieved by three different indicators: comments on MRR, timeliness on P5, and semantics on P10.

Next, we shift our attention to combinations of indicators (the bottom part of Table 8). From these results we observe two things. First, the combined blog-level indicators do not improve over the baseline run on any metric, which is disappointing, but expected given the scores of individual indicators on this level. Second, the combined post-level indicators have the highest scores on the precision metrics, but improvements are not significant.

As an aside, given the strong performance of the comments indicator, it is natural to wonder what would happen if this blog level indicator were included with the post level indicators. That is, we take all post-level indicators and combine these with the comments indicator only. Using this combination we achieve the following scores: MRR 0.8280; P5 0.7280; P10 0.7167; and MAP 0.3744. Here, we find that performance on all metrics is still slightly below post-level indicators only.

Summarizing, we see that the Credibility-inspired reranking approach works well for post-level indicators, although it is hard to obtain significant improvements. The blog- level indicators, with the exception of comments, perform rather disappointing. Given the fact that we completely ignore the retrieval score once we start the reranking process, the results obtained by post-level indicators are quite remarkable and show the possibilities of taking ideas from the credibility framework on board as precision enhancement.

6.3 Combined reranking

Completely ignoring the initial retrieval score sounds like a "bad" idea: there is a reason why certain posts get assigned a higher retrieval score than others and we probably should be using these differences in scores. In this section we take another approach to incorporating ideas from the credibility framework in ranking blog posts: we combine the original retrieval score and the credibility-inspired score of posts to rerank the baseline ranking. We, again, look only at the top 20 results of the original ranking and multiply the retrieval score of each document by the (normalized) score on each credibility-inspired indicator. We present the results similar to the previous section: (1) the baseline and upperbound, (2) the individual post-level indicators, (3) the individual blog-level indicators, and (4) the combinations of indicators. The results are listed in Table 9.

Table 9. Results for Combined reranking using a combination of retrieval and credibility scores, and reranking the top 20 results based on this score for all 150 topics. Significance tested against the baseline

Run	MRR	P5	P10	MAP
Baseline	0.7722	0.6947	0.6960	**0.3893**
Upperbound	0.9806	0.9507	0.8787	0.3976
Post-level indicators				
Quality	0.7986$^{\vartriangle}$	0.7120	0.7020	0.3768$^{\triangledown}$
Document length	0.8009	0.7107	0.7013	0.3768$^{\triangledown}$
Timeliness	0.8151$^{\vartriangle}$	0.7253$^{\vartriangle}$	**0.7147**	0.3781$^{\triangledown}$
Semantics	0.8210$^{\vartriangle}$	**0.7347**$^{\vartriangle}$	0.7173	0.3779$^{\triangledown}$
Blog-level indicators				
Comments	**0.8311**$^{\vartriangle}$	0.7200	0.7093	0.3754$^{\triangledown}$
Pronouns	0.7796	0.7093	0.7027	0.3772$^{\triangledown}$
Coherence	0.7531	0.6760	0.6707$^{\triangledown}$	0.3757$^{\triangledown}$
Regularity	0.7624	0.6787	0.6787	0.3743$^{\blacktriangledown}$
Expertise	0.7608	0.6827	0.6827	0.3782$^{\triangledown}$
Combinations				
Post level	0.8098$^{\vartriangle}$	0.7227$^{\vartriangle}$	0.7113	0.3771$^{\triangledown}$
Blog level	0.7622	0.6827	0.6747	0.3766$^{\triangledown}$
All	0.7895	0.7160	0.7027	0.3769$^{\triangledown}$

Results show that most post-level indicators are able to improve over the baseline on precision metrics. Especially scores on MRR improve significantly and both the timeliness and semantics indicators show large improvements on MRR and P5 compared to the baseline. Compared to the Credibility-inspired reranking approach in the previous section, we observe better performance on the precision at 5 and 10 metrics, as well as more significant (stable) improvements. Looking at the individual blog-level indicators we see a similar pattern as before: the comments indicator works well on MRR, but coherence, regularity, and expertise cannot improve over the baseline on any metric. An interesting difference with the previous approach is that both the pronouns and regularity indicators, which dropped significantly in performance compared to the baseline in Sect. 6.2 are now comparable to the baseline.

When combining the credibility-inspired indicators on our two levels we notice that scores for the post-level combination are, in absolute sense, slightly below the results of Credibility-inspired reranking, but they do show significant improvements over the baseline on precision metrics, indicating a more stable improvement.

Given the below-baseline performance of some of the blog-level indicators, we experiment by excluding them from the final (all) combination. Table 10 shows the results of using only comments and using both comments and pronouns in this final combination. Results here show that we can indeed improve over the combined post-level indicators when adding comments and pronouns to the combination. The final two runs show a (strong) significant improvement over the baseline on MRR and precision at 5.

Table 10. Results for combining post-level indicators and one or two blog-level indicators. Significance tested against the baseline

Run	MRR	P5	P10	MAP
Baseline	0.7722	0.6947	0.6960	**0.3893**
Post level	$0.8098^{\triangle}$	$0.7227^{\triangle}$	**0.7113**	$0.3771^{\triangledown}$
Post level + comments	$0.8107^{\blacktriangle}$	$\mathbf{0.7253}^{\triangle}$	0.7100	$0.3770^{\triangledown}$
Post level + comments + pronouns	$\mathbf{0.8113}^{\blacktriangle}$	$0.7240^{\triangle}$	0.7107	$0.3770^{\triangledown}$

Summarizing, we find that Combined reranking resembles a "smoothed" version of Credibility-inspired reranking: It takes away the outliers, leading to slightly lower absolute scores than for Credibility-inspired reranking, but the improvements over the baseline are more often significant. Again, post-level indicators are the better performing ones, although this time we find that combining these with two blog-level indicators (comments and pronouns) leads to even better performance. Combined reranking is a powerful way of incorporating ideas from the credibility framework, resulting in stable improvements.

In the analysis section (Sect. 7), we often look at the two best performing runs from both approaches. For Credibility-inspired reranking this is the post-level combination run, and for Combined reranking it is the post-level + comments + pronouns run.

7 ANALYSIS AND DISCUSSION

We presented the overall results of our two credibility-inspired reranking approaches in the previous section. These results, however, hide a lot of detail, which could be important to understanding what exactly is happening. In this section we perform extensive analyses on our results from four perspectives. First, in Sect. 7.1, we look at the performance of our spam classifier. In Sect. 7.2 we acknowledge the fact that we are looking at reranking strategies and give more details on how our approaches really affect ranking by looking at swaps, the positions of relevant posts, and specific (relevant) posts that move significantly up or down the ranking. Sect. 7.3 deals with per-topic analyses of our indicators and reranking approaches and compares various runs on a per-topic basis and explores which specific topics show improvement or drops in performance. We discuss the setting of n, the number of results we rerank, in Sect. 7.4, and finally, we explore the interplay between credibility-inspired ranking and relevance in Sect. 7.5.

7.1 Spam classification

The official collection was purposefully injected with spam by gathering blog posts from known splogs. In total, 17,958 splogs were followed during the 11 week period of crawling. As mentioned before, we use a relatively simple approach to splog detection based on a rather small training set and a limited set of features (unigrams). From the 6,412 blogs classified as splogs, 4,148 are really splogs (precision 65%). The recall for our classifier is rather low, with 4,148 out of 17,958 splogs identified (recall 23%).

7.2 Changes in ranking

Our two approaches for incorporating credibility-inspired indicators are based on reranking an initial ranking of posts. Besides looking at scores produced by each of the (re)rankings, we can also look at the rankings themselves and explore how they differ between runs. First, we look at the number of swaps in the top 20 after reranking. The higher this number, the more changes in positions between the baseline and the reranked result lists. We compare the various indicators and also the two reranking approaches, in Table 11. Note that for most analyses in this section the numbers for the timeliness indicators might seem out of the ordinary, but this is because this indicator only affects 50 of the 150 topics, which influences the averages quite a bit.

Table 11. Average number of swaps (changes in ranking) per topic between each run and the (spam-filtered) baseline

	Swaps	
Indicator	Reranking	Combining
Quality	19.0	15.1
Document length	18.9	15.6
Timeliness	6.2	6.1
Semantics	17.2	16.5
Comments	19.0	18.4
Pronouns	19.0	7.2
Coherence	19.0	18.2
Regularity	19.0	17.7
Expertise	18.7	17.9
Post level	18.8	14.9
Blog level	18.7	16.5
All	18.8	14.8

We observe that in the Credibility-inspired reranking approach more swaps are generated than in the Combined reranking approach, although in some cases (e.g., timeliness) the difference is only marginal. The reason for the difference between the two approaches is that in the Combined reranking approach the initial retrieval score acts as a kind of "smoothing," making the changes less radical. In general we see that most of the results in the top 20 get a different position after applying our reranking techniques.

To examine how successful the swaps are, we combine the swaps with relevance information; Tables 12 (Credibility-inspired reranking) and 13 (Combined reranking) show the average number of *relevant* posts per topic that go up or down in the ranking after reranking has been applied and the average number of positions each of these posts gains or loses. We should note that relevant posts going down in the ranking is not necessarily a problem, as long as the posts crossing them are relevant too.

Table 12. Credibility-inspired reranking: average number of *relevant* posts per topic that go up or down the ranking after reranking, and the average number of positions these posts go up or down. Also: the ratio of rising vs. dropping relevant posts per indicator

Indicator	Up		Down		Ratio up/down
	Posts	Positions	Posts	Positions	
Quality	6.43	7.03	6.63	6.75	0.97
Document length	6.24	6.31	6.71	6.26	0.93
Timeliness	1.91	2.47	2.48	1.84	0.77
Semantics	6.19	5.36	5.63	5.68	1.10
Comments	6.55	6.61	6.51	6.43	1.01
Pronouns	6.18	6.33	6.89	6.75	0.90
Coherence	6.23	6.43	6.84	6.63	0.91
Regularity	6.41	6.53	6.69	6.96	0.96
Expertise	6.09	6.09	6.79	6.38	0.90
Post level	6.65	6.56	6.29	6.45	1.06
Blog level	6.06	6.04	6.81	6.41	0.89
All	6.37	6.33	6.55	6.56	0.97

Table 13. Combined reranking: average number of *relevant* posts per topic that go up or down the ranking after reranking, and the average number of positions these posts go up or down. Also: the ratio of rising vs. dropping relevant posts per indicator

Indicator	Up		Down		Ratio up/down
	Posts	Positions	Posts	Positions	
Quality	7.02	2.38	3.37	5.11	2.08
Document length	5.40	2.91	5.32	3.17	1.02
Timeliness	2.13	2.21	2.24	1.88	0.95
Semantics	5.75	4.41	5.46	4.29	1.05
Comments	6.68	5.65	5.95	6.08	1.12
Pronouns	2.39	1.12	2.45	1.31	0.98
Coherence	6.39	5.25	6.13	6.13	1.11
Regularity	6.35	4.25	5.78	5.18	1.10
Expertise	5.89	5.18	6.41	5.31	0.92
Post level	6.37	2.54	3.96	3.85	1.61
Blog level	5.56	3.50	5.82	4.09	0.96
All	5.63	2.54	4.67	3.47	1.21

Comparing the two approaches on these numbers, we observe that all the numbers (except the ratios) are higher for Credibility-inspired reranking than for Combined reranking: more relevant posts go up, more relevant posts go down and for both the average number of positions is higher. The only numbers that are consistently higher for Combined reranking are the ratios of number of relevant posts going up vs. relevant posts going down. Here, we see that for most indicators this ratio is above 1 for Combined reranking, whereas it is above 1 for only two indicators for Credibility-inspired reranking.

Looking at the individual indicators for Combined reranking, we notice some interesting differences. The quality indicator has by far the highest ratio of relevant posts up vs. down, but the average number of positions is almost the lowest over all indicators. The comments indicator on the other hand has a mediocre up vs. down ratio, but the average number of positions relevant posts move (either up or down) is much higher than most other indicators.

7.2.1 Per-post analysis

Next, we drill down to the level of individual posts and look at example posts that show "interesting" behavior. First we look at posts that move up or go down most when comparing our approaches to the baseline. Table 14 shows the average of these maxima per topic for two selected indicators and the best performing run per approach. We observe that Credibility-inspired reranking leads to posts going up and also going down a lot, whereas Combined reranking is more modest in both cases.

Table 14. Average maximum number of positions per topic a relevant post goes up or down the top 20 of the ranking for two individual indicators and the best run per approach

Approach	Indicator	Avg. max. up	Avg. max. down
Credibility-inspired	Quality	14.6	15.0
	Comments	14.6	14.1
	Post level	14.0	14.1
Combined	Quality	4.5	9.2
	Comments	12.7	13.5
	Post level + comments + pronouns	5.2	7.4

We zoom in and look at the posts themselves. Table 15 shows four examples of posts that are relevant to a topic and that show the largest "bump" for that topic after using Combined reranking (with post-level + comments + pronouns). For each example post we give the topic to which it is relevant, the change in positions, the ID, a part of the post's text, and the reasons why this post went up in the ranking.

The example posts show that we are able to push more credible posts up the ranking. As to the indicators that matter most in these examples, we observe that most have a high (text) quality (few spelling mistakes, correct use of punctuation and capitalization), have many comments, are timely (i.e., published on the day of the related event), and share semantics with related news articles.

Table 15. Examples of relevant posts helped by credibility after reranking using Combined reranking (post-level + comments + pronouns)

Topic	Ann Coulter (854)
Change in positions	3 (5 to 2)
Post ID	BLOG06-20060131-018-0031501574
Conservative commentator Ann Coulter has come under media fire yet again, this time for joking that U.S. Supreme Court Justice John Paul Stevens should be poisoned so that conservatives can gain a majority on the high court. Coulter is an articulate conservative and an outspoken Christian, but it is becoming increasingly clear that her "bomb throwing" style does more harm than good to these cause.	
Why?	Many comments
	High quality
	Few pronouns
Topic	Cheney hunting (867)
Change in positions	10 (20–10)
Post ID	BLOG06-20060213-013-0027595552
Today the AP reported: WASHINGTON - Vice President Dick Cheney accidentally shot and wounded a companion during a weekend quail hunting trip in Texas, spraying the fellow hunter in the face and chest with shotgun pellets. Vice President Cheney explained the shooting this way: "I was tracking a covey of quail with my gun barrel. Suddenly Whittington just popped up from the grass, directly in the way, so I shot him. I know my critics on the left will point out that Whittington is not a bird, but he was between the quail and my gun.	
Why?	Very timely
	Many comments
	High quality
	Few pronouns
Topic	Seahawks (882)
Change in positions	6 (12–6)
Post ID	BLOG06-20060207-025-0012517965
DETROIT – Shoulders slumped. Eyes drooped, some red with the hint of earlier tears. Heads sagged. The Seahawks' locker room was a sad and somber place. In many of their minds, the Seahawks were the better team in Super Bowl XL. The scoreboard at Ford Field said differently, however, and that was all that mattered. The greatest Seahawks season ended in bitter disappointment Sunday, a 21-10 loss to the Pittsburgh Steelers. The way the Seahawks lost—with mistake after mistake—left them disconsolate.	
Why?	Very timely
	High quality
	Proper semantics
Topic	Qualcomm (884)
Change in positions	4 (6–2)
Post ID	BLOG06-20060212-028-0007415694
A federal district court in California permanently barred chip maker Broadcom from prosecuting several of its patent infringement claims against Qualcomm before the International Trade Commission, ruling that the dispute must be resolved under the court's own jurisdiction in San Diego. Judge Rudi M. Brewster said in his ruling the week of Feb. 6 that Broadcom cannot pursue two individual claims from its patent case with the ITC in Washington, or in another California District Court, based on the details of a licensing agreement signed by the companies related to the legal dispute.	
Why?	Proper semantics
	High quality
	Few pronouns

We perform a similar analysis for relevant posts that drop in the ranking after using Combined reranking. Table 16 shows four of these posts, again with a snippet from the post and the reasons why the system believes these posts should drop.

Table 16. Examples of relevant posts hurt by credibility after reranking using Combined reranking (post-level + comments + pronouns)

Topic	Hybrid car (879)
Change in positions	−15 (1–16)
Post ID	BLOG06-20051219-075-0006828953
If your goal is to find out whether a hybrid car is right for you or your biggest desire is reducing your impact on the environment buy using a hybrid car, then take advantage of the advantages of hybrid car material that we have pulled together. Browse the site for additional Hybrid Cars information.	
Why?	Few comments Short Improper semantics
Topic	Qualcomm (884)
Change in positions	−4 (2 to 6)
Post ID	BLOG06-20051211-081-0015735208
I have been analyzing wireless communications for 26 years. I am president of Wireless Internet & Mobile Computing, a pioneering consulting firm that helps create new and enhance existing wireless data businesses in the United States and abroad. Previously, I created the world's first wireless data newsletter, wireless data conference, cellular conference and FM radio subcarrier newsletter. I was instrumental in creating and developing the world's first cellular magazine. I also helped create and run the first association in the U.S. for the paging and mobile telephone industries.	
Why?	Few comments Improper semantics Many pronouns
Topic	Oprah (895)
Change in positions	−14 (6–20)
Post ID	BLOG06-20060211-010-0023506187
George: I appreciate that. Fighting evil, it's hard work. I, um . . . my SUV, um . . . Oprah: George, you just go ahead, cry if you want to. I'm not ashamed to tell you that when I watched your speech, I cried. George: I really appreciate that, Oprah. Oprah: But George, I have to be straight with you now. I . . . I have to say it is difficult for me to talk to you because I also feel really duped.	
Why?	Not timely Low quality Improper semantics
Topic	Lance Armstrong (940)
Change in positions	−2 (3 to 5)
Post ID	BLOG06-20051209-083-0015483759
When is enough, well. . . enough? Lance Armstrong "was" possibly the most tested athlete of all time never being tested positive once for using performance enhancing drugs yet the European press simply will not let it go. Again the press have attacked Lance Armstrong for using a drug called "EPO" which increases performance in athetes. Maybe we can let Armstrong retire a champ instead continuing down this road. . . ??	
Why?	Few comments Low quality Short

Looking at these posts, we feel that, although relevant, they are less credible than the posts in Table 15. The first post is a collection of links to other sources and contains in itself not much information, which is reflected by its short length and lack of comments. The second post sounds more credible, but is quite biased (i.e., a high number of pronouns) and has again only few comments. The third post is a fake "conversation" between Oprah and George Bush and is considered less credible because improper semantics and low text quality. Finally, the fourth post is characterized by punctuation "abuse" (..., ??), short length, and very few comments.

In general we see that Credibility-inspired reranking is a more radical reranking approach, leading to many changes in the ranking and many (relevant) posts moving up and down. This is risky; it can lead to high gains, but also to large drops in performance. Combined reranking is a more careful, "smoothed" approach, which shows (slightly) fewer changes and moves in the ranking, but is more stable in its improvements (i.e., the ratio of posts going up and down), leading to significant improvements.

Looking at examples of relevant posts that are helped or hurt by credibility-inspired indicators, we find that posts that are pushed up the ranking are indeed more credible, whereas the posts that are pushed down seem to be less credible (although still relevant). There is not one indicator that leads to these changes, but it is always a combination of indicators (like comments, timeliness, semantics, and quality). We revisit the influence of individual indicators and the interplay between credibility-inspired ranking and relevance in Sect. 7.5.

7.3 Per topic analysis

Performance numbers averaged over 150 topics hide a lot of details. In this section we analyze the performance of our approaches on a per-topic basis and see how their behavior differs for various topics. We start by looking at the results of our best performing Credibility-inspired reranking and Combined reranking runs as compared to the baseline. The plots in Figure 4 show the increase or decrease on precision metrics for each topic when comparing thetwo approaches to the baseline.

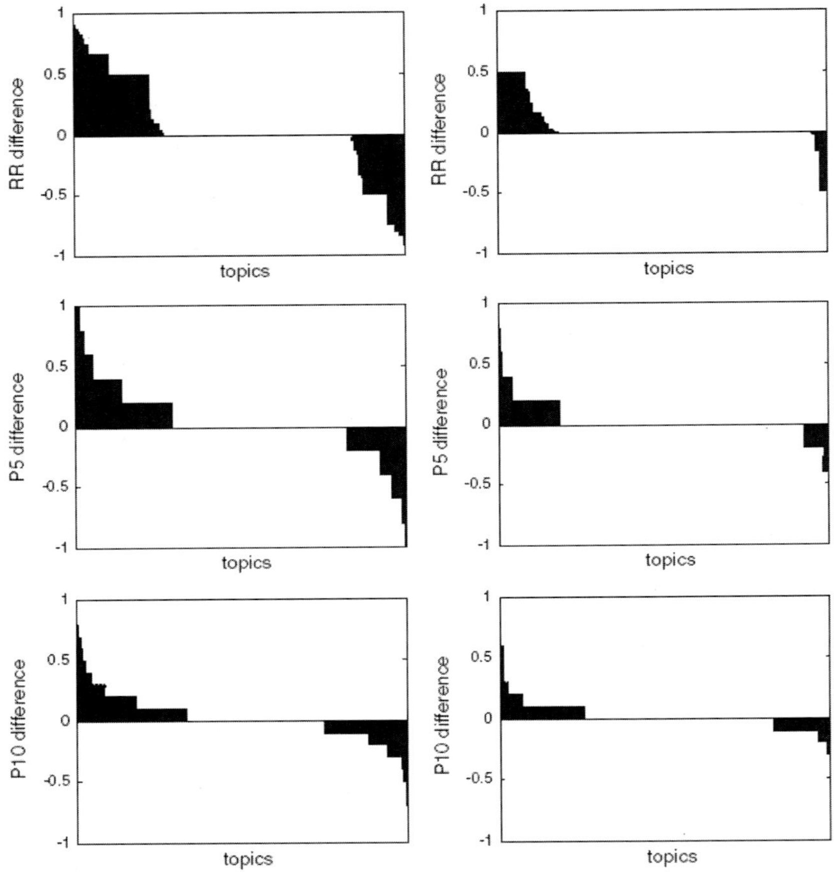

Figure 4. Comparing the baseline against (*Left*) Credibility-inspired reranking (post-level indicators) and (*Right*) Combined reranking (post-level + comments + pronouns). A *positive bar* indicates the topic improves over the baseline, a *negative bar* indicates a drop compared to the baseline

The plots show some interesting differences between the two reranking approaches. First, both approaches have topics on which they improve over the baseline, as well as topics for which the baseline performs better. In general, we observe that Credibility-inspired reranking has more topics that improve over the baseline than Combined reranking, but also more topics that drop in performance. Both gains and losses are higher for Credibility-inspired reranking compared to Combined reranking. The actual number of topics going up or down for both approaches compared to the baseline are listed in Table 17.

Table 17. Number of topics that increase or decrease as compared to the baseline for both approaches on precision metrics

Approach	RR		P5		P10	
	Up	Down	Up	Down	Up	Down
Credibility-inspired reranking	42	24	44	27	50	38
Combined reranking	29	9	28	12	38	26

We move on to the analysis of a selection of individual indicators. Figure 5 shows similar plots as before for four individual indicators; We only show precision at 5, to keep the number of plots limited.

The quality indicator shows similar behavior as the combinations of indicators: numbers for Credibility-inspired reranking are higher across the board. This pattern is, however, not so strong for timeliness and comments, where both approaches show similar behavior (i.e., equal number of topics increasing and decreasing compared to the baseline). We included the expertise indicator to show that, although overall performance of this indicator was below the baseline, we can improve over the baseline for a number of topics (32 topics for Credibility-inspired reranking and 30 for Combined reranking).

Finally, we compare the two reranking approaches in the same way: per topic. Figure 6 shows the number of topics that prefer either Credibility-inspired reranking ("negative" bars) or Combined reranking ("positive" bars) on the precision metrics.

The plots show that both reranking approaches have topics on which they clearly outperform the other, although in general the Credibility-inspired reranking is preferred for slightly more topics. To be precise, Credibility-inspired reranking is preferred for 30 (RR), 34 (P5), and 40 (P10) topics, whereas Combined reranking is preferred for 26 (RR), 27 (P5), and 34 (P10) topics.

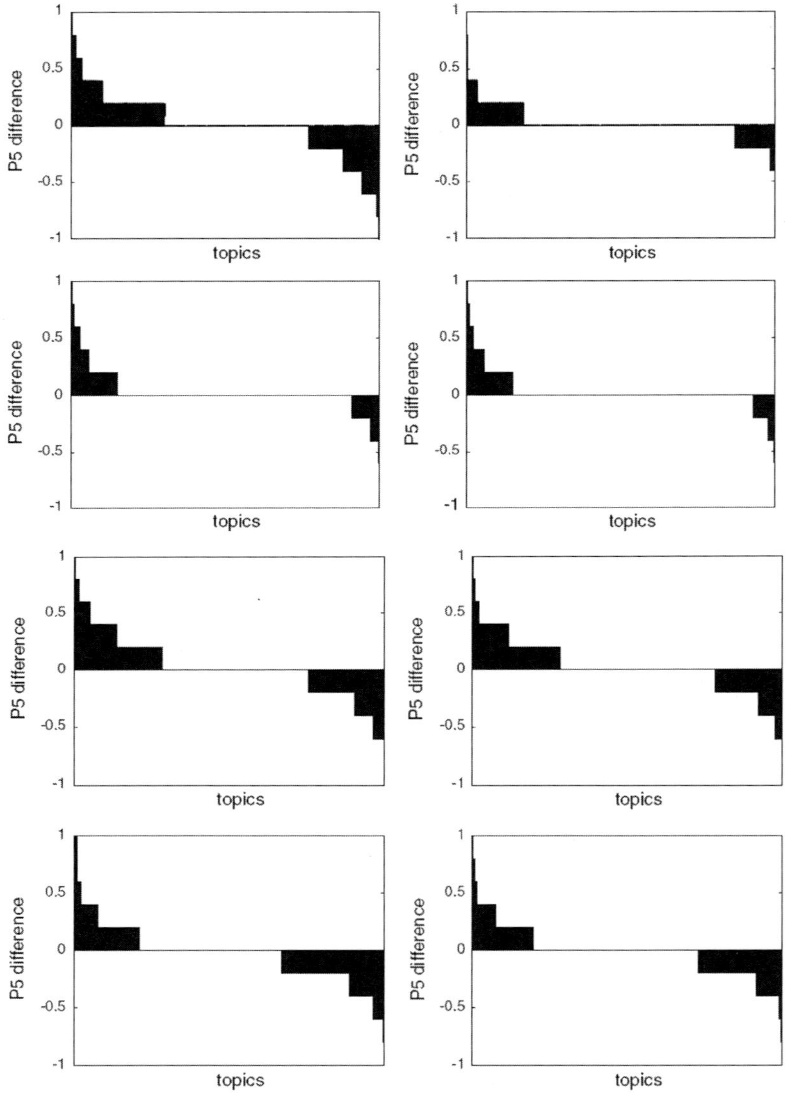

Figure 5. Comparing the baseline against (*Left*) Credibility-inspired reranking (*post-level* indicators) and (*Right*) Combined reranking (post-level + comments + pronouns) on precision at 5 for four individual indicators: (1) quality, (2) timeliness, (3) comments, and (4) expertise. A *positive bar* indicates the topic improves over the baseline, a *negative bar* indicates a drop compared to the baseline

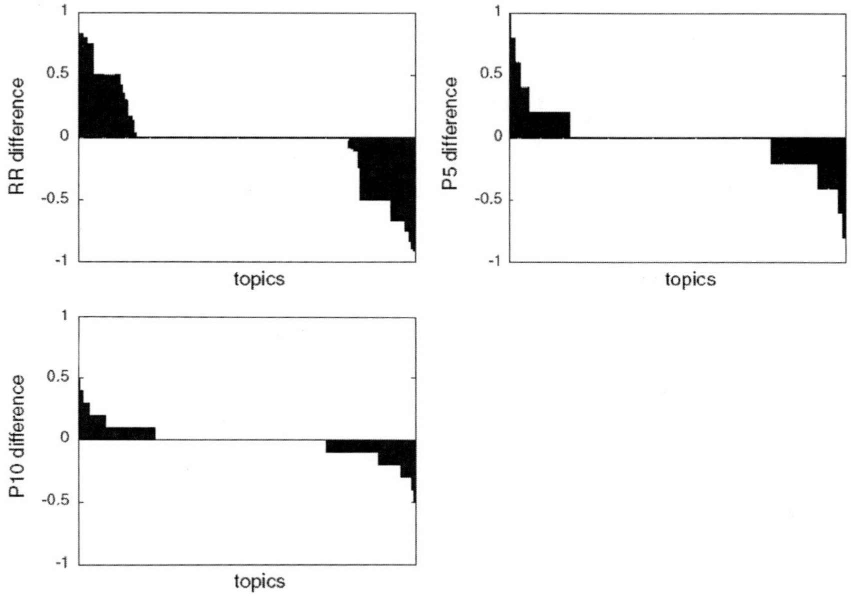

Figure 6. Comparing Credibility-inspired reranking (*post-level* indicators), as baseline, to Combined reranking (post-level + comments + pronouns) on (*Top left*) RR, (*Top right*) P5, and (*Bottom*) P10. A *positive bar*indicates that Combined reranking makes the topic improve over Credibility-inspired reranking, a*negative bar* indicates the opposite

7.3.1 Very early precision

We shift focus to MRR, the ability to rank the first relevant post as high as possible. We see that our Combined reranking approach is capable of moving the first relevant post from position 2 to position 1 for 13 topics, while another 16 topics show an increase in RR as well. On the other hand, only 9 topics show a decrease in RR. Table 18 shows on the left hand side the topics that improve the most after reranking and on the right the topics that drop the most.

Table 18. Topics that increase or decrease most on RR using Combined reranking (post-level indicators + comments + pronouns), compared to the baseline

Increase			Decrease		
#	Topic	ΔRR	#	Topic	Δ RR
942	Lawful access	0.5000	929	Brand manager	−0.7500
1,018	Mythbusters	0.5000	921	Christianity today	−0.5000
1,011	Chipotle restaurant	0.5000	943	Censure	−0.5000
1,023	Yojimbo	0.5000	869	Muhammad cartoon	−0.5000
903	Steve jobs	0.5000	870	Barry bonds	−0.1667
885	Shimano	0.5000	893	Zyrtec	−0.1666
913	Sag awards	0.5000	1,038	Israeli government	−0.0250
895	Oprah	0.5000	1,012	Ed norton	−0.0139
873	Bruce bartlett	0.5000	881	Fox news report	−0.0047
947	Sasha cohen	0.5000			
879	Hybrid car	0.5000			
878	Jihad	0.5000			
1,042	David irving	0.5000			

Table 19. Topics that increase or decrease most on RR using Credibility-inspired reranking (post-level indicators) compared to the baseline

Increase			Decrease		
#	Topic	ΔRR	#	Topic	Δ RR
1,034	Ruth rendell	0.9167	921	Christianity today	−0.9167
1,012	Ed norton	0.8750	1,014	Tax break for hybrid automobiles	−0.8333
940	Lance armstrong	0.8571	937	Lexisnexis	−0.8333
923	Challenger	0.8333	950	Hitachi data systems	−0.8000
1,035	Mayo clinic	0.8000	1,039	The geek squad	−0.8000
887	World trade organization	0.7500	1,022	Subway sandwiches	−0.7500
941	Teri hatcher	0.7500	1,025	Nancy grace	−0.7500
1,007	Women in saudi arabia	0.6667	1,019	China one child law	−0.7500
1,013	Iceland european union	0.6667	915	Allianz	−0.5000
933	Winter olympics	0.6667	855	Abramoff bush	−0.5000
880	Natalie portman	0.6667	943	Censure	−0.5000
890	Olympics	0.6667	918	Varanasi	−0.5000
1,008	Un commission on human rights	0.6667	938	Plug awards	−0.5000
1,047	Trader joe's	0.6667	867	Cheney hunting	−0.5000
893	Zyrtec	0.6667	866	Whole foods	−0.5000
900	Mcdonalds	0.6667	925	Mashup camp	−0.5000

We perform the same comparison between Credibility-inspired reranking using post-level indicators and the baseline. Table 19 shows the topics that show the largest difference on RR between the two runs. In total, 42 topics go up in RR, and 24 go down.

Some interesting observations can be made from the tables with topics. E.g., we notice that for topic 921 ("christianity today") it is hard to maintain a relevant post at the first position for both approaches and the same goes for topic 943 ("censure"). Credibility-inspired reranking is capable of pushing the first relevant result quite a bit up for topics 893 ("zyrtec") and 1012 ("ed norton"), whereas these drop for Combined reranking. All other topics that either increase or decrease are different between both approaches, which again supports the notion that certain topics are helped by Credibility-inspired reranking and others by Combined reranking.

7.4 Impact of parameters on precision

So far, we have looked at the results of reranking only the top 20 of the initial ranking. What happens if we change the value of *n* and rerank not 20, but the first 15 or 500 results of the ranking? We first explore the impact of different values of*n* on Credibility-inspired reranking on precision metrics, and then look at Combined reranking.

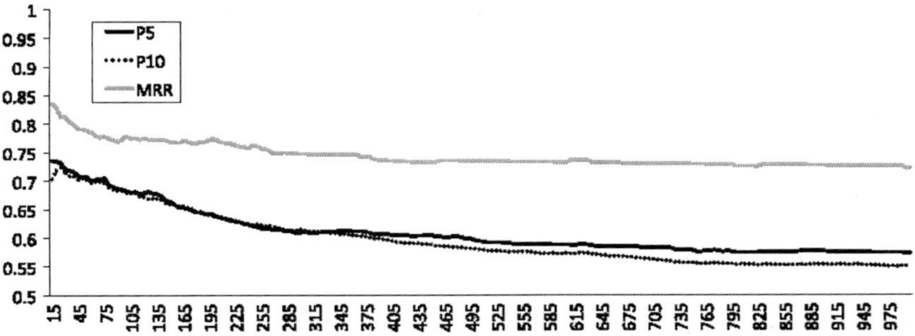

Figure 7. Influence of reranking top *n* (x-axis) on precision at 5 (P5) and 10 (P10) and MRR for Credibility-inspired reranking using post-level indicators

The plot in Figure 7 shows the change in performance for Credibility-inspired reranking on precision when using increasing values of *n*. We start at *n* = 15, so that we can measure a difference in P10 after reranking. On all metrics performance drops quite rapidly with *n* going up and it keeps dropping all the way up to *n* = 1,000.

The best performance for Credibility-inspired reranking is achieved using either*n* = 15 (for P5 and MRR) or *n* = 25 (for P10). Results of these two runs and the baseline are reported in Table 20. The results for MRR using *n* = 15 are higher than before and show a significant increase over the baseline. For P5 and P10 the results are slightly higher, but are still not significantly better.

Table 20. Results for the best values of *n* (15 and 25), our baseline, and the run presented before (*n* = 20) for Credibility-inspired reranking (using post-level indicators). Significance tested against the baseline

Run	MRR	P5	P10	MAP
Baseline	0.7722	0.6947	0.6960	**0.3893**
$n = 15$	**0.8364**$^{\triangle}$	**0.7360**	0.7033	0.3754$^{\triangledown}$
$n = 20$	*0.8289*	*0.7347*	*0.7193*	*0.3748*$^{\blacktriangledown}$
$n = 25$	0.8134	0.7320	**0.7233**	0.3723$^{\blacktriangledown}$

Looking at Combined reranking we find a very stable performance on all metrics over all *n*'s. Smoothing the credibility scores with the initial retrieval score leads to improvements, but the ranking does not change anymore going further down the ranking than position 15–20. The best performance is already achieved using*n* = 20 and there is no need to present further results here.

7.5 Credibility-inspired ranking vs. relevance ranking

We have seen that the effects of using credibility-inspired indicators on blog post retrieval are positive, but why this is the case? One issue that we should raise is the fact that assessors in the blog post retrieval task are asked to judge whether a blog post is *topically relevant* for a given topic. This relevance is assessed regardless of other factors that could otherwise influence judgements (e.g., readability, opinionatedness, quality). If we would follow this line of reasoning, we might wonder why credibility-inspired indicators have an effect on the performance at all. In order to gain a better understanding of this matter, we explore the topics that show the biggest increase or decrease in terms of precision at 10 and identify reasons for the change in performance. Below we list the factors that are most influential in performance changes.

Spam filtering:

We already discussed the issue of spam classification in Sect. 7.1. In this analysis we find that spam filtering is one of the main contributors to both improvements and drops in performance. By removing spam blogs, proper blog posts are promoted to higher ranks, leading to better results. Similarly, when spam classification fails and non-spam blogs are filtered out, non-relevant blog posts might take their place in the ranking, leading to a drop in performance.

Timeliness:

For topics that are time sensitive, the timeliness indicator is very influential. It often leads to relevant blog posts being pushed up in the ranking, while non-relevant blog posts are pushed down. Since this indicator is topic-dependent it does not influence all topics.

Semantics:

Another topic-dependent indicator, semantics, shows a large degree of influence on performance. As with the other indicators, semantics can make relevant posts move up the ranking and non-relevant posts down, but also the other way around.

Comments:

We observe that the number of comments a post receives is among the more influential indicators. One of the reasons why this indicator has so much influence could be that the text of the comments is considered to be part of the blog post and thus is being considered when determining relevance. A larger number of comments leads to extra text associated with the post and possibly to a better match between blog post and topic.

Post length:

The influence of the length of a document has attracted a lot of interest over the years (see e.g., Losada and Azzopardi 2008; Singhal et al. 1996), and its influence on retrieval performance is well-studied. In this chapter we also find that post length is one of the indicators with most influence on performance.

We observe that the credibility-inspired indicators each have their own reasons for improving (topical) blog post retrieval performance. However, the credibility framework offers us a principled way of combining these indicators and leaves space to include other indicators as well. Moreover, although we do not have the test collections to prove it, anecdotes suggest that the credibility-inspired indicators do indeed push more credible posts up the ranking.

8 CONCLUSIONS

In this paper we explore the use of ideas from a credibility framework in blog post retrieval. Based on a previously introduced credibility framework for blogs, we define several credibility-inspired indicators. These indicators are divided into post-level and blog-level indicators. Post-level indicators include spelling mistakes, correct capitalization, use of emoticons, punctuation abuse, document length, timeliness (when related to a news event), and how its semantics matches formal (news) text. On the blog level we introduce the following indicators: average number of comments, average number of pronouns, regularity of posting, coherence of the blog, and the expertise of the blogger.

Since the task at hand is precision-oriented and we expect credibility to help on precision, we propose to use inspiration from the credibility framework in a reranking approach and we introduce two ways of incorporating the credibility-inspired indicators in our blog post retrieval process. The first approach, Credibility-inspired reranking, simply reranks the top *n* of a baseline based on the credibility-inspired score. The second approach, Combined reranking, multiplies the credibility-inspired score of the top *n* results by their retrieval score and reranks based on this score.

Results show that Credibility-inspired reranking leads to larger improvements over the baseline than Combined reranking, but both approaches are capable of improving over an already strong baseline. For Credibility-inspired reranking the best performance is achieved using a combination of all post-level indicators. Combined reranking works best using the post-level indicators combined with comments and pronouns. The blog-level indicators expertise, regularity, and coherence do not contribute positively to the performance, although analysis shows that they can be useful for certain topics.

Analyses revealed that reranking on credibility-inspired scores alone (Credibility-inspired reranking) leads to higher gains and higher drops: its absolute scores are higher than for Combined reranking, but less stable. Combined reranking managed to improve significantly over the baseline on MRR and P5 and Credibility-inspired reranking can only do that after optimizing n to 15. Examples of posts that are affected by the reranking approaches indicated that we get the desired effect of moving credible posts up the ranking, but this is not always reflected in retrieval performance, as our test collection does not allow for direct measurement of credibility. We identified the most influential indicators and explained why these indicators lead to improvements in retrieval performance.

Concluding, in this paper we have shown that we can translate certain credibility indicators to measurable indicators from blog posts and their blogs. Applying two reranking approaches shows that the (early) precision of blog post retrieval can benefit from incorporating credibility-inspired indicators. Interestingly, ignoring the original retrieval score when reranking leads to the highest scores, although combining the two scores leads to more significant improvements in precision. The credibility framework offers us a principled way of adding indicators to a retrieval model, although the real effect on credibility ranking needs to be examined when an appropriate collection is available. Future work focuses around the blog-level indicators, that have proven to be harder to estimate than post-level indicators. We believe that blog-level indicators are important, but that we need other ways of estimating coherence, regularity, an expertise. An important future direction is the direct measurement of credibility using our indicators; for this, we need new collections or assessments.

FOOTNOTES

[1]http://odur.let.rug.nl/~vannoord/TextCat/.

[2]We used Lemur version 4.10, http://www.lemurproject.co.

ACKNOWLEDGMENTS

We are grateful to our reviewers and the editors of the journal for providing valuable comments and feedback. This research was supported by the European Union's ICT Policy Support Programme as part of the Competitiveness and Innovation Framework Programme, CIP ICT-PSP under grant agreement nr 250430 (GALATEAS), the 7th Framework Program of the European Commission, grant agreements no. 258191 (PROMISE) and no. 288024 (LiMoSINe), the DuOMAn project carried out within the STEVIN programme which is funded by the Dutch and Flemish Governments under project nr STE-09-12, the Netherlands Organisation for Scientific Research (NWO) under project nrs 612.-061.-814, 612.-061.-815, 640.-004.-802, 380-70-011, the Center for Creation, Content and Technology (CCCT), the Hyperlocal Service Platform project funded by the Service Innovation & ICT program, the WAHSP project funded by the CLARIN-nl program, under COMMIT project Infiniti, and by the ESF Research Network Program ELIAS.

REFERENCES

1. Agichtein, E., Castillo, C., Donato, D., Gionis, A., Mishne, G. (2008). Finding high-quality content in social media. In *Proceedings of the 1st ACM international conference on web search and data mining (WSDM 2008)*, (pp. 183–194), New York, NY: ACM.

2. AQUAINT-2. Guidelines. (2007).

3. Baeza-Yates, R., & Ribeiro-Neto, B. (2010). *Modern information retrieval: The concepts and technology behind search*. Boston: Addison Wesley.

4. Castillo, C., Mendoza, M., & Poblete, B. (2011) Information credibility on twitter. In *Proceedings of the 20th international conference on World Wide Web (WWW 2011)* (pp. 675–684), New York, NY: ACM.

5. Chafe, W. (1986). Evidentiality in English conversion and academic writing. In W. Chaf & J. Nichols (Eds.), *Evidentiality: The linguistic coding of epistemology* (Vol. 20, pp. 261–273). New York: Ablex Publishing Corporation.

6. Chen, M., & Ohta, T. (2010). Using blog content depth and breadth to access and classify blogs. *International Journal of Business and Information, 5*(1), 26–45.

7. Croft, W. B., & Lafferty, J. (Eds.) (2003). *Language modeling for information retrieval*. Berlin: Kluwer.

8. Diakopoulos, N., & Essa, I. (2010). Modulating video credibility via visualization of quality evaluations. In*Proceedings of the 4th workshop on information credibility on the Web (WICOW 2010)* (pp. 75–82). New York, NY: ACM.

9. Diaz, F., & Metzler, D. (2006). Improving the estimation of relevance models using large external corpora. In:*Proceedings of the 29th international ACM SIGIR conference on research and development in information retrieval (SIGIR 2006)* (pp. 154–161). New York, NY: ACM.

10. Hawking, D., & Craswell, N. (2002). Overview of the TREC-2001 Web track. In *The 10th text REtrieval conference proceedings (TREC 2001)*. Gaithersburg, USA: NIST.

11. He, J., Larson, M., & de Rijke, M. (2008). Using coherence-based measures to predict query difficulty. In*Advances in information retrieval—30th European conference on IR research (ECIR 2008), volume 4956 of Lecture Notes in Computer Science* (pp. 689–694). Berlin: Springer.

12. He, J., Weerkamp, W., Larson, M., & de Rijke, M. (2009). An effective coherence measure to determine topical consistency in user generated content. *International Journal on Document Analysis and Recognition, 12*(3), 185–203.

13. Hearst, M. A., & Dumais, S. T. (2009). Blogging together: An examination of group blogs. In *Proceedings of the 3rd international conference on weblogs and social media (ICWSM 2009)*. Menlo Park: AAAI Press.

14. Hofmann, K., & Weerkamp, W. (2008). Content extraction for information retrieval in blogs and intranets. Technical report, University of Amsterdam, 2008. URL http://ilps.science.uva.nl/biblio/content-extraction-information-retrieval-blogs-and-intranet.

15. Java, A., Kolari, P., Finin, T., Joshi, A., & Martineau, J. (2007). The blogVox opinion retrieval system. In*Proceedings of the 15th text REtrieval conference (TREC 2006)*. Gaithersburg, USA: NIST.

16. Juffinger, A., Granitzer, M., & Lex, E. (2009). Blog credibility ranking by exploiting verified content. In *Proceedings of the 3rd workshop on information credibility on the Web (WICOW 2009)* (pp. 51–58). New York, NY: ACM.

17. Klewes, J., & Wreschniok, R. (2009). *Reputation capital*. New York: Springer.

18. Kolari, P., Finin, T., Java, A., & Joshi, A. (2006). Splog blog dataset. http://ebiquity.umbc.edu/resource/html/id/212/Splog-Blog-Datase.

19. Lavrenko, V., & Croft, W. B. (2001). Relevance-based language models. In *Proceedings of the 14th international ACM SIGIR conference on research and development in information retrieval (SIGIR 2001)* (pp. 120–127). New York, NY: ACM.

20. Lee J. H. (1995). Combining multiple evidence from different properties of weighting schemes. In *Proceedings of the 18th international ACM SIGIR conference on research and development in information retrieval (SIGIR 1995)*(pp. 180–188). New York, NY: ACM.

21. Liu, B. (2007). *Web data mining*. Heidelberg: Springer.

22. Losada, D. E., & Azzopardi, L. (2008). An analysis on document length retrieval trends in language modeling smoothing. *Information Retrieval Journal, 11*(2), 109–138.

23. Lu, Y., Tsaparas, P., Ntoulas, A., & Polanyi, L. (2010). Exploiting social context for review quality prediction. In*Proceedings of the 19th international conference on World Wide Web (WWW 2010)* (pp. 691–700), New York, NY: ACM.

24. Macdonald, C., & Ounis, I. (2006). *The TREC Blogs06 collection: Creating and analyzing a blog test collection. Technical report TR-2006-224*: Department of Computer Science, University of Glasgow.

25. Macdonald, C., Ounis, I., & Soboroff, I. (2008a) Overview of the TREC 2007 blog track. In *Proceedings of the 16th text REtrieval conference (TREC 2007)*. Gaithersburg, USA: NIST.

26. Macdonald, C., Ounis, I., & Soboroff, I. (2008b) Overview of the TREC 2007 blog track. In *Proceedings of the 16th text REtrieval conference (TREC 2007)*. Gaithersburg, USA: NIST.

27. Mandl, T. (2006). Implementation and evaluation of a quality-based search engine. In: *Proceedings of the 17th conference on hypertext and hypermedia* (pp. 73–84). New York, NY: ACM.

28. Manning, C., Raghavan, P., & Schütze, H. (2008). *Introduction to information retrieval*. Cambridge: Cambridge University Press.

29. Massoudi, K., Tsagkias, M., de Rijke, M., & Weerkamp, W. (2011). Incorporating query expansion and quality indicators in searching microblog posts. In: *Advances in information retrieval—33rd European conference on IR research (ECIR 2011), Vol. 6611 of Lecture Notes in Computer Science* (pp. 362–367). Berlin/Heidelberg: Springer.

30. Metzger, M. (2007). Making sense of credibility on the Web: models for evaluating online information and recommendations for future research. *Journal of the American Society for Information Science and Technology, 58*(13), 2078–2091.

31. Mishne, G. (2007a) Using blog properties to improve retrieval. In *Proceedings of the 1st international conference on weblogs and social media (ICWSM 2007)*. Menlo Park: AAAI Press.

32. Mishne, G. (2007b) *Applied text analytics for blogs*. PhD thesis, Amsterdam: University of Amsterdam.

33. Mishne, G., & de Rijke, M. (2006). A study of blog search. In *Advances in information retrieval—28th European conference on IR research (ECIR 2006), Vol. 3936 of Lecture Notes in Computer Science* (pp. 289–301), Berlin/Heidelberg: Springer.

34. Mishne, G., & Glance, N. (2006) Leave a reply: An analysis of weblog comments. In *Proceedings of the WWW 2006 workshop on weblogging ecosystem: Aggregation, analysis and dynamics.*

35. O'Mahony, M. P., & Smyth, B. (2009) Learning to recommend helpful hotel reviews. In *Proceedings of the 3rd ACM conference on recommender systems (RecSys 2009)* (pp. 305–308). New York, NY: ACM.

36. O'Mahony, M. P., & Smyth, B. (2010). Using readability tests to predict helpful product reviews. In *Proceedings of the 9th*

international conference on adaptivity, personalization and fusion of heterogeneous information (RIAO 2010)(pp. 164–167).

37. Ounis, I., de Rijke, M., Macdonald, C., Mishne, G., & Soboroff, I. (2006). Overview of the TREC-2006 blog track. In *Proceedings of the 15th text REtrieval conference (TREC 2006)*. Gaithersburg, USA: NIST.

38. Ounis, I., Macdonald, C., & Soboroff, I. (2009). Overview of the TREC-2008 blog track. In *Proceedings of the 7th text REtrieval conference (TREC 2008)*. Gaithersburg, USA: NIST.

39. Rubin, V., & Liddy, E. (2006). Assessing credibility of weblogs. In *Proceedings of the AAAI spring symposium: Computational approaches to analyzing weblogs (CAAW)*.

40. Singhal, A., Buckley, C., & Mitra, M. (1996). Pivoted document length normalization. In *Proceedings of the 19th international ACM SIGIR conference on research and development in information retrieval (SIGIR 1996)* (pp. 21–29). New York, NY: ACM.

41. Sriphaew, K., Takamura, H., & Okumura, M. (2008). Cool blog identification using topic-based models. In*Proceedings of the 2008 IEEE/WIC/ACM international conference on Web intelligence and intelligent agent technology (WIIAT 2008)* (pp. 402–406). Washington, DC: IEEE Computer Society.

42. Stanford, J., Tauber, E., Fogg, B., & Marable, L. (2002). Experts vs online consumers: A comparative credibility study of health and finance web sites, http://www.consumerwebwatch.org/dynamic/web-credibility-reports-experts-vs-online-abstract.cf.

43. Su, Q., Huang, C.-R., & Yun Chen, K. (2010). Evidentiality for text trustworthiness detection. In *Proceedings of the 2010 workshop on NLP and linguistics: Finding the common ground (NLPLING 2010)*, (pp. 10–17), Stroudsburg, PA: Association for Computational Linguistics.

44. Tsagkias, M., Larson, M., & de Rijke M. (2010). Predicting podcast preference: An analysis framework and its application. *Journal of the American Society for Information Science and Technology, 61*(2), 374–391.

45. Van House, N. (2004). Weblogs: Credibility and collaboration in an online world, people.ischool.berke-ley.edu/*vanhouse/Van%20House%20trust%20workshop.pdf.

46. Weerkamp, W. (2011). *Finding people and their utterances in social media*. PhD thesis, University of Amsterdam.

47. Weerkamp, W., & de Rijke, M. (2008). Credibility improves topical blog post retrieval. In *Proceedings of the 46th annual meeting of the association for computational linguistics (ACL 2008)* (pp. 923–931), Stroudsburg, PA: Association for Computational Linguistics.

48. Weerkamp, W., Balog, K., & de Rijke M. (2009). A generative blog post retrieval model that uses query expansion based on external collections. In *Proceedings of the joint conference of the 47th annual meeting of the ACL and the 4th international joint conference on natural language. Processing of the AFNLP (ACL-IJCNLP 2009)* (pp. 1057–1065). Stroudsburg, PA: Association for Computational Linguistics.

49. Weerkamp, W., Balog, K., & de Rijke, M. (2011). Blog feed search with a post index. *Information Retrieval Journal, 14*(5), 515–545.

50. Weimer, M., Gurevych, I., & Mehlhauser, M. (2007). Automatically assessing the post quality in online discussions on software. In *Proceedings of the ACL 2007 demo and poster sessions*, pp. 125–128.

5

CHAPTER

Increasing Cheat Robustness of Crowdsourcing Tasks

Carsten Eickhoff[1], Arjen P. de Vries[2]

[1]*Delft University of Technology, Delft, The Netherlands*

[2]*CWI, Amsterdam, The Netherlands*

ABSTRACT

Crowdsourcing successfully strives to become a widely used means of collecting large-scale scientific corpora. Many research fields, including Information Retrieval, rely on this novel way of data acquisition. However, it seems to be undermined by a significant share of workers that are primarily interested in producing quick generic answers rather than correct ones in order to optimise their time-efficiency and, in turn, earn more money. Recently, we have seen numerous sophisticated schemes of identifying such workers. Those, however, often require additional resources or introduce artificial limitations to the task. In this work, we take a different approach by investigating means of a priori making crowdsourced tasks more resistant against cheaters.

Keywords: Crowdsourcing; User experiments; Stability; Human factors

1 INTRODUCTION

Many scientific fields including information retrieval, artificial intelligence, machine translation or natural language processing rely heavily on large-scale corpora for system building, training and evaluation. The traditional approach to acquiring these data collections is employing human experts to annotate or create the relevant material. A well-known example from the area of information retrieval is the series of extensive corpora created in the context of the NIST's *Text REtrieval Conference* (TREC) (Harman 1993). Since the manual creation of such resources typically requires substantial amounts of time and money there have long been advances into using automatically generated or extracted resources (Riloff 1996; Lesher and Sanelli 2000; Soboroff et al. 2001; Amitay et al. 2004). While there are several promising directions and methods that are reported to correlate well with human judgements, for many applications that require high precision, human judgements are still necessary (Marcus et al. 1993).

Especially in novel or niche areas of research for which there are little or no existing resources that could be re-used, the demand for an alternative way of data acquisition becomes apparent. With the advent of commercial crowdsourcing, a new means of satisfying this need for large-scale human annotations emerged. Starting in 2005, Amazon Mechanical Turk (MTurk 2011) and others provide platforms on which task requesters can reach a large number of freelance employees to solve *human intelligence tasks* (HITs). The payment is typically done on micro level, e.g., a few US cents per quickly solvable HIT. This process is now widely accepted and represents the basis for data collection, resource annotation or validation in many recent research publications (Ambati et al. 2010; Kittur et al.2008).

Over the years crowdsourcing became substantially more popular among both requesters and workers. As a consequence, the relatively small initial crowd of workers that was mainly attracted by the prospect of completing odd or entertaining tasks as a diversion, changed. Nowadays, the number of users who are mainly attracted by the monetary reward represents a significant share of the crowd's workforce (Baio 2008; Kaufmann et al. 2011; Ross et al. 2010). At the same time we observe a significant share of cheaters entering the market. Those workers try to maximise their financial gains by submitting quick generic, non-reflected answers that, in turn, serve for weak or altogether compromised corpus quality. In response to this trend, research work based on crowdsourcing nowadays has to pay careful attention to monitoring result quality. The accepted way of addressing cheat submissions in crowdsourcing is the use of high quality gold standard data or inter-annotator agreement ratios to check on and if necessary reject deceivers. In this work we present an alternative approach by designing HITs that are less attractive for cheaters. Based on the experience gained from several previous crowdsourcing tasks and a number of dedicated experiments, this work aims to quantify the share of deceivers as well as to identify criteria and methods to make tasks more robust against this new form of annotation taint.

The remainder of this work is structured as follows: Sect. 2 gives an overview of related work in the domain of crowdsourcing. In Sect. 3, we analyse commonly observed cheating strategies in crowdsourcing environments. Section 4 describes a number of experiments that were conducted in order to measure the current extent of crowdsourcing scam as well as the remedial effect of several design criteria. Finally, Sect. 5 concludes with a summary of our findings and an outlook on future directions in countering cheaters and thus preserving result quality.

2 RELATED WORK

Despite the fact that crowdsourcing is being widely used to create and aggregate data collections for scientific and industrial use, the current amount of research work dedicated to methodological evaluations of crowdsourcing is relatively limited. One of the early studies by Sorokin and Forsyth in (2008) investigated the possibility of using crowdsourcing for image annotation.

They found an interesting non-monotonic dependency between the assigned monetary reward per HIT and the observed result quality. While very low pay resulted in sloppy work, gradually increasing the reward improved annotation quality up to a point where further increases even deteriorated performance due to attracting more cheaters. In the same year, Kittur et al. (2008) published their influential overview on the importance of task formulation to obtaining good results. Their main conclusion was that a task should be given in such a way, that cheating takes approximately the same time as faithfully completing it. The authors additionally underline the importance of clearly verifiable questions in order to reject deceivers.

In the course of the following year, several independent research groups studied the performance of experts versus non-experts for various natural language processing tasks such as paraphrasation, translation or sentiment analysis (Snow et al. 2008; Hsueh et al. 2009). The unanimous finding, also confirmed by Alonso and Mizzaro (2009), was, that a single expert is typically more reliable than a single non-expert. However, aggregating the results of several cheap non-experts, the performance of an expensive professional can be equalled at significantly lower cost. In the same year, Little et al. (2009) released TurkIt, a framework for iterative programming of crowdsourcing tasks. In their evaluation, the authors mention relatively low numbers of cheaters. This finding is somewhat conflicting with most publications in the field, that report higher figures. We suspect that there is a strong connection between the type of task at hand and the type of workers attracted to it. In this work we will carefully investigate this dependency through a series of experiments.

There is a line of work dedicated to studying HIT design in order to facilitate task understanding and worker efficiency. Examples are Khanna et al. (2010)'s investigation of the influence of HIT interface design on Indian workers' ability to successfully finish a HIT or Grady and Lease's (2010) study of human factors in HIT design. The interface-related study in Sect. 4.3 inspects a very different angle by using interface design as a means of making cheating less efficient and therefore less tempting.

We can conclude that there are numerous good publications that detail tailor-made schemes to identify and reject cheaters in various crowdsourcing scenarios. Snow et al. (2008) do not treat cheaters explicitly, but propose modelling systematic worker bias and subsequently correcting for it. For their sentiment analysis of political blog posts, Hsueh et al. (2009) rely on a combination of gold standard labels and majority voting to ensure result quality. Soleymani and Larson 2010) use a two-stage process. In a first round, the authors offer a pilot HIT as recruitment and manually invite well-performing workers for the actual task. Hirth et al. (2010) describe a sophisticated workflow in which one (or even potentially several) subsequent crowdsourcing step is used in order to check on the quality of crowdsourced results. In her recent work, Gabriella Kazai discusses how the HIT setup influences result quality, for example through pay rate, worker qualification or worker type (Kazai 2011; Kazai et al. 2011).

In this article, we take a different approach from the state of the art by (1) Aiming at discouraging cheaters rather than detecting them. While there is extensive work on the posterior identification and rejection of cheaters, we deem these methods sub-optimal as they still bind resources such as time or money. Instead, we try to find out what makes a HIT look appealing to cheaters and subsequently aim to remedy these aspects. (2) While there are many publications *also* detailing the authors' cheater detection schemes, we are not aware of comprehensive works on cheat robustness that are applicable to a wide range of HIT types. By giving a broad overview of frequently encountered adversarial strategies as well as established countermeasures, we hope to close this gap.

3 HOW TO CHEAT

Before proceeding to our experimentally supported inspection of various cheat countering strategies, we will spend some thought on the nature of cheating on large-scale crowdsourcing platforms. The insights presented in this section are derived from related work, discussions with peers, as well as our own experience as HIT providers. They present, what we believe is an overview of the most frequently encountered adversarial strategies in the commercial crowdsourcing field. While one could theorize about many more potential exploits, especially motivated by the information security domain (e.g., Pfleeger and Pfleeger 2007; Moore et al. 2001), we try to concentrate on giving an account of the main strategies HIT designers have to face regularly.

As we will show in more detail, the cheaters' methods are typically straightforward to spot for humans, but, given the massive HIT volume, such a careful manual inspection is not always feasible. Cheating as a holistic activity can be assumed to follow a breadth-first strategy in that the group of cheating workers will explore a wide range of naive cheats and move on to a different HIT if those prove to be futile. When dealing with cheating in crowdsourcing, it is important to take into consideration the workers' different underlying motivations for taking up HITs in the first place

(Ipeirotis 2010b). We believe that there are two major types of workers with fundamentally different motivations for offering their work force. Entertainment-driven workers primarily seek diversion by taking up interesting, possibly challenging HITs. For this group the financial reward plays a minor role. The second group are money-driven workers. These workers are mainly attracted by monetary incentives. We expect the latter group to contain more cheating individuals as an optimization of time efficiency and, subsequently, an increased financial reward, is clearly appealing given their motivation. In this work, we also regard any form of automated HIT submission, i.e., bots, scripts, etc. to originate from money-driven workers. We could get an interesting insight into the organization of the money-driven crowdsourcing subculture when running a HIT that involved filling a survey with personal information (Eickhoff et al. 2011) (See Figure 4 in the Appendix). For this HIT we received multiple submissions by unique workers that contained largely contradictory statements. We suspect these workers to be organised in large-scale offices from where multiple individuals connect to the platform under the same worker id. While this rather anecdotal observation is not central to our work and demands further evidence in order to be quantifiable, we consider it an interesting one, worth sharing with the research community.

Our following overview of cheating approaches will be organised according to the types of HITs and quality control mechanisms they are aimed at.

3.1 Closed class questions

Closed class questions are probably the most frequently used HIT elements. They require the worker to choose from a limited, pre-defined list of options. Common examples of this category include radio buttons, multiple choice question, check boxes and sliders. There are two widely-encountered cheating strategies targeting closed-class tasks: (1) Arbitrarily picked answers can often easily be rejected by using good gold standard data or by inspecting agreement with redundant submissions by multiple workers, either in terms of majority votes or more sophisticated combination schemes (Dawid and Skene 1979). (2) Some clever cheaters may learn from previous HITs and come up with educated guesses based on the answer distribution underlying the HIT. An example could be the typically sparsely distributed relevance in web search scenarios for which a clever cheater might learn that arbitrarily selecting only a very small percentage of documents closely resembles meaningful judgements. This is often addressed by introducing a number of very easy to answer gold standard awareness questions. A user that fails to answer those questions can be immediately rejected as he is clearly not trying to produce sensible results.

3.2 Open class questions

Open questions allow workers to provide less restricted answers or perform creative tasks. The most common example of this class are text fields but it potentially includes draw boxes, file uploads or similar. Focussing on the widely used text fields, there are three different forms of cheats: (1) Leaving the field blank can be disabled during HIT design. (2) Entering generic text blocks is easily detectable if the same text is used repeatedly. (3) Providing unique (sometimes even domain-specific) portions of natural language text copied from the Web is very hard to detect automatically.

3.3 Internal quality control

Most current large-scale crowdsourcing platforms collect internal statistics of the workers' reliability in order to fend off cheaters. Reliability is, to the best of our knowledge, measured by all major platforms in terms of the worker's share of previously accepted submissions. There are two major drawbacks of this approach: (1) Previous acceptance rates fail to account for the high share of submissions that are uniformly accepted by the HIT provider and are post-processed and filtered, steps, to which the platform's reputation system has no access. (2) Previous acceptance rates are prone to gaming strategies such as rank boosting (Ipeirotis2010a) in which the worker simultaneously acts as a HIT provider. He can then artificially boost his reliability by requesting and submitting small HITs. This gaming scheme is very cheaply implementable as the cycle only loses the service fee deducted by the crowdsourcing platform.

In addition to these theoretical considerations concerning the shortcomings of current quality control mechanisms, Sect. 4.4 will show an empirical evaluation backing the assumption that we need better built-in quality measures than prior acceptance rates.

3.4 External quality control

Some very interactive HIT types may require more sophisticated technical means than offered by most crowdsourcing platforms. During one of our early experiments, we dealt with this situation by redirecting workers to an external, less restricted web page on which they would complete the actual task and receive a confirmation code to be entered on the original crowdsourcing platform. Despite this openly announced completion check, workers tried to issue made-up confirmation codes, to resubmit previously generated codes multiple times or to submit several empty tasks and claim that they did not get a code after task completion. While such attempts are easily fended off, they offer a good display of deceiver strategies. They will commonly try out a series of naive exploits and move on to the next task if they do not succeed.

4 EXPERIMENTS

After our discussion of adversarial approaches and common remedies, this section will give a quantitative experimental overview of various cheating robustness criteria of crowdsourcing tasks. The starting point of our evaluation are two very different HITs that we originally requested throughout 2010 and that showed substantially different cheat rates. The first task is a straightforward binary relevance assessment between pairs of web pages and queries. The second task asked the workers to judge web pages according to their suitability for children of different age groups and to fill a brief survey on their experience in guiding children's web search (Eickhoff et al. 2011). Examples of both tasks can be found in the Appendix.

All experiments were run through CrowdFlower 1 in 2010 and 2011. The platform incorporates the notion of "channels" to forward HITS to third party platforms. To achieve broad coverage and results representative of the crowdsourcing market, we chose all available channels, which at that time were Amazon Mechanical Turk 2(AMT), Gambit 3, SamaSource 4 as well as the GiveWork smartphone application jointly run by Samasource and CrowdFlower. Table 1 shows the overall distribution of received submissions according to the channels from which they originated. The figures are reported across all HITs collected for this study, as there were no significant differences in distribution between HIT types. The vast majority of submissions came from AMT. We are not are not aware of the reason why we did not receive any submissions from the GiveWork app. HITs were offered in units of 10 at a time with initial batch sizes of 50 HITS. Each HIT was issued to at least 5 independent workers. Unless stated differently, all HITs were offered to unrestricted audiences with the sole qualification of having achieved 95% prior HIT acceptance, the default setting on most platforms. The monetary reward per HIT was set to 2 US cents per relevance assessment and 5 US cents per filled web page suitability survey. We did not change the reward throughout this work. Previous work, e.g., by Harris (2011), has shown the influence of different financial incentive models on result quality. Statistical significance of results was determined using a Wilcoxon Signed Rank test with $\alpha < 0.05$.

A key aspect of our evaluation is identifying cheaters. There is a wide range of indicators for this purpose, including: (1) Agreement with trusted gold standard data can be used to measure the general quality of an answer. (2) Agreement with other workers enables us to identify hard tasks on which even honest workers occasionally fail. (3) HIT completion times (either compared per HIT or HIT type) give an estimate of how much effort the worker put into the task. (4) Simple task awareness questions that are correctly and unambiguously answerable for every worker can be introduced to identify distracted or cheating individuals. Mistakes on this kind of question are typically penalized heavily in cheater detection schemes. 5The concrete scheme chosen in this work will be formally detailed in the following section.

Table 1. Submission distribution for all HITs

Channel	Absolute	Relative share (%)
Amazon mechanical turk	4285	85
Samasource	454	9
Gambit	303	6
GiveWork	0	0

Our analysis of methods to increase cheating robustness was conducted along four research questions: (1) How does the concrete task type influence the number of observed cheaters? (2) Does interface design affect the share of cheaters? (3) Can we reduce fraudulent tendencies by explicitly filtering the crowd? (4) Is there a connection between the size of HIT batches and observed cheater rates?

4.1 What qualifies a cheater?

Before beginning our inspection of different strategies to fend off cheaters in crowdsourcing scenarios, let us dedicate some further consideration to the definition of cheaters. Following our previous HIT experience we can extend the worker classification scheme by Kittur et al. (2008) to identify several dysfunctional worker types. *Incapable workers* do not fulfil all essential requirements needed to create high quality results. *Malicious workers* try to invalidate experiment results by submitting wrong answers on purpose. *Distracted workers* do not pay full attention to the HIT which often results in poor quality. The source of this distraction will vary across workers and may be of external or intrinsic nature. The exclusively money-driven cheater introduced in Sect. 3 falls into the third category, as he would be capable of producing correct results but is distracted by the need to achieve the highest possible time-efficiency. As a consequence, we postulate the following formal definition of cheaters for all subsequent experiments in this work:

Definition 1

A cheater is a worker who fails to correctly answer simple task awareness questions or who is unable to achieve better than random performance given a HIT of reasonable difficulty.

In the concrete case of our experiments we measure agreement as a simple majority vote across a population of at least 5 workers per HIT. Disagreeing with this majority decision for at least 50% of the questions asked will flag a worker as a cheater. Additionally, we inject task awareness questions that require the worker to indicate whether the resource in question is written in a non-English language (each set of 10 judgements that a worker would complete at a time would contain one known non-English page). Awareness in this context represents that the worker actually visited the web page that he is asked to judge. Failing to answer this very simple question will also result in being considered a cheater. The cheater status is computed on task level (i.e., across a set of 10 judgements in our setting) in order to result in comparable reliability. Computing cheater status on batch level or even globally would serve for very strict labels as a single missed awareness question would brand someone a cheater even if the remainder of his work in the batch or the entire collection were valuable. Our approach can be considered lenient as cheaters are "pardoned" at the end of each task. Our decision is additionally motivated by the fact that the aim of this study is to gauge the proportion of cheaters attracted by a given HIT design rather than achieving high confidence at identifying individuals to be rejected in further iterations. At the same time, we are confident that a decision based on 10 binary awareness questions and the averaged agreement across 10 relevance judgements produces reliable results that are hard to bypass for actual cheaters.

This approach appears reasonable as also it focuses on workers that are distracted to the point of dysfunctionality. In order to not be flagged as a cheater, a worker has to produce at least mediocre judgements and not fail on any of the awareness questions. Given the relative simplicity of our experiments we do not expect incapability to be a major hindrance for well-meaning workers in our setting. Truly malicious workers, finally, can be seen as a rather theoretical class given the large scale of popular crowdsourcing platforms on the web. This worker type is expected to be more predominant in small-scale environments where their activity has higher detrimental impact. We believe that our definition is applicable in a wide range of crowdsourcing scenarios due to its generality and flexibility. The concrete threshold value of agreement to be reached as well as an appropriate type of awareness question should be selected depending on the task at hand.

4.2 Task-dependent evaluation

As a first step into understanding the dynamics of cheating on crowdsourcing platforms, we compare the baseline cheater rate for the two previously introduced HIT types. The main differences between the two tasks are task novelty and complexity. Plain relevance judgements are frequently encountered on crowdsourcing platforms and can be assumed to be well-known to a great number of workers. Our suitability survey, on the other hand, is a novel task that requires significantly more consideration. Directly comparing absolute result quality across tasks would not be meaningful due to the very different task-inherent difficulty. Table 2 shows the observed share of cheaters for both tasks before and after using gold standard data.

Table 2. Task-dependent share of cheaters before and after using gold standard data

Task	Before gold (%)	After gold (%)
Suitability	2.2	1.6
Relevance	37.3	28.4

We can find a substantially higher cheater rate for the straightforward relevance assessment. The use of gold standard data reduced cheater rates for both tasks by a comparable degree (27.3% relative reduction for the suitability HIT and 24% for the relevance assessments). With respect to our first research question, we note that more complex tasks that require creativity and abstract thinking attract a significantly smaller percentage of cheaters. We assume this observation to be explained by the interplay of two processes: (1) Money-driven workers prefer simple tasks that can be easily automated over creative ones. (2) Entertainment-seekers can be assumed to be more attracted towards novel, enjoyable and challenging tasks. For all further experiments in this work we will exclusively inspect the relevance assessment task as it has a higher overall cheater rate that is assumed to more clearly illustrate the impact of the various evaluated factors.

4.3 Interface-dependent evaluation

We have shown how innovative tasks draw a higher share of faithful workers that are assumed to be primarily interested in diversion. However, in the daily crowdsourcing routine, many tasks are of rather straightforward nature. In this section, we will evaluate how interface design can influence the observed cheater rate even for well-known tasks such as image tagging or relevance assessments. Traditional interface design commonly tries to not distract the user from the task at hand (Shneiderman 1997). As a consequence, the number of context changes is kept as low as possible to allow focused and efficient working. While this approach is widely accepted in environments with trusted users, crowdsourcing may require a different treatment. A smooth interaction with a low number of context changes makes a HIT prone to automation, either directly by a money-driven worker or by scripts and bots. We investigate this connection at the example of our relevance assessment task.

Table 3 shows the results of this comparison. In the first step, we present the workers with batches of 10 web page/query pairs using gold standard data. In order to keep the number of context changes to a minimum we asked the workers to visit a single web page 6 and create relevance judgements for that page given 10 different queries. The resulting share of cheaters turns out to be substantial (28.4%). Now we increase the amount of interaction in the HIT by requiring the worker to create 10 judgements for query/document pairs in which we keep the query constant and require visiting 10 unique web pages. Under this new setting the worker is required to make significantly more context changes between different web pages. While in a controlled environment with trusted annotators this step would be counterproductive, we see a significant relative decline of 23% to a proportion of 21.9% cheaters. In a final step, we issue batches of 10 randomly drawn query/document pairs. As a result, the proportion of cheaters decreases by another 15 to 18.5%. The general HIT interface remains unchanged from the original example shown in Figure 3, only the combinations of query/document pairs vary. With respect to our second research question, we find that greater variability and more context changes discourage deceivers as the task appears less susceptible to automation or cheating, and therefore less profitable.

Table 3. Interface-dependent percentage of cheaters for variable queries, variable documents and fully variable pairs

Interface type	Observed cheater rate (%)
Variable queries	28.4
Variable documents	21.9
Both variable	18.5

4.4 Crowd filtering

In this section, we will address our third research question by inspecting a number of commonly used filtering strategies to narrow down the pool of eligible workers that can take up a HIT. In order to make for a fair comparison, we will regard two settings as the basis of our juxtaposition: (1) The initial cheat-prone relevance assessment setup with 10 queries and 1 document, using gold standard verification questions. (2) The previous best performance that was achieved using gold standard verification sets as well as randomly drawn query/document pairs as described in Sect. 4.3 Please note that the crowd filtering experiment were exclusively run on AMT as not all previously used platforms offer the same filtering functionalities. The HITs created in this section are not shown in Table 1, as they would artificially boost AMT's prominence even further.

4.4.1 By prior performance

In the course of this document we argued that the widely used prior acceptance rates are not an optimal means of assessing worker reliability. In order to evaluate the viability of our hypothesis we increase the required threshold accuracy to 99% (The default setting is 95%). Given a robust reliability measure, this, at least seemingly very strict standard should result in highest result quality.

4.4.2 By origin

Offering the HIT exclusively to inhabitants of certain countries or regions is a further commonly-encountered strategy for fending off cheaters and sloppy workers. Following our model of money-driven and entertainment-driven workers we assume that offering our HITs to developed countries should result in lower cheater rates. In order to evaluate this assumption we repeat the identical HIT that was previously offered unrestrictedly, on a pure US crowd.

4.4.3 By recruitment

Recruitment (sometimes also called qualification) HITs are a further means of a priori narrowing down the group of workers. In a multi-step process, workers are presented with preparatory HITs. Workers that achieve a given level of result quality are eligible to take up the actual HIT. In our case we presented workers with the identical type of HIT that was evaluated later and accepted every worker that did not qualify as a cheater (according to Definition 1) for the final experiment.

4.4.4 Results

The first two columns of Table 4 shows an overview of the three evaluated filtering dimensions. Raising the threshold of prior acceptance from the 95% default to 99% only gradually lowered the observed cheater rate. Filtering depending on worker origin was able to cut cheater rates down to less than a third of the originally observed 28.4%. However, this substantial reduction comes at a cost. The run time of the whole batch increased from 5 hours to slightly under one week as we limit the crowd size. Providers of time-sensitive or very large HIT batches may have to consider this trade-off carefully. The introduction of a recruitment step prior to the actual HIT was able to reduce the cheater rate, however, the cheat reduction vs. increase in completion time is worse than for origin-based filtering. To further confirm and understand these trends, columns 3 and 4 of the same table display the same statistics for the varied HIT setting in which we assigned random query/document pairs. In general, the effect of filtering turned out to be largely independent of the previously applied interface changes. The relative merit of the applied methods was found to be comparable for both the initial and the high-variance interface.

Table 4. Effect of crowd filtering on cheater rate and batch processing time

Filtering method	Cheaters (initial) (%)	Time (initial) (h)	Cheaters (varied) (%)	Time (varied) (h)
Baseline	28.4	3.2	18.5	5.2
99% prior acc.	26.2	3.8	17.7	7.6
US only	8.4	140	5.4	160
Recruitment	19	145	12.2	144

The conclusion towards our third research question is twofold: (1) We have seen how prior crowd filtering can greatly reduce the proportion of cheaters. This narrowing down of the workforce may however result in longer completion times. (2) Additionally, we could confirm the assumption that a worker's previous task acceptance rate can not be seen as a robust stand-alone predictor of his reliability.

4.5 The influence of batch sizes

Crowdsourced HITs are typically issued on large scale in order to collect significant amounts of data. Currently, HIT batch sizes are typically adjusted according to practical or organizational needs but with little heed to result quality. Wang et al. (2011) gave a first intuition of an instrumental use of batch sizes by showing that small batches typically have longer per-HIT completion times than large ones. We assume that this tendency is explained by large HIT batches being more attractive for workers interested time-efficiency. A batch of only 2 HITs has a relatively large overhead of reading and understanding the task instructions before completing actual work. For large batches, workers have a significantly higher reuse potential. The same holds true for cheating. Investing time into finding a way to game a 5-HIT batch is far less attractive than doing the same for a batch of 100 HITs. As a consequence, we expect large HIT batches to attract relatively higher cheater rates than small batches. Previously, all HITs were offered in batches of 50. In order to evaluate our hypothesis we issued several batches of relevance assessment HITs (see Figure 3 in the Appendix) and compared the observed cheater rates depending on the batch size. For each setting, we collected judgements for 100 query/document pairs. Except for the batch size, all experiment parameters were kept at the settings described in Sect. 4. Batches were requested one at a time. Only after a batch's completion would we publish the following one. In this way we aim to avoid giving the impression that there was a large amount of similar HITs available to be preyed on by cheaters. As a consequence, we do not expect major external effects caused by the resulting higher number of batches offered as they are never available at the same time. Figure 1 shows the result of this comparison. The figure represents the mean observed cheater rate for each batch size *s* across a population of n=100sn=100s batches. We can note a statistically significant (using Wilcoxon signed Rank test with $\alpha < 0.05$) increase in cheating activity for batch sizes of at least 10 HITs. As a consequence of determining cheater status at task level, we do not expect any influence of the batch size on the confidence of our cheater detection since the number of HITs per task remained unchanged across batch size settings.

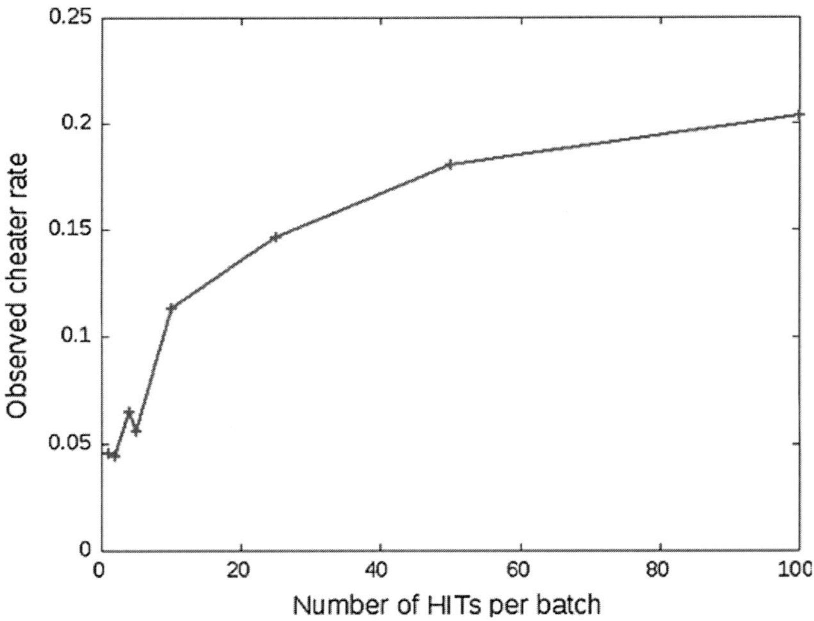

Figure 1. Observed percentage of cheaters for HIT batches of variable size

As a further piece of evidence, let us investigate how the cheater rate develops within a batch as HIT submissions arrive. The previously made observations would imply that, as the batch approaches completion, the arrival of new cheaters should become less frequent as the batch of available HITs shrinks in size. To pursue this intuition, workers were ordered according to their time of first submission to the batch. Subsequently, we determined the maximum likelihood estimate of encountering a new cheater, $p(c)$ given an original batch size and a degree of completion as:

$$p(c|s,\omega) = \frac{|C_{s,\omega}|}{|W_{s,\omega}|}$$

where |Cs,ω||Cs,ω| is the number of new cheaters observed for size *s* at degree of completion ω, and |Ws,ω||Ws,ω| is the overall number of new workers arriving at that time. Figure 2 shows the resulting distributions. For significantly large *s*, we can clearly see our intuition confirmed. As the number of remaining HITs declines, new cheaters are observed less and less frequently. For settings of $s < 25$ the distributions are near uniform and we could not determine significant changes over time.

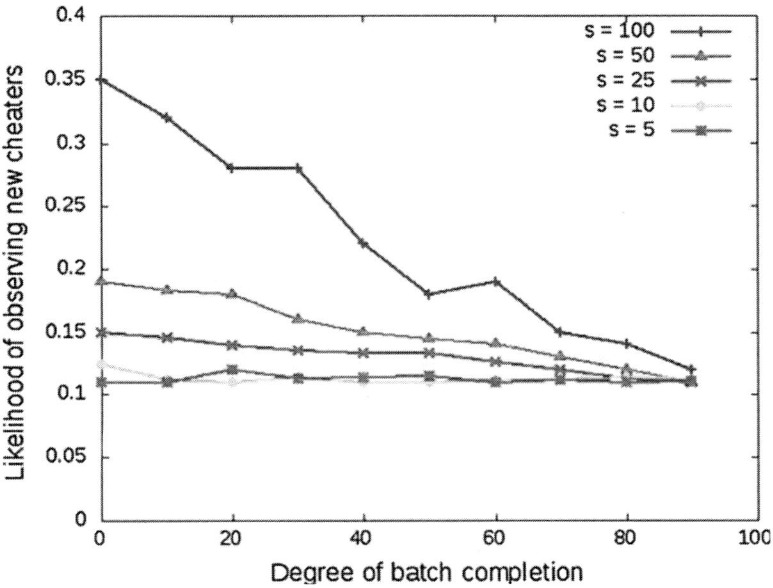

Figure 2. Likelihood of observing new cheaters as batches approach completion

With respect to our fourth research question, we conclude that larger batches indeed attract more cheaters as they offer greater potential of automation or repetition. This finding holds interesting implications for HIT designers, who may consider splitting up large batches into multiple smaller ones.

5 DISCUSSION AND CONCLUSION

In this work we investigated various ways of making crowdsourcing HITs more robust against cheat submissions. Many state of the art approaches to deal with cheating rely on posterior result filtering. We choose a different focus by trying to design and formulate HITs in such a way that they are less attractive for cheaters. The factors evaluated in this article are: (1) The HIT type. (2) The HIT interface. (3) The composition of the worker crowd. (4) The size of HIT batches.

Based on a range of experiments, we conclude that cheaters are less frequently encountered in novel tasks that involve creativity and abstract thinking. Even for straightforward tasks we could achieve significant reductions in cheater rates by phrasing the HIT in a non-repetitive way that discourages automation. Crowd filtering could be shown to have significant impact on the observed cheater rates, while filtering by origin or by means of a recruitment step were able to greatly reduce the amount of cheating, the batch processing times multiplied. We are convinced that implicit crowd filtering through task design is a superior means to cheat control than excluding more than 80% of the available workers from accessing the HIT. An investigation of batch sizes further supported the hypothesis of fundamentally different worker motivations, as the observed cheater rates for large batches that offer a high reuse potential, were significantly higher than those for small batches.

Finally, our experiments confirmed that prior acceptance rates, although widely used, cannot be seen as a robust measure of worker reliability. Recently, we have seen a change in paradigms in this respect. In June 2011, Amazon introduced a novel service on AMT that allows to issue HITs to an selected crowd of trusted workers, so-called Masters (at higher fees). Master status is granted per task type and has to be maintained over time. For example, as a worker reliably completes a high number of image tagging HITs, he will be granted Master status for this particular task type. Currently, the available Master categories are “Photo Moderation” and “Categorization”. Due to the recency of this development, we were not able to set up a dedicated study of the performance-cost trade-off of Master crowds versus regular ones.

Novel features like this raise an important general question to be addressed by future work: Temporal instability is a major source of uncertainty in current crowdsourcing research results. The crowdsourcing market is developing and changing at a high pace and is connected to the economical situation outside the cloud. Therefore, it is not obvious whether this year’s findings about worker behaviour, the general composition of the crowd or HIT design would still hold two years from now. Besides empirical studies, we see a clear need for explicit models of the crowd. If we could build a formal representation of the global (or, depending on the application, local) crowd, including incentives and external influences, we would have a reliable predictor of result quality, process costs and required time at our fingertips, where currently the process is trial-and-error-based.

One particularly interesting aspect of such a model of crowdsourcing lies in a better understanding of worker motivation, gained for example through activity log analyses and usage history, can solicit more sophisticated worker reliability models. To this end, we are currently investigating the use of games in commercial crowdsourcing tasks. There are different fundamental motivations for offering one’s labour on a crowdsourcing platform. Following previous experience, we hypothesise that workers who are mainly entertainment-driven and for whom the financial reward only plays a subordinate role, are less likely to cheat during the task. Using games, such workers can be rewarded more appropriately by representing HITs in engaging and entertaining ways. Ultimately, this should lead to better results and greater cost-efficiency of crowdsourcing.

FOOTNOTES

[1]http://www.crowdflower.com

[2]http://www.mturk.com

[3]http://getgambit.com/

[4]http://samasource.org/

[5]The original suggestion of this trick resulted from personal communication between the authors, Mark Sanderson and William Webber.

[6]The pages used in this study originate from the ClueWeb'09 collection (http://lemurproject.org/clueweb09.php/) and the queries and gold standard judgements for topics 51-57 from NIST's TREC 2010 Web track adhoc task (Clarke 2009).

ACKNOWLEDGMENTS

This research is part of the PuppyIR project (PuppyIR (2011). It is funded by the European Community's Seventh Framework Programme FP7/2007-2013 under grant agreement no. 231507.

REFERENCES

1. Alonso, O., & Mizzaro, S. (2009). Can we get rid of TREC assessors? Using mechanical turk for relevance assessment. In *Proceedings of the SIGIR 2009 workshop on the future of IR evaluation* (pp. 15–16). Citeseer.

2. Ambati, V., Vogel, S., & Carbonell, J. (2010). Active learning and crowd-sourcing for machine translation.*Language Resources and Evaluation (LREC), 7*, 2169–2174.

3. Amitay, E., Carmel, D., Lempel, R., & Soffer, A. (2004). Scaling IR-system evaluation using term relevance sets. In *Proceedings of the 27th annual international ACM SIGIR conference on research and development in information retrieval* (pp. 10–17), ACM.

4. Baio, A. (2008). The faces of mechanical turk. http://waxy.org/2008/11/the_faces_of_mechanical_turk.

5. Clarke, C. (2009). *Overview of the trec 2009 web track*. Technical report, Waterloo University.

6. Dawid, A., & Skene, A. (1979). Maximum likelihood estimation of observer error-rates using the EM algorithm.*Journal of the Royal Statistical Society Series C (Applied Statistics), 28*(1), 20–28.

7. Eickhoff, C., Serdyukov, P., & de Vries, A. (2011). A combined topical/non-topical approach to identifying web sites for children. In *Proceedings of the 4th ACM international conference on Web search and data mining* (pp. 505–514). ACM.

8. Grady, C., & Lease, M. (2010). Crowdsourcing document relevance assessment with mechanical turk. In*Proceedings of the NAACL HLT 2010 workshop on creating speech and language data with Amazon's mechanical turk* (pp. 172–179). Association for Computational Linguistics.

9. Harman, D. (1993). Overview of the first trec conference. In *Proceedings of the 16th annual international ACM SIGIR conference on research and development in information retrieval* (pp. 36–47). ACM.

10. Harris, C. (2011). Youre hired! An examination of crowdsourcing incentive models in human resource tasks.*Crowdsourcing for search and data mining* (*CSDM 2011*) (p. 15).

11. Hirth, M., Hoßfeld, T., & Tran-Gia, P. (2010). *Cheat-detection mechanisms for crowdsourcing*. Technical report, University of Würzburg.

12. Hsueh, P., Melville, P., & Sindhwani, V. (2009). Data quality from crowdsourcing: A study of annotation selection criteria. In *Proceedings of the NAACL HLT 2009 workshop on active learning for natural language processing* (pp. 27–35). Association for Computational Linguistics.

13. Ipeirotis, P. (2010a). Be a top mechanical turk worker: You need $5 and 5 minutes. http://behind-the-enemy-lines.blogspot.com/2010/10/be-top-mechanical-turk-worker-you-need.html.

14. Ipeirotis, P. (2010b). *Demographics of mechanical turk*. Center for Digital Economy Research, NYU Stern School of Business, Working paper.

15. Kaufmann, N., Schulze, T., & Veit, D. (2011). More than fun and money. Worker motivation in crowdsourcing—A study on mechanical turk. In *Proceedings of the 17th Americas Conference on Information Systems*.

16. Kazai, G. (2011). In search of quality in crowdsourcing for search engine evaluation. *Advances in Information Retrieval, 6611*, 165–176.

17. Kazai, G., Kamps, J., & Milic-Frayling, N. (2011). Worker types and personality traits in crowdsourcing relevance labels. In *Proceedings of 20th International Conference on Information and Knowledge Management (CIKM)*. ACM.

18. Khanna, S., Ratan, A., Davis, J., & Thies, W. (2010). Evaluating and improving the usability of mechanical turk for low-income workers in india. In *Proceedings of the first ACM symposium on computing for development* (p. 12). ACM.

19. Kittur, A., Chi, E., & Suh, B. (2008). Crowdsourcing user studies with mechanical turk. In *Proceeding of the 26th annual SIGCHI conference on human factors in computing systems* (pp. 453–456). ACM.

20. Lesher, G., & Sanelli, C. (2000). A web-based system for autonomous text corpus generation. In *Proceedings of ISSAAC*.

21. Little, G., Chilton, L., Goldman, M., & Miller, R. (2009). Turkit: Tools for iterative tasks on mechanical turk. In*Proceedings of the ACM SIGKDD workshop on human computation* (pp. 29–30). ACM.

22. Marcus, M., Marcinkiewicz, M., & Santorini, B. (1993). Building a large annotated corpus of english: The penn treebank. *Computational linguistics 19*(2), 313–330.

23. Moore, A., Ellison, R., & Linger, R. (2001). *Attack modeling for information security and survivability*. Technical report, Carnegie-Mellon University, Software Engineering Institute.

24. MTurk. (2011). *Amazon mechanical turk—Artificial artificial intelligence*. https://www.mturk.com/.

25. Pfleeger, C., & Pfleeger, S. (2007). *Security in computing* (Vol. 604). New Yok: Prentice Hall.

26. PuppyIR. (2011). PuppyIR: An open source environment to construct information services for children. http://www.puppyir.eu.

27. Riloff, E. (1996). Automatically generating extraction patterns from untagged text. In *Proceedings of the national conference on artificial intelligence* (pp. 1044–1049).

28. Ross, J., Irani, L., Silberman, M., Zaldivar, A., & Tomlinson, B. (2010). Who are the crowdworkers? Shifting demographics in mechanical turk. In *Proceedings of the 28th of the international conference extended abstracts on human factors in computing systems* (pp. 2863–2872). ACM.

29. Shneiderman, B. (1997). *Designing the user interface: strategies for effective human-computer interaction*. Addison-Wesley Longman Publishing Co., Inc. Boston, MA, USA.

30. Snow, R., O'Connor, B., Jurafsky, D., & Ng, A. (2008). Cheap and fast—But is it good? Evaluating non-expert annotations

for natural language tasks. In *Proceedings of the conference on empirical methods in natural language processing* (pp. 254–263). Association for Computational Linguistics.

31. Soboroff, I., Nicholas, C., & Cahan, P. (2001). Ranking retrieval systems without relevance judgments. In*Proceedings of the 24th annual international ACM SIGIR conference on research and development in information retrieval* (pp. 66–73). ACM.

32. Soleymani, M., & Larson, M. (2010). *Crowdsourcing for affective annotation of video: Development of a viewer-reported boredom corpus.* In *Proceedings of the ACM SIGIR 2010 workshop on crowdsourcing for search evaluation* (*CSE 2010*) (pp. 4–8).

33. Sorokin, A., & Forsyth, D. (2008). Utility data annotation with amazon mechanical turk. In *Computer vision and pattern recognition workshops, 2008. CVPRW'08. IEEE computer society conference on IEEE* (pp. 1–8).

34. Wang, J., Faridani, S., Ipeirotis, P. (2011). Estimating the completion time of crowdsourced tasks using survival analysis models. *Crowdsourcing for search and data mining* (*CSDM 2011*) (p. 31).

6

CHAPTER

Establishing a Research Information System as Part of an Integrated Approach to Information Management: Best Practice at the Karlsruhe Institute of Technology (KIT)

Frank Scholze[1], Jan Maier[2]

[1]Karlsruhe Institute of Technology (KIT), KIT Library, Karlsruhe, Germany

[2]Avedas, Karlsruhe, Germany

ABSTRACT

The Karlsruhe Institute of Technology (KIT) is one of the largest research and higher education organisations in the world focusing on engineering and natural sciences. At present KIT, under the chairmanship of its executive board, is installing an extensive current research information system (CRIS) covering all institutes and facilities of the organisation.

The assumption underlying the project is that a consistent overview of research performance has become fundamental for the international competitiveness of research institutions and is increasingly important for strategic decisions at the executive level. Ultimately, it also leads to better data and control in rankings at higher education assessments.

The new research information system systematically maps all of KIT's processes and instruments to obtain, connect, present and utilise the research metadata of active researchers. This reduces the documentation workload for researchers, for the executive level and central units such as the library, and at the same time allows for and facilitates an overall view and the aggregation and visualisation of research metadata.

Our vision is to build a federally structured network of systems that gathers information on KIT's publications, research competence, research projects, patents and technological offers by retrieving data from external and internal sources as well as directly from the researchers. The network facilitates linking and aggregating of data and provides unique identifiers for individual researchers and organizational units. With its consistent data model the research information system also fosters the organisational development of KIT, which was formed in 2009 by the merger of a university and a national research centre.

The researchers and their activities are at the core of the research information system. The system substantially reduces their administrative burden in documenting project information and publications. Automatic data import from external online sources and repositories has the big advantage that publication data are acquired and validated only once and can be used subsequently for manifold purposes such as websites, CVs, publication lists and reference management software.

Due to the complexity of workflows, internal and external sources and the organisational infrastructure that is required for such an implementation, KIT has chosen a commercial software solution (by AVEDAS AG) as the basic installation, and in cooperation with AVEDAS will expand it and adjust it to a tailor-made system that covers the entire KIT publication and research life cycle. The CRIS at KIT is part of a larger integrated and service-oriented approach to information management (Karlsruhe Integrated Information Management — KIM).

Keywords: research; information system; information management

THE KARLSRUHE INSTITUTE OF TECHNOLOGY (KIT)

The Karlsruhe Institute of Technology (KIT) is a German academic research and education institution resulting from a merger between the University (Universität Karlsruhe) and the Research Centre (Forschungszentrum) Karlsruhe. The university, also known as

Fridericiana, was founded in 1825. In 2009 it merged with the former national nuclear research centre founded in 1956 as the Kernforschungszentrum Karlsruhe (FZK). KIT is a unique initiative as it combines the mission of a University funded by the State of Baden-Württemberg with the mission of a national research centre funded by the Federal Government. A special law had to be passed to make this happen. From a historical perspective, however, it was a logical step, as both institutions look back on a long tradition of research and education with many parallels in terms of content and organisation. KIT is one of nine German Excellence Universities and positions itself as an institution with excellent research and teaching in natural and engineering sciences on an international scale, and with scientific excellence as a global cutting-edge university in research, teaching and innovation. As a member of the Helmholtz Association, the largest science organisation in Germany, KIT makes major contributions to top national and international research.

KARLSRUHE INTEGRATED INFORMATION MANAGEMENT (KIM)

The concept of 'Karlsruhe Integrated Information Management (KIM)' pursues the goal of increasing excellence in research and teaching at the Karlsruhe Institute of Technology (Hartenstein et al., 2007). Therefore, it strives for a continuous and sound integration of relevant legacy systems and data as well as for increasing the accessibility and transparency of related business processes. The KIM project's technical realisation is based on a service- oriented aAchitecture (SOA) model which was termed 'KIM integrated Service Oriented Architecture (KIM iSOA)' (Freudenstein et al., 2006).

KIM consists of a series of associated sub-projects (Figure 1). Among them are 'Management of courses, examinations and study assistance (KIM-CM)' and 'Identity management (KIM-IDM)'. The results of these projects have led to services which are accessible through the portals 'studium.kit.edu' and 'intra.kit.edu'. Furthermore, provisioning all KIT employees and students on the basis of their associated KIT accounts not only facilitates innovative IT services, but contributes substantially to giving people in the university and in the large-scale research sector a sense of solidarity.

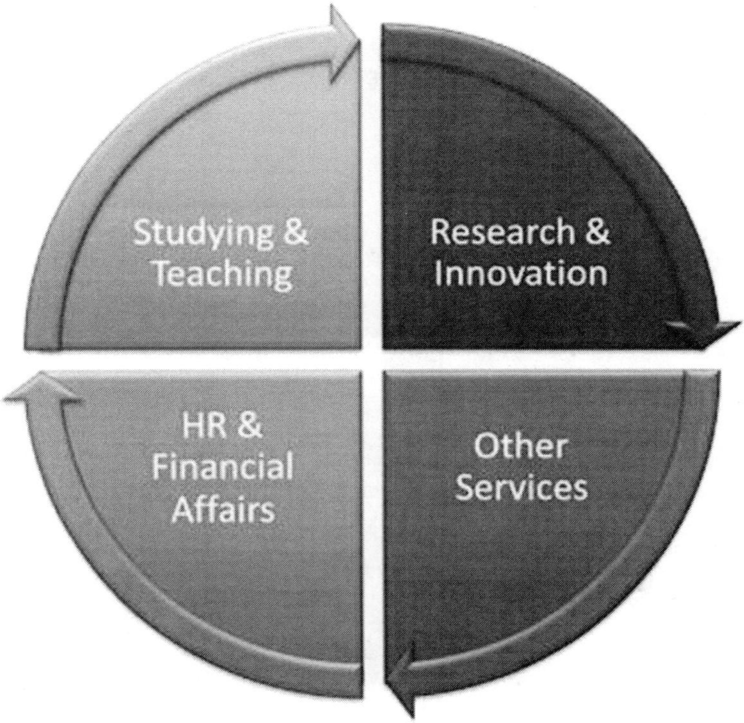

Figure 1. Project Portfolio within Karlsruhe Integrated Information Management (KIM).

In order to co-ordinate information provision and processing, and to ensure that organisational and cultural change associated with the KIM projects is managed properly, co-ordination structures have been established at KIT. Among these are the position of a 'Chief Information Officer (CIO)' as a member of the executive board in order to promote the integration and co-ordination of information provision and processing in all fields of the KIT at the top management level; and the 'Committee on Information Provision and Processing (IVA)', which was established by the senate and the executive board chaired by the CIO and gives recommendations to the president's office and the senate on all questions concerning the processing or provision of information at KIT, especially in matters of general importance. There are two sub-committees established by the IVA, one for information provision (A-IVS) and one for information processing (A-IFE). Two more will follow: one dealing with the 'application of new media in research, teaching, study, further education and administration (A-ILS)' and one for 'information processing in administration (A-IVD)' (Figure 2).

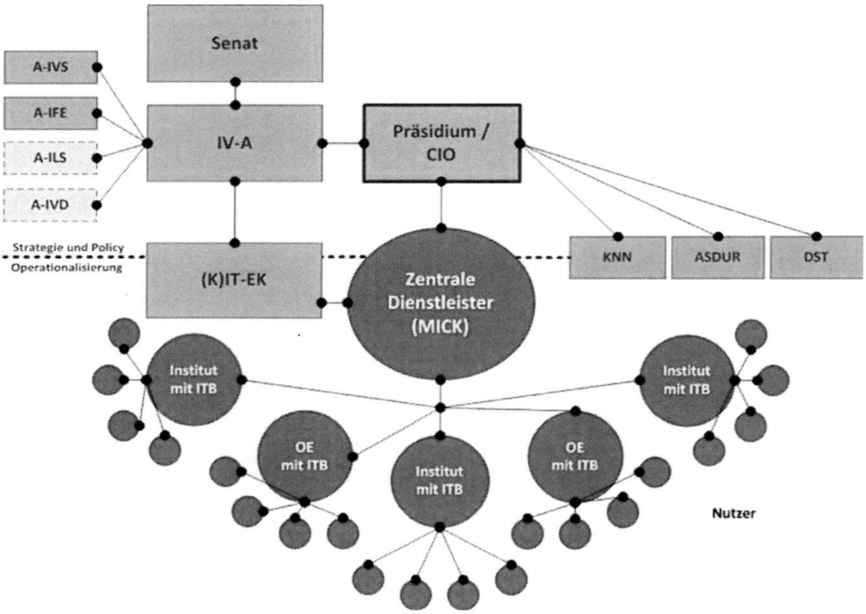

Figure 2. Governance within Karlsruhe Integrated Information Management (KIM).

Guidelines for these sub-committees form user governance: the sub-committees represent the interests of users in the respective fields, advise the operational officers and give appropriate recommendations for strategic development. Integration with the IVA is guaranteed by the fact that the respective chairmen of the subcommittees have to be members of the IVA. At the operational level, all relevant organisational units are represented in the 'Media and Information Service Centre Karlsruhe (MICK)'. MICK is organised co-operatively by the Steinbuch Centre for Computing, KIT Library and the administrative units dealing with information provision and processing. It pools all competencies and services in this domain. On the other hand, it does not break up or absorb the computing centre, library or administration as distinctive organisational units, as they have unique tasks and missions which do not overlap.

CRIS AND REPOSITORIES

CRIS (Current Research Information Systems) have existed since the 1960s and have been designed to manage information related to research. This includes input and output data like publications, patents, products, prices as well as projects, equipment and facilities. At the European level, there exists a standardised data model called CERIF (Common European Research Information Format) which is maintained and developed by euroCRIS.[1]

Repositories were developed in the 1990s as part of the movement to secure open access to scholarly publications. Therefore they concentrated on providing free and unrestricted access to publications and not to the contextual data resulting from the research processes which led to these publications. As discussions and developments have matured, repositories have become much more aware of the importance of contextual information. The discussion now focuses on publication management, virtual research environments and research data.[2] Critics say this is due to the fact that, despite numerous initiatives and incentives,[3] repositories are not as well filled with full-text publications as promoters of the idea had hoped they would be.[4]

After initial discussions within the Knowledge Exchange (Razum et al., 2007), there is now a wider uptake of the question as to how and to what purpose CRIS and repositories should integrate or interact. Three main lines of discourse can be distinguished. Some think that a repository will develop into a CRIS (Carr, 2010), adding more contextual and standardised metadata about persons, projects, funders etc. The majority within both communities think that a parallel development will continue, and consequently there has to be some kind of interface between the systems depending on local requirements — be it one or bi-directional (Sheppard, 2010).[5] As a third perspective, some argue that a CRIS already has the ability to contain full-text publications and has to be enhanced accordingly to act as a repository. Their main argument is that a CRIS already has a rich and contextual data model which can express temporal roles and relationships between entities (Jeffery et al., 2010).

KIM-FIS — THE CURRENT RESEARCH INFORMATION SYSTEM AT KIT

Information about the research output and the context of research at KIT is currently held in numerous systems run by different organisational units using different formats and data models. It is not possible to combine, aggregate or integrate this rich information, whether it regards scientists, institutes or other characteristic features. This became all the more evident when the University and Research Centre Karlsruhe merged to form KIT. Both organisations had developed their own policies and daily practices in collecting, managing and evaluating research information.

These heterogeneous 'cultures' make it difficult if not impossible to gain a consistent overview of and insight into the research performance of KIT. However, such an overview is of crucial importance for KIT because it is competing with the top research institutions on an international level.

Therefore, in March 2010, the executive board of KIT initiated a project to build an integrated research information system as one of the sub-projects of KIM called KIM-FIS. This means that it will be part of the service-oriented concepts developed within iSOA. In a tendering process, KIT decided to choose Converis (by AVEDAS AG)[6] as a software platform for building its CRIS. Converis fulfilled most of the requirements which had been defined and both parties were interested in a strategic partnership promoting agile development on the one hand and long-term development of the product on the other. After the decision to acquire Converis in July 2010, a demonstrator was built which focused on managing information about publications and projects. KIT library is responsible for the former, the research department for the latter. The project is co-ordinated by the CIO and there is a steering committee in which the library, research department and the department for planning and control are represented. The researchers and their activities are at the core of both sub-projects within KIM-FIS. A key challenge is to automate data collection and integration as much as possible. This includes migration of the existing publication databases, repositories and project databases within the former University and the former Research Centre, which are not integrated in researchers' workflows very well. In KIM-FIS, data is acquired and validated only once and then they can be used for manifold purposes, such as websites, CVs, publication lists and reference management software. In December 2010 the demonstrator was presented successfully to different stakeholder groups within KIT, namely researchers, the executive board and the Committee on Information Provision and Processing (IVA).

Publication Management

Publication management within KIM-FIS is also part of the open access strategy of KIT. As researchers strive for impact and visibility for their published results, they are willing to provide full-text files as long as they can be sure that copyright issues and other administrative burdens are taken care of. This is underpinned by a rigorous publication policy within the former research centre. It states that all publications have to be approved by the chair of the respective institute before they can be handed over to a publisher. The approval workflow ensures that coverage of the publication database of the former research centre is nearly 100%. The database has existed since 1956 and it holds about 75,000 records. At the former University, a publications database has existed on a voluntary basis since 1968 and it contains about 60,000 records. Currently a general publication policy for KIT is in the making which tries to combine the best of both worlds. The central idea is that the chair of an institute can decide if he/she wants to approve publications planned, as he/she is responsible for the scientific output of his/her unit. KIM-FIS will support the workflows which are currently being tested and rolled out to selected researchers and institutes. A first production release of the system was scheduled for August 2011. For the remainder of 2011, more institutes will gradually use KIM-FIS and give feedback, allowing for one or more iterations in development if necessary. The general roll-out of the system is scheduled for 2012.

From the very beginning, it became obvious that KIM-FIS was strongly linked to the identity management system already established in KIM-IDM.[7] It provides single-sign-on facilities for a wide variety of internal and external services at KIT. Roles and rights management must be clearly defined and the unique identification of researchers, funders and organizational units must be warranted. Internationally standardised persistent identifier systems for these and other entities are a natural requirement within projects like KIM-FIS, as they will greatly help the mobility of researchers' portfolios. However, there is not even a consensus about which persistent identifier systems should be deployed on a global scale for publications and which services should be supplied by them

(Hakala, 2010). ORCID[8] and other activities in this domain are carefully monitored; for the time being a pragmatic 'bag of identifiers' approach seems most promising for KIT. This means that maybe more than one (persistent) identifier will be attached to a person or a publication.

In addition to the publication databases, two open access repositories have been developed locally, one at the former University and one at the former Research Centre Karlsruhe. KIT is a strong actor in open access. It has passed an institutional policy endorsing the green and gold routes. It has signed the Berlin Declaration on Open Access to Knowledge in the Sciences and Humanities and has established a fund to support open access publication charges.[9] It also runs KIT Scientific Publishing,[10] an institutional open access publishing house which actively engages in the Association of European University Presses (AEUP).

It soon became obvious that none of the locally developed repositories would be the long-term solution to supporting the green road to open access at KIT. Two options remained: to migrate to a new repository platform like dspace or fedora, or to expand the possibilities to handle full-text publications within Converis. As has been said before, one of the main arguments in favour of full integration is that Converis already supports a rich and contextual data model which can express temporal roles and relationships between entities. Therefore, it seems natural to follow an integrated approach which avoids the need to develop and maintain interfaces between the CRIS and a repository.

As KIM-FIS is gradually being deployed at KIT during the second half of 2011, a separate project (KIM-FIS Repository) will develop additional functionality to turn Converis into an open access repository. The benchmark will be the DINI Certificate for Document and Publication Services (Dobratz and Scholze, 2006).[11] DINI, the German Initiative for Networked Information, is a coalition formed by German Higher Education infrastructure and service institutions, such as libraries, computing centres and media centres, as well as by scientific learned societies. The DINI Certificate aims at networking document and publication repositories by promoting the use of standards, interoperability and co-operation between Higher Education institutions. It formulates requirements and recommendations covering technical, organisational and policy aspects like visibility, author support, legal issues, indexing and interfaces, access statistics and long-term availability. Looking at the technical parts of the DINI Certificate, the main focus in development will be on external interfaces, like OAI-PMH, SWORD, OpenAire and others, adding to the visibility of publications which is not a traditional feature of a CRIS. From a researcher's perspective this makes perfect sense. A research information system is the back end in which his/her whole research portfolio is available for re-use and external communication. It should provide publication lists for his/her website, for project proposals as well as for his/her CV or for scholarly communication with peers. From this perspective, separating a CRIS from a repository seems is much like erecting an artificial barrier, although the historical development is clear. A CRIS will always have an internal side which is used for evaluation and reporting. This does not prevent its rich and networked data from being displayed externally to achieve maximum visibility. When it comes to publications, it enables storage of all full-text articles and then display of links to the publisher website or internal or external repositories depending on the publisher's open access policy and the user's rights and roles (Figure 3).

Figure 3. KIM-FIS demonstrator with links to the published and the repository version of a publication.

PERSPECTIVES

The motto for developing KIM-FIS is 'think big in small steps'. Therefore a CERIF-based rich data model has been implemented, although, as first steps, only the publication and project information modules will go into production service. Patents, prices and other assets of research output will follow later in 2012 and 2013. By this time, publication management including repository functionality will be operational for some time and will play its part in a large-scale evaluation exercise within the Helmholtz Association of Research Centres, the so-called Programme Oriented Funding (POF).[12] Indicators based on publications will be calculated for comparing the Research Centres (KIT being one of them). KIM-FIS will then be the backbone for this exercise at KIT.

ACKNOWLEDGEMENTS

The authors would like to thank Karlsruhe Institute of Technology (KIT) and the Ministry for Science, Research and the Arts of Baden-Württemberg (MWK) for supporting this work.

NOTES

1 http://www.eurocris.org

2 See the talks at the DINI-Helmholtz-Workshop: *Repositorien — Praxis und Vision*, Berlin 2010, http://www.dini.de/ veranstaltungen/ workshops/ dinihelmholtzworkshop-repositorien-praxis-und-vision/programm/

3 http://ec.europa.eu/research/science-society/index.cfm? Fuseaction =public.

topic&id=1294&lang=1

[4] (Björk *et al.*, 2010) show that repositories in the STM field cover about 12% of the published Journal articles. Cf. Paul Jump: Research intelligence — Empty buckets or pure gold? In: *Times Higher Education* 17 March 2011.

[5] Workshop on CRIS, CERIF and Institutional Repositories. 10–11th May 2010, Rome, Italy. http://www.irpps. cnr.it/it/eventi/workshop-on-cris-cerif-and-nstitutionalrepositories 2nd WORKSHOP ON CRIS, CERIF AND INSTITUTIONAL REPOSITORIES 'Integrating Research Information: CRIS+OAR' 23–24th May 2011, Rome, Italy. http://www.irpps. cnr.it/it/eventi/ 2nd-workshop-on-cris-cerif-andinstitutional- repositories-integrating-research-information-crisoar.

[6] http://www.avedas.com/en/converis.html.

[7] http://kim.cio.kit.edu/138.php.

[8] http://www.orcid.org.

[9] http://www.bibliothek.kit.edu/cms/english/publishing.php.

[10] http://www.ksp.kit.edu.

[11] http://www.dini.de/dini-zertifikat/english/.

[12] http://www.helmholtz.de/en/about_us/programme_oriented_funding/.

REFERENCES

1. Björk, B-C., P. Welling, M. Laakso, P. Majlender, T. Hedlund, *et al.* (2010): 'Open Access to the Scientific Journal Literature: Situation 2009'. *PLoS One*, 5(6), e11273. doi:10.1371/journal.pone.0011273.

2. Carr, L. (2010): 'EPrints: A Hybrid CRIS/Repository'. In: *Workshop on CRIS, CERIF and Institutional Repositories*, 10–11th May 2010, Rome, Italy. http://eprints.ecs.soton. ac.uk/21048/.

3. Dobratz, S. and F. Scholze (2006): 'DINI Institutional Repository Certification and Beyond'. In: *Library Hi Tech*. pp. 583–594.

4. Freudenstein, P., L. Liu, F. Majer, A. Maurer, C. Momm, D. Ried and W. Juling (2006): 'Architektur für ein universitätsweit integriertes Informations- und Dienstmanagement'. In: *Proceedings of INFORMATIK 2006 — Informatik für Menschen, 36. Jahrestagung der Gesellschaft für Informatik*. Dresden. pp. 50–54.

5. Gaedke, M., J. Meinecke and M. Nussbaumer (2005): 'Aspects of Service-Oriented Component Procurement in Web-Based Information Systems'. *International Journal of Web Information Systems* (*IJWIS*), 1(1), 15–24.

6. Hakala, J. (2010): 'Persistent identifiers — an overview'. *KIM Technology Watch Report* 2010. http://metadaten-twr.org/2010/10/13/persistent-identifiers-an-overview/.

7. Hartenstein, H., W. Juling and A. Maurer (2007): 'Karlsruhe Integrated Information Management — KIM'. In: *Changing Infrastructures for Academic Services. Information Management in German Universities. Göttingen*: DINI — Deutsche Initiative für Netzwerkinformation, http://www.dini.de/fileadmin/docs/DINI_Informationsinfrastrukturen.pdf.

8. Jeffery, K.G., A. Asserson and D. Luzi (2010): *State of the Art and Roadmap for Current Research Information Systems and Repositories*. euroCRIS White Paper. http://www.irpps.cnr.it/it/system/files/PositionPaperRoadMap20100610.doc.

9. Razum, M., E. Simons and W. Horstmann (2007): Institutional Repository Workshop Strand Report — Exchanging Research Information. http://www.driver-repository.be/media/docs/KEIRstrandreportExchangingResearchInfoFINALFeb07.pdf

10. Sheppard, N. (2010): 'Learning How to Play Nicely: Repositories and CRIS'. In: *Ariadne* Issue 64 http://www.ariadne.ac.uk/issue64/wrn-repos-2010-05-rpt/.

7

CHAPTER

The Uncertain Representation Ranking Framework for Concept-Based Video Retrieval

Robin Aly[1], Aiden Doherty[3], Djoerd Hiemstra[1], Franciska de Jong[2], Alan F. Smeaton[3]

[1]*Database Group and Human Media Interaction Group, University of Twente, Enschede, The Netherlands*

[2]*British Heart Foundation Health Promotion Research Group, University of Oxford, Oxford, UK*

[3]*CLARITY: Centre for Sensor Web Technologies, Dublin City University, Dublin, Ireland*

ABSTRACT

Concept based video retrieval often relies on imperfect and uncertain concept detectors. We propose a general ranking framework to define effective and robust ranking functions, through explicitly addressing detector uncertainty. It can cope with multiple concept-based representations per video segment and it allows the re-use of effective text retrieval functions which are defined on similar representations. The final ranking status value is a weighted combination of two components: the expected score of the possible scores, which represents the risk-neutral choice, and the scores' standard deviation, which represents the risk or opportunity that the score for the actual representation is higher. The framework consistently improves the search performance in the shot retrieval task and the segment retrieval task over several baselines in five TRECVid collections and two collections which use simulated detectors of varying performance.

Keywords: Representation uncertainty; Concept-based representation; Video retrieval

1 INTRODUCTION

Concept-based video retrieval has many advantages over other content-based approaches (Snoek and Worring 2009). In particular, it is more straightforward to define ranking functions on concept-based representations than for most other content-based representations (Naphade et al. 2006). For example, the definition of a ranking function for the query "Find me tigers" is intuitively more straightforward based on the concept *Animal* in a (video-) segment 1 than based on the color distribution in an example image. As the current state-of-the art in automatic concept detection is not mature enough for ranking functions directly using the binary concept labels occurs/absent (Hauptmann et al. 2007), concept-based search engines use the confidence score of a detector that the concept occurs. However, the uncertainty introduced by the use of confidence scores makes the definition of effective and robust ranking functions again more difficult. This paper presents a general framework for the definition of concept-based ranking functions for video retrieval that fulfill these requirements.

Research in concept-based retrieval currently focuses on the retrieval of video shots, which are segments of roughly five seconds length. According to Kennedy et al. (2008) the main problem here is the definition of query-specific ranking functions, which are often modeled as weighted sums of confidence scores. But the estimation of weights based on semantic distance of the concept to the query or on relevance feedback has proven difficult, which leads to poor performance (Aly et al. 2009). Another approach learns weights for a set of query classes based on relevance judgments for training queries (Yan 2006). However, the gathering of relevance judgments for training queries is expensive and it is unclear how to define a suitable set of query classes. Additionally, although de Vries et al. (2004) find that users do not only search for shots but also for longer segments, concept-based search engines do not support this retrieval task. A likely reason is that a single confidence score per segment does not sufficiently discriminate relevant from nonrelevant segments. However, it is not straightforward to define a more discriminative document representation based on confidence scores. Therefore it is an important challenge to come up with a framework to define ranking functions for varying retrieval tasks that are *effective* for arbitrary queries.

The performance of detectors changes significantly with the employed detection technique and the considered collection (Yang and Hauptmann 2008). If a ranking function strongly depends on a particular distribution of confidence scores, its performance varies, which is clearly undesirable. For example, the confidence scores of the concept *Animal* in relevant shots for the query "Find me tigers" can be high in one collection and low in another collection. Now, if a ranking function assumes that confidence scores for the concept *Animal* in relevant shots are high, its performance will be poor for the second collection. Because current ranking functions are weighted sums of confidence scores they rely on the weight estimation to adapt the weights according to the score distribution of the considered collection. However, how could we estimate these weighted for arbitrary detectors and collections? Therefore it is also an important challenge to define*robust* ranking functions over detectors of varying performance.

In this paper, we propose the uncertain representation ranking (URR) framework which describes a general way to define ranking functions which meet the following challenges:

- they are *effective* for arbitrary queries, and
- they are *robust* over detector techniques and collections.

The framework uses a basic ranking function defined on representations of binary concept labels and addresses the uncertainty of the concept detectors separately. In this paper, we adapt *effective* ranking functions from text retrieval. To address detector uncertainty, the framework considers multiple representations for each document. Applying the basic ranking function to each representation leads to multiple possible retrieval scores for each document. The final score is a combination of the expected score, which represents a good guess of the score of a known representation, and the scores' standard deviation, which represents the chance that the score is actually higher or lower.

Taking into account the expected score makes the performance *robust* against changes of detectors and collections. This paper focuses on the definition of concept-based ranking functions. For this purpose we use results of existing work for the setting of the ranking functions' parameters.

To demonstrate that the framework produces effective and robust ranking functions, we show that this is the case for the shot retrieval task and the segment retrieval task. Note that the ranking functions used for these tasks originate from ideas which we proposed earlier. In Aly et al. (2008) we propose to rank shots by the probability of relevance given the confidence scores, marginalizing over all possible concept occurrence. The ranking function obtained through marginalization is equal to the expected score used in the URR framework. The expected score allows us to additionally model the risk of choosing a certain score. Furthermore, in Aly et al. (2010) we propose a ranking function for segment retrieval, where the idea of ranking by the expected score and the scores' standard deviation is used for the first time for a concept language model ranking function and a document representation in terms of concept frequencies. The URR framework generalizes this idea to arbitrary ranking functions and representations.

The remainder of this paper is structured as follows. First in Sect. 2 related work on treating uncertainty in information retrieval is presented. In Sect. 3 we describe the proposed URR framework. In Sects. 4 and 5 the framework is applied to shot and segment retrieval respectively. Then Sect. 6 describes the experiments which we undertook to evaluate the URR framework. Section 7 discusses the experimental results. Finally, Sect. 8 presents the conclusions.

2 RELATED WORK

In this section we describe how related work approaches uncertainty, both in concept-based video retrieval and in text retrieval. Note that there are significant bodies of research on the storage of uncertainties in databases, see for example Benjelloun et al. (2006), and on the exploitation of uncertain knowledge representations for the inference of new knowledge, see for example Ding and Peng (2004), which lie outside the scope of this paper.

2.1 Concept-based video ranking functions

Most concept-based video ranking functions use confidence scores of detectors built from support vector machines. To ensure comparability of confidence scores among concepts, confidence scores are usually normalized. Platt (2000) provides a method to transform a confidence score into a posterior probability of concept occurrence given the confidence score, which we refer to as probabilistic detector output.

Figure 1 shows a classification of existing concept-based ranking functions into principle ways of dealing with detector uncertainty, to which we refer to as uncertainty classes. On the left the figure shows the confidence scores **o** for the three concepts of a shot together with their ranks within the collection. The confidence scores are then used to determine the posterior probability of each possible concept representations. At the bottom the occurrence probabilities for each concept are combined into the expected concept occurrence. In the following we will describe well-known methods of each uncertainty class.

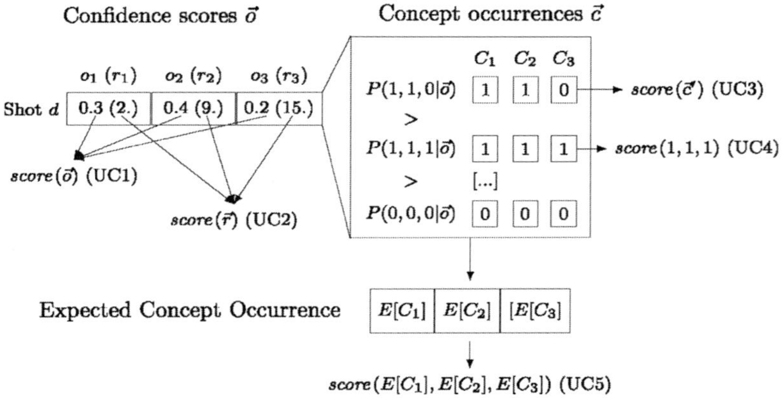

Figure 1. Uncertainty classes (UC1–UC5) of video shot ranking functions *score* using three concepts: confidence score-based (**o**) (UC1), on the rank of confidence scores (**r**) based (UC2), based on the most likely concept representation (**c**′) (UC3), based on the probability that all concepts occur (UC4), and based on the expected concept occurrences (UC5)

In uncertainty class UC1, ranking functions (indicated by *score*) take confidence scores as arguments. Most ranking functions are weighted sums or products of confidence scores, where the used weights carry no particular interpretation (Snoek and Worring 2009). Yan (2006) proposes the Probabilistic Model for combining diverse knowledge sources in multimedia. The proposed ranking function is a discriminative logistic regression model, calculating the posterior probability of relevance given the observation of the confidence scores. Here the confidence score weights are the coefficients of the logistic regression model. The ranking functions of uncertainty class UC1 mainly have the problem that they require knowledge about the confidence score distributions in relevant shots, which is difficult to infer. Additionally, if a concept detector changes, the distribution of confidence scores changes, making existing knowledge obsolete.

In uncertainty class UC2, ranking functions are based on the (inverse) rank of the confidence scores within the collection (McDonald and Smeaton 2005; Snoek et al.2007). As only the ranks of confidence scores are taken into account, estimating weights for this uncertainty class only requires knowledge over the distribution of confidence scores in relevant shots relative to other shots. Otherwise UC2 suffers from the same drawbacks as UC1.

In uncertainty class UC3, ranking functions take a vector of the most probable concept representation as arguments. To the best of our knowledge, no method of this class was proposed in concept-based video retrieval so far, most likely due to the weak performance of concept detectors. Nevertheless, we include this uncertainty class in our discussion because methods of this class have been used in spoken document retrieval, where the most probable spoken sentence is considered (Voorhees and Harman 2000), and once concept detectors improve, ranking functions from this class might become viable.

In uncertainty class UC4, ranking functions use a particular concept representation, not necessarily the most probable, together with its probability. Zheng et al. (2006) propose the point-wise mutual information weight (PMIWS) ranking function. As we showed in Aly et al. (2008), the PMIWS can be seen to rank by the probability of relevance given the occurrence of all selected concepts multiplied by the probability that these concepts occur in the current shot. The main problem of instances of uncertainty class UC4 is that concepts which only occur sometimes in relevant shots cannot be considered. To see this, let us assume perfect detection, a concept that occurs in 50 % of the relevant shots, and a ranking function that only rewards shots in which this concept occurs. Here, relevant shots, in which the concept does not occur, receive zero score.

In uncertainty class UC5, ranking functions take the expected components of concept occurrences as parameters. Li et al. (2007) propose an adaptation of the language modeling framework (Hiemstra 2001) to concept-based shot retrieval. We show in (Aly 2010, p. 32) that the ranking function by Li et al. (2007) can also be interpreted as using the expected concept occurrence in the language modeling framework where concepts (terms) either appear or not. Instead of focusing on one representation, as done by UC3 and UC4, this uncertainty class combines all possible representations into the expected values of a representation, which is then used in a ranking function. The ranking functions of uncertainty class UC5 are limited to arguments of real numbers because they are defined on expectations, which are real numbers. But some existing effective probabilistic ranking functions, for example the binary independence model (Robertson et al. 1981), are defined on binary arguments, and therefore cannot be used. Furthermore, the ranking functions in uncertainty class UC5 result in a single score, which abstract from the uncertainty that is involved by using this result.

The URR framework proposed in this paper can be seen as a general ranking framework of a new uncertainty class (UC6) of ranking functions that are defined on the distribution of all possible concept-based representations of a document. The URR framework uses a basic ranking function to calculate a score for each possible representation. The final ranking score value of a document is then calculated by combining the expected score and the scores' standard deviation according to the probability distribution over the possible representations for this document. This procedure has the following advantages. Compared to the uncertainty classes UC1 and UC2, the basic ranking function of the URR framework does not require knowledge about the distribution of confidence scores in relevant segments. In contrast to the uncertainty classes UC3 and UC4, which both only use a single concept-based representation, the URR framework takes into account all possible representations, which reduces the risk of missing the actual representation of a document. Finally, compared to uncertainty class UC5, the basic ranking functions in the URR framework are defined on concept-based representations, which allow us to re-use existing, effective ranking functions from text retrieval. Additionally, the scores' standard deviation in the URR framework can be seen as a measure of the riskiness of score, which we show can be used in ranking.

2.2 **Uncertainty in text retrieval**

We are not the first to address uncertainty in information retrieval, which has been done before in text retrieval, for example, in probabilistic indexing and in the recently proposed mean-variance analysis framework for uncertain scores, as well as in several other areas. We describe the former two approaches in the following.

2.2.1 Probabilistic indexing

In probabilistic indexing for text retrieval, the assignment of an index terms to a document is only probabilistically known. Croft (1981) approaches this uncertainty by ranking documents according to the expected score of the binary independence ranking function (Robertson et al. 1981). However, Fuhr (1989) shows that, although the binary independence ranking function is a rank preserving simplification of the probability of relevance function, the expected binary independence score is not rank preserving to the expected probability of relevance score. Instead, Fuhr (1989) ranks by the probability of relevance given the confidences of indexers as a ranking function, marginalizing over all possible index term assignments. This marginalization is equivalent to ranking by the expected probability of relevance, which we use as a ranking component of our URR framework in Sect. 4.

Note that there is a difference in interpretation between the marginalization and the expected score used in the URR framework, which we discuss in the following. The marginalization approach considers for each document the probability of relevance of *any* document with the same indexer confidences, which are similar to confidence scores in concept-based video retrieval. On the other hand, the URR framework uses the expected score of a *particular* document. This allows us to consider the scores' standard deviation, which represents the risk or opportunities of ranking a document by its expected score. Additionally, Fuhr assumes that the true index term assignments of a document are always unknown, but for the URR framework concept occurrences are only uncertain because of the uncertainty of detectors. Indeed, the URR framework could be extended to handle the case where the occurrences of some concepts are known, which we propose for future work. Additionally to the expected score, the URR framework considers a component to represent the risk inherent to a retrieval model when ranking a document.

2.2.2 Mean-variance analysis

Wang (2009) proposes the mean-variance analysis framework for managing uncertainty in text retrieval, which is based on the Portfolio Selection Theory (Markowitz 1952) in finance. We believe that the processes in finance are more intuitive, therefore we first describe the Portfolio Selection Theory and describe its application to text retrieval afterwards.

The Portfolio Selection Theory finds efficient portfolios based on the uncertain future win of companies in a portfolio. The win of a portfolio is:

$$Win = \sum_{j=1}^{N} p_j \, d_j.Win \tag{1}$$

where *Win* is the random variable of the total win of the portfolio, $d_j.Win > 0$ is the random variable of company d_j's win 2, and p_j (with $0 \le p_j \le 1$ and $\sum_j p_j = 1$) is the percentage of the available budget invested in company d_j. The Portfolio Selection Theory assumes that analysts can predict the following statistical components for a company d_j:

1. The *expected* win, $E[d_j.Win]$ ("What win is to be expected from the company *d*?").
2. The *variance* of the win, $var[d_j.Win]$ ("How widely do the possible wins vary?").

3. The *co-variance* between the win of company d and any other company d_j, cov[d_j.*Win*, d_i.*Win*] ("How does the win of company d_j influence the win of company d_i?").

The above statistical components are then used to find an efficient portfolio, a set of percentages (p1,...,pN)(p1,...,pN), which optimizes the following expression:

$$E[Win] - b\ \mathrm{var}[Win] \tag{2}$$

where b is the *risk parameter* which represents the risk-attitude of the analysts. If$b > 0$, analysts are *risk-averse*. For $b = 0$, analysts would only invest in the company of the highest expected win, which Markowitz (1952) identified as unreasonable in finance as the whole budge would be invested in the company with the highest expected win. If $b < 0$, analysts like to take risks, which we informally call *risk-loving*. Figure 2 shows an example of the win distributions of two companies d_1 and d_2 ignoring the co-variance between their wins. Intuitively,*risk-averse* and *risk-neutral* analysts invest everything into company d_2 ($p_1 = 0, p_2 = 1$) because it has a higher expected win. However, *risk-loving* analysts speculate on a win of company d_1 in the area denoted by "Opportunity for d_1" and therefore will increase p_1.

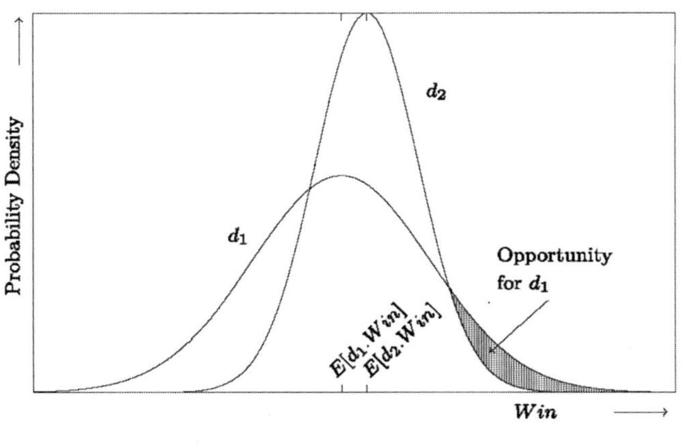

Figure 2. The win distributions of company d_1 and company d_2. The area marked as "Opportunity for d_1" shows the reason why a risk-loving investor ($b < 0$), would buy companies of d_1 ($E[d.Win]$ is the expected win and the variance of the win is implicitly specified by the shape of the Gaussian)

In the mean-variance analysis framework, a document *d* is equivalent to a company and the uncertain score *d.S* of document *d* is equivalent to the uncertain win *d. Win* of the company *d*. For a ranking function *s* the mean-variance analysis assumes that the expected score of a document is $E[d.S] = score(\mathbf{f})$, where **f** is the known representation of document *d*. Wang (2009) transforms the Portfolio Selection criterion from Eq. (2) into a document ranking problem by fixing a percentage p_i to rank *i* rather than to a document and requires that weights monotonically decrease ($p_i > p_{i+1}$). Therefore, it is no longer a question as to what percentage to invest, but how to rank documents. In contrast to the Portfolio Selection Theory, where a risk-neutral attitude $b = 0$ leads to unwanted results, a risk-neutral attitude is an intuitive solution in the mean-variance analysis framework because the expected value is an unbiased estimator of the actual score (Papoulis1984). Therefore, the scores' variance only adds something on top of an already reasonable solution rather than making the solution reasonable, which is the case in the Portfolio Selection Theory. For the transformed Portfolio Selection Theory formula in Eq. (2) to the document ranking problem with fixed percentages, Wang (2009) proposes a greedy algorithm as a solution, which ranks a document d^* at rank *j* which has the highest mean-variance trade-off:

$$d^* = \text{argmax}_d \left(E[d.S] - b\, p_j\, \text{var}[d.S] - 2b \sum_{k=1}^{j-1} p_j\, p_k\, \text{cov}[d.S, d_k.S] \right) \qquad (3)$$

where d1,...,dj−1d1,...,dj−1are the previously ranked documents. In an analogy to the Portfolio Selection Theory, the mean-variance analysis requires estimations for the variance and co-variance of the ranking status value, which Wang (2009), Wang and Zhu (2009) provide.

The URR framework uses a similar ranking algorithm to the one proposed in Eq. (3), using the scores' standard deviation instead of its variance. In the mean-variance analysis, the reason for the uncertainty of a document's score is unspecified. On the other hand, in the URR framework the scores' standard deviation originates from the uncertain document representation. Similar to the mean-variance analysis, the URR framework could also take into account correlations between document representations, to influence the standard deviation of the score. For example, videos usually follow a story and the occurrence of concepts in nearby shots are correlated (the fact that an *Animal* occurs in a shot influences the probability of an *Animal* in a nearby shot). Yang and Hauptmann (2006) are the first to explore the exploitation of such correlations in videos. As until now only oracle models trained on the test collection were able to achieve significant improvements, we leave the consideration of co-variances, although promising, to future work.

3 THE UNCERTAIN REPRESENTATION RANKING FRAMEWORK

This section describes the URR framework which ranks segments by considering uncertain concept-based representations in a similar way as the Mean-Variance framework (Wang 2009)3.

3.1 Intuitive example

Before we formally define the URR framework we introduce an intuitive example using a particular document representation and ranking function. Let us consider a collection of two documents and $n = 2$ concepts. Furthermore, let us assume that an effective ranking function based on known concept occurrences for the current query would be the following:

$$score(\mathbf{c}) = \sum_{i=1}^{n} w_i \, c_i \tag{4}$$

where $\mathbf{c}$ is a binary vector of concept occurrences, $score(\mathbf{c})$ is the ranking function, c_i is a concept occurrence state of concept i ($c_i = 1$ if it occurs), and w_i is the weight for concept i. For this example, let $w_1 = 20$ and $w_2 = 40$. We denote the uncertain concept occurrences in document d by the random variable $d.C$. We assume that concept detectors can predict the occurrence of a concept probabilistically. For example, given a confidence score $o_{d,i}$ for document d, the probabilistic output of a concept detector for concept i, would be $P(d.C_i | o_{d,i})$. For each document, there are 2^n possible combinations of n concept occurring or being absent, which we jointly denote by a vector of random variables $d.\mathbf{C}$. The probabilities of the occurrence of each of the n concepts given the confidence scores **o** can then be combined to the posterior probability of each combination concept stats **c** (a binary vector), $P(d.\mathbf{C} = \mathbf{c}|\mathbf{o})$. According to the ranking function in Eq. (4), each state combination **c** results in a score. We denote the uncertain score of each document d as $d.S = score(d.\mathbf{C})$, a function of random variables, which is again a random variable4. From the above, we can calculate the expected score of a document d, $E[d.S|\mathbf{o}]$, and it's standard deviation $\sqrt{\text{var}[d.S|\mathbf{o}]}$. Figure 3visualizes this scenario (the standard deviation is represented by the spread of the distribution).

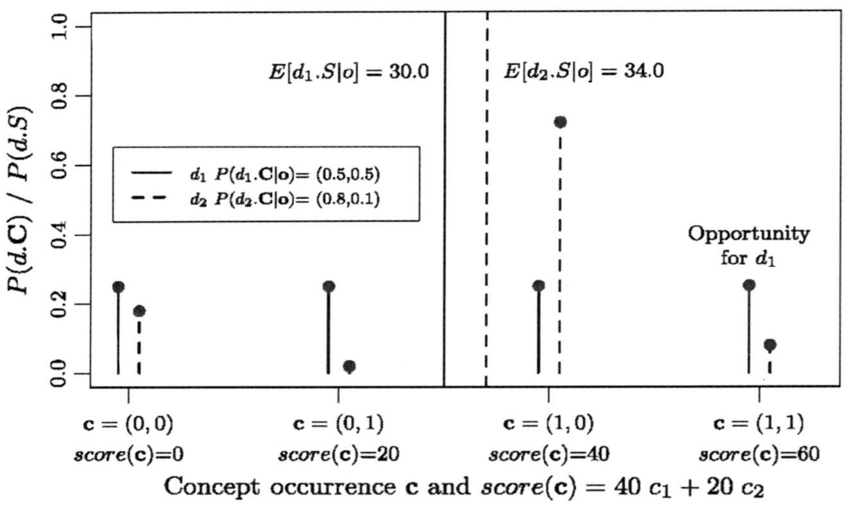

Figure 3. The score distributions for document d_1 and document d_2 considering two concepts. $P(d.\mathbf{C} = \mathbf{c}|\mathbf{o})$ is the probability that the actual concept occurrences are **c**

A search engine in a risk-neutral will rank document d_2 above document $d_1$because it has a higher expected score. However, similar to the analysts in the previous section, the search engine in a risk-loving setting might prefer document d_1 over document d_2 because of the higher probability that the document has the highest score of 60. In the following section we define the URR framework, which generalizes this intuitive case to arbitrary score functions defined on arbitrary concept representations.

3.2 Definitions

Because the URR ranking framework is not specific to a particular type of feature, let F=(F1,...,Fn)F=(F1,...,Fn) be the considered representation of documents for the current query consisting of *n* features (or representation). Formally, each feature F_i is a random variable, a function of documents to feature values. For example, the ranking functions in this paper consider concept occurrences, denoted by *C*s, and concept frequencies, denoted by *CF*s, as features. For the query "Find me tigers", a search engine might consider the frequencies of the concept *Animal* and the concept *Jungle* $\mathbf{CF} = (CF_1, CF_2)$ as features where $CF_1(d)$ and $CF_2(d)$ yield the frequency of the concept *Animal* and the concept *Jungle* in document *d*respectively.

Furthermore, let score: rng(**F**)→IR be a ranking function which maps known feature values to scores, where rng(·) denotes the range of a function. For example, the simple ranking function in Eq. (4), score(f∈ rng(F))=∑iwifiscore w_i is the weight feature value f_i, is such a score function. Note that we adopt the common notation of random variables and denote random variables and functions in the same way as their range, therefore leaving out rng(·) in the following (Papoulis 1984).

Because the feature values of documents are uncertain, we introduce the random variable *d*.**F** for the feature values of document *d*. Furthermore, let*d.S* = *score*(*d*.**F**) be the random variable for the score of document *d* which results from the application of the ranking function *score* on *d*'s uncertain feature values*d*.**F**. For example, if a segment contains *m* shots and the considered representation consists of *n* concept frequencies, the random variable of the uncertain concept frequencies $\mathbf{CF}\ d$ ranges over $(m + 1)^n$ possible frequency combinations, and the random variable *d.S* ranges over the scores obtained from the application of *score* on each combination.

It is important to note the difference between the random variables **F** and the ranking function *score* on the one hand, and its document-specific counter parts*d*.**F** and *d.S* on the other hand. For example, *score*(**F**(*d*)) is the actual score of document *d* based on the known features **F**(*d*). On the other hand, *d*.**F** and *d.S* are random variables for the possible feature values and their corresponding scores of document *d*.

We denote the posterior probability of a document *d* having representation values f∈d.Ff∈d.F given the confidence scores **o** as $P(d.\mathbf{F} = \mathbf{f}|\mathbf{o})$, which we use to calculate the expected score and its standard deviation.

3.3 **Ranking framework**

Using the above definitions we now define statistical components of the URR framework, the expected score and the scores' variance. The most important component of the URR framework is the expected score of a document *d*. That is, if we consider the representation of *d* to be random, what score do we expect on average. As the score *d.S* is a function of its representation *d*.**F**, the expected score can be calculated by using the distribution of *d*.**F** given the confidence scores of the document (Papoulis 1984):

$$E[d.S|\mathbf{o}] = \sum_{\mathbf{f} \in d.\mathbf{F}} score(\mathbf{f})\ P(d.\mathbf{F} = \mathbf{f}|\mathbf{o}) \tag{5}$$

where $E[d.S|\mathbf{o}]$ is the expected score given the confidence scores **o**. Furthermore, the scores' variance is (Papoulis 1984):

$$\text{var}[d.S|\mathbf{o}] = E[d.S^2|\mathbf{o}] - E[d.S|\mathbf{o}]^2 \tag{6}$$

with

$$E[d.S^2|\mathbf{o}] = \sum_{\mathbf{f} \in d.\mathbf{F}} score(\mathbf{f})^2\ P(d.\mathbf{F} = \mathbf{f}|\mathbf{o}) \tag{7}$$

where $E[d.S^2|\mathbf{o}]$ is the expected squared score. Similar to the greedy algorithm in Eq. (3) of the mean-variance analysis framework, the URR framework finally ranks documents by the expected score plus a weighted expression of the scores' standard deviation:

$$RSV(d) = E[d.S|\mathbf{o}] - b\sqrt{\text{var}[d.S|\mathbf{o}]} \tag{8}$$

where $RSV(d)$ is the final ranking status value by which document d is ranked, $E[d.S|\mathbf{o}]$ is the expected score of document d in Eq. (5), b represents the risk-attitude of the search engine, and $\sqrt{\mathrm{var}[d.S|\mathbf{o}]}$ is the scores' standard deviation in Eq. (6). Equation (8) is the general ranking framework proposed in this paper. In the following Sects. 4 and 5 we adapt the URR framework for two particular basic ranking functions for particular representations.

4 SHOT RETRIEVAL

In this section we describe an adaptation of the URR framework to shot retrieval in which the expected score component is equivalent to the Probabilistic Framework of Unobservable Binary (PRFUBE), which was originally proposed by Aly et al. (2008). Additional to the expected score, we define the scores' standard deviation. For consistency reasons we use the name PRFUBE for our method for shot retrieval, despite the additional consideration of the scores' standard deviation.

4.1 Representation and ranking function

The PRFUBE considers binary concept-based representations, where each concept either occurs or is absent in shot. By using the analogy of concept occurrences in shots and index term assignments to documents, PRFUBE re-uses the probability of relevance given index term assignments (Robertson et al. 1981) as a ranking function:

$$score(\mathbf{c}) = P(R|\mathbf{C}{=}\mathbf{c}) = \frac{P(\mathbf{C}{=}\mathbf{c}|R)\ P(R)}{P(\mathbf{C}{=}\mathbf{c})} \tag{9}$$

where $P(R|\mathbf{C} = \mathbf{c})$ is the probability of relevance given that the concept occurrences $\mathbf{c}$ of the concept-based representation $\mathbf{C}$, $P(\mathbf{C} = \mathbf{c}|R)$ is the probability of the concept occurrences $\mathbf{c}$ given relevance, $P(\mathbf{C} = \mathbf{c})$ is the prior of the concept occurrences $\mathbf{c}$, and $P(R)$ is the relevance prior. Because of the uncertainty of concept occurrences $\mathbf{c}$, we use the ranking function in Eq. (9) as a basic ranking function in the URR framework.

4.2 Framework integration

The integration of the ranking function in Eq. (9) into the URR framework requires the definition of a random variable for the uncertain representation and its expected score. Let $d.\mathbf{C}$ be the uncertain binary concept-based representation of document d, and let $d.S = score(d.\mathbf{C})$ be the uncertain score of document d define in Eq. (9). We now define the expected score and the expected squared score which we used in the URR framework in Eq. (5) and in Eq. (7). The expected score of document d is:

$$E[d.S|\mathbf{o}] = \sum_{\mathbf{c} \in d.\mathbf{C}} score(\mathbf{c})\ P(d.\mathbf{C} = \mathbf{c}|\mathbf{o}) \qquad (10)$$

where $\mathbf{c}$ is one of $|d.\mathbf{C}| = 2^n$ possible representations of n considered concepts, and$\mathbf{o}$ are the confidence scores for document d. Note that the calculation in Eq. (10) has a run-time complexity of $O(2^n)$, which makes it inapplicable to realistic numbers of concepts. We make the following independence assumptions to make the computation efficient:

$$P(\mathbf{C}|R) = \prod_i^n P(C_i|R) \qquad (11)$$

$$P(\mathbf{C}) = \prod_i^n P(C_i) \qquad (12)$$

$$P(d.\mathbf{C}|\mathbf{o}) = \prod_i^n P(d.C_i|o_i) \qquad (13)$$

where Eq. (11) assumes conditional independence of all random variables C_i given relevance, which is a common assumption in text retrieval. Following Fuhr (1989), Eq. (12) assumes that concept variables are independent in the whole collection. Finally, Eq. (13) assumes that the occurrence of concepts is independent from the occurrence of other concepts $(P(C_1, C_2|o_1, o_2) = P(C_1|o_1, o_2)\ (P(C_2|o_1, o_2))$ and from confidence scores of other concepts $(P(C_1|o_1,o_2) = P(C_1|o_1))$. Using the above independence assumptions, the expected score in Eq. (10) can be expressed as follows:

$$E[d.S|\mathbf{o}] = P(R) \sum_{\mathbf{c} \in d.\mathbf{C}} \prod_{i}^{n} \frac{P(C_i = c_i|R)}{P(C_i = c_i)} P(d.C_i = c_i|o_i) \tag{14}$$

where we can ignore the query-specific constant $P(R)$. Additionally, because **c** is a vector of binary values, the generalized distributive law can be applied (Aji and McEliece 2000). This results in the expected score, which has a linear run-time complexity in the number of concepts:

$$E[d.S|\mathbf{o}] = \prod_{i=1}^{n} \left[\underbrace{\frac{P(C_i|R)}{P(C_i)} P(d.C_i|o_i)}_{C_i \text{ occurs}} + \underbrace{\frac{1 - P(C_i|R)}{1 - P(C_i)} (1 - P(d.C_i|o_i))}_{C_i \text{ isabsent}} \right] \tag{15}$$

where $P(C_i|R)$ is the probability of concept C_i occurring in relevant shots, $P(C_i)$ is the prior of concept C_i, and o_i is the confidence score for concept C_i. Here, the probability $P(C|R)$ is a weight which has to be defined for each query, and the prior$P(C)$, which can be estimated from the data, see Sect. 6. Furthermore, for the calculation of the scores' standard deviation in Eq. (6), we also require the expected squared score:

$$E[d.S^2|\mathbf{o}] = \sum_{\mathbf{c} \in d.\mathbf{C}} score(\mathbf{c})^2 P(d.\mathbf{C} = \mathbf{c}|\mathbf{o}) \tag{16}$$

The calculation in Eq. (16) also has a run-time complexity of $O(2^n)$. Using similar assumptions and derivations as in Eq. (14) and in Eq. (15), we can derive a more efficient function for the expected squared score:

$$E[d.S^2|\mathbf{o}] = \prod_{i=1}^{n} \left[\left[\frac{P(C_i|R)}{P(C_i)} \right]^2 P(d.C_i|o_i) + \left[\frac{1 - P(C_i|R)}{1 - P(C_i)} \right]^2 (1 - P(d.C_i|o_i)) \right] \tag{17}$$

where the parameters are the same as in Eq. (15). The expected score in Eq. (15) and the standard deviation [calculated using the expected squared score in Eq. (17)] can then be used to calculate the URR retrieval score in Eq. (8).

5 SEGMENT RETRIEVAL

In this section we describe the Uncertain Concept Language Model (UCLM) ranking function for segment retrieval, which was originally presented in Aly et al. (2010). While the original publication already contained the main ideas of the URR framework, it was specific to the representation of document representations of concept frequencies and concept language model as a ranking function. In this paper, we describe the UCLM as an instance of the URR framework.

5.1 Representation and ranking function

We model a long segment, for example a news item, as a sequence of shots. Figure 4 shows the analogy between spoken text consisting of three spoken words, and a segment consisting of the occurrence of three shots. We denote the *j*th shot of a segment *d* as $d.s_j$, and the occurrence of a concept C_i in $d.s_j$ as $C_i(d.s_j) \in \{0, 1\}$. If we know the concept occurrences in each shot of a segment, we can represent a segment by its concept frequencies, in an analogy to the term frequency of a spoken text, as a sum of occurrences: $CF_i(d) = \sum_j^{dl} C_i(d.s_j)$, where *dl* is the segment length in the number of shots. For example, the segment in Figure 4 would be represented by the concept frequency vector $\mathbf{CF}(d) = (5, 3, 1)$ meaning that there are five concept occurrences of the first concept, three of the second concept, and one of the third concept.

Based on the representation of concept frequencies, we define a ranking function, which is derived from the language modeling framework (Hiemstra 2001). The basic idea behind our approach is to consider the occurrence and absence of a concept as two concept words of the language of this concept, and instead of a single stream of terms, we have multiple concept streams. We then use the language model ranking function with Dirichlet smoothing (Zhai and Lafferty 2004) as a ranking function:

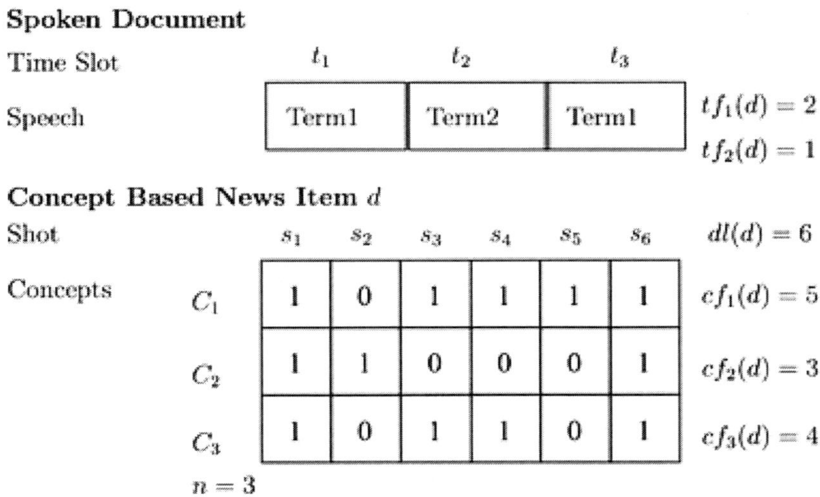

Figure 4. A concept-based segment representation and its analogy to a spoken document. Note that, compared to the main text, we use here the shorter notation s_j for shot $d.s_j$

$$score(\mathbf{cf}) = \prod_{i}^{n} \frac{cf_i + \mu\, P(C_i|\mathcal{D})}{dl + \mu} \tag{18}$$

where **cf** is a vector of n concept frequencies, C_i refers to the ith selected concept, cf_i is the concept frequency of concept Ci,P(Ci|D)Ci,P(Ci|D) is the prior of encountering concept C_i, dl is the segment length (in numbers of shots), and μ is the Dirichlet parameter. Note that in this setting, the segment length dl is always known, since we assume a perfect segmentation of videos.

5.2 **Framework integration**

Because the concept occurrences in each shot are uncertain, the concept frequencies of the surrounding segment are also uncertain. Therefore, we introduce for each segment d a random variable for its representation consisting of concept frequencies $d.\mathbf{CF} = (d.CF_1, \ldots, d.CF_n)$, where $d.CF_i$ is the uncertain concept frequency of concept C_i. As the representation of segment d is uncertain, so is the concept language score in Eq. (18), for which we introduce the random variable $d.S = score(d.\mathbf{CF})$. The expected score and the expected squared score are:

$$E[d.S|\mathbf{o}] = \sum_{\mathbf{cf} \in d.\mathbf{CF}} score(\mathbf{cf})\, P(d.\mathbf{CF} = \mathbf{cf}|\mathbf{o}) \quad (19)$$

$$E[d.S^2|\mathbf{o}] = \sum_{\mathbf{cf} \in d.\mathbf{CF}} score(\mathbf{cf})^2\, P(d.\mathbf{CF} = \mathbf{cf}|\mathbf{o}) \quad (20)$$

where **cf** is one of $|d.\mathbf{CF}| = (dl + 1)^n$ possible concept frequency representations of n concepts in a segment with dl shots, $P(d.\mathbf{CF} = \mathbf{cf}|\mathbf{o})$ is the probability that segment d has the concept frequencies **cf**. For example, the probability of a concept frequency one for a concept C_i in segment d with segment length $dl = 3$ is:

$$P(d.CF_i = 1|\mathbf{o}) = P(d.\mathrm{C}_i = (1,0,0)|\mathbf{o}) + P(d.\mathrm{C}_i = (0,1,0)|\mathbf{o}) + P(d.\mathrm{C}_i = (0,0,1)|\mathbf{o}) \quad (21)$$

where $d.\mathbf{C}$ is a short form for (d.s1.C,d.s2.C,d.s3.C). Because of the independence assumptions in Eq. (13), the probability of a sequence of concept occurrences **c** in a segment in Eq. (21) for concept C is:

$$P(d.\mathbf{C} = \mathbf{c}|\mathbf{o}) = \prod_{j=1}^{dl} P(d.s_j.C = c_j|o(d.s_j))$$

where $o(d.s_j)$ is the confidence score of concept C in shot $d.s_j$. Finally, the probability that a segment has the concept frequency representation **cf** can be calculated as follows:

$$P(d.\mathbf{CF} = \mathbf{cf}|\mathbf{o}) = \prod_{i}^{n} P(d.CF_i = cf_i|\mathbf{o}) \quad (22)$$

where $P(d.CF_i = cf_i|\mathbf{o})$ is calculated according to Eq. (21). In general, Eq. (22) can be used to calculate the expected score in Eq. (19) and expected squared score in Eq. (20) which to rank segments according to the URR ranking function in Eq. (8). However, the high number of possible representations prohibits a direct calculation of the above formulae. To reduce the computational costs, we use the Monte Carlo Sampling method (Liu 2002) to approximate the expectations in Eq. (19) and in Eq. (20): we first generate *NS* random samples of concept frequency representations, $\mathbf{cf}^1, \ldots, \mathbf{cf}^{NS}$, from the distribution $P(d.\mathbf{CF}|\mathbf{o})$. We generate a sample of a concept frequency of concept C_i for segment *d* by using the concept occurrence probabilities of each shot:

$$cf_i^k = \sum_{j=1}^{dl} [(rnd() < P(d.s_j.C_i|\mathbf{o})) \ ? \ 1 \ : \ 0]$$

where *k* is the index of the sample, C_i is the considered concept, and *rnd*() generates a uniform random number in the interval [0:1]. The notation $(X) \ ? \ Y : Z$ has the following meaning: if the generated random number is lower than the probability of concept occurrence in shot *j* (*X*), we increase the concept frequency of the sample by 1 (*Y*), otherwise the frequency is left unchanged (*Z*). We repeat this procedure for all considered concepts in the representation for each of the *NS* samples. Note that the samples can be generated at indexing time to reduce computational costs at query time. The Monte Carlo estimate for the expected score in Eq. (19) and the expected squared score in Eq. (20) is then:

$$E[d.S|\mathbf{o}] \simeq \frac{1}{NS} \sum_{k=1}^{NS} score(\mathbf{cf}^k)$$

$$E[d.S^2|\mathbf{o}] \simeq \frac{1}{NS} \sum_{k=1}^{NS} score(\mathbf{cf}^k)^2$$

where both approximations have a linear run-time complexity in the number of samples *NS*. Because the standard error of the Monte Carlo estimate is in the order of $1/\sqrt{NS}$, a good estimate is already achieved with relatively few samples. Note that there are more advanced sampling methods which further reduce the required samples, for example importance sampling (Liu 2002). But here we focus on the qualitative results of sampling and leave more advanced sampling methods for future work.

6 EXPERIMENTS

In this section we present the experiments which we undertook to evaluate the performance of the URR framework. We investigated two retrieval tasks in connection with the annual TRECVid evaluation workshop (Smeaton et al. 2006): the automatic shot retrieval task, which is a standard task in TRECVid, and the segment retrieval task, which we proposed earlier to accommodate the user's need to search for longer segments (Aly et al. 2010). Note that because we focus on purely concept-based search the performance figures presented in this section are not directly comparable with figures reported elsewhere which also use features such as text and visual similarity.

6.1 Experiment setup

In the following we describe the general experimental setup. Table 1 shows statistics of the collections used. We used the output of state-of-the-art concept detectors which were released by participants of the TRECVid workshops. For the segment retrieval task, we used a segmentation of broadcast news videos into news items from the tv05t and tv06t collection, which was provided by Hsu et al. (2006). The segmentation resulted in 2,451 news items and 5,380 news items respectively.

Table 1. Statistics of the collections used in the experiments

Collection	Shots	Domain	Queries	Detectors sets	Number of concepts	Training collection for ADCS
tv05t	45,765	News	24	MM101	101	tv05d
tv06t	79,484	News	24	Vireo	374	tv05d
tv07t	18,142	G.TV	24	Vireo	374	tv05d
tv08t	35,766	G.TV	48	Vireo	374	tv05d
tv08t	35,766	G.TV	48	MM09	64	tv07d
tv09t	61,384	G.TV	24	MM09	64	tv07d

tvXXt TRECVid test collection of year 20XX, *News* Broadcast News, *G.TV* General Dutch Television. The detector sets are described in the following publications: MM101 (Snoek et al. 2006), Vireo (Jiang et al. 2010), MM09 (Snoek et al. 2008)

Some ranking functions use concept priors in their formula, which we estimated from the data:

$$P(C) = \frac{\sum_d P(d.C|\mathbf{o})}{N}$$

where $P(C)$ is the concept prior of concept C, $P(d.C|\mathbf{o})$ is the posterior probability of concept C in shot d, and N is the number of shots in the collection.

Before we execute a query we first needed to select concepts and estimate the corresponding ranking function parameters. We used the Annotation-Driven Concept Selection (ADCS) which showed good performance on several collections (Aly et al. 2009). The ADCS method is based on a collection with known concept occurrences and textual shot descriptions. The probability of a concept occurrence given relevance was estimated by executing the textual query on the shot descriptions and using the known concept occurrences for the estimation of the probability (Aly et al. 2009). The shot descriptions consisted of the automatic speech recognition output together with the corresponding Wikipedia articles of the occurring concepts. We used the general-purpose retrieval engine PF/Tijah (Hiemstra et al. 2006) to rank the shot descriptions in the training collection. The parameter m of the ADCS method states the numbers of top-ranked shot descriptions we assume are relevant. For each concept, the method estimates the probability of the concept's occurrence given relevance, $P(C|R)$. To select concepts, we used these estimates together with the concept priors to calculate the Mutual Information between a concept and relevance which was identified by Huurnink et al. (2008) as a measure of usefulness. From the resulting ranked list of concepts, we selected the first n concepts.

The performance of current concept detectors is still limited, and the resulting search performance is low compared to, for example, performance figures from text retrieval. Therefore we also used our simulation-based approach (Aly et al.2012) to investigate the search performance of the considered ranking functions with increased detector performance. This is in line with work reported in Toharia et al. (2009) which artificially varied the quality of concept detector performance in order to study the impact of improving or degrading this, on retrieval.

In the simulation the confidence scores of the positive and the negative class of known concept occurrences are modeled as Gaussian distributions. Changes in detector performance are simulated by changing the Gaussians' parameters. For each concept in each shot we generated confidence scores randomly from the Gaussian corresponding to the concept occurrence status. On the resulting collection of confidence scores, we executed the considered ranking functions, resulting in the average precision of each method with these confidence scores. We repeated this procedure 25 times, yielding an estimation of the search performance we would expect for retrieval using detectors with these parameters. To keep our discussion focused, we only investigate the search performance when changing the confidence scores' mean of the positive class—therefore making the detector on average more confident about the concept occurrences. For a more detailed description of this simulation approach, we refer the interested reader to Aly et al. (2012).

6.2 **Shot retrieval**

In this section we describe the evaluation of our shot retrieval model PRFUBE described in Sect. 4. Table 2 shows the ranking functions to which we compared the PRFUBE. Note that it would have been interesting to compare PRFUBE with the Probabilistic Model for combining diverse Knowledge Sources in Multimedia by Yan (2006). However, we were not able to include this ranking function because it required confidence scores on a development collection which are only available for the text collection tv05t. In the following, we present the results from first investigating the influence of the risk parameter b on the search results, the results of using the user study for concept selection and the results from using automatic concept selection via the ADCS method.

6.2.1 Risk parameter study

Figure 5 shows the influence of the risk parameter b on the search performance of PRFUBE in the tv05t collection. For a risk-averse attitude, $b > 0$, the search performance quickly decreases to virtually zero and for a risk-loving or risk-neutral attitude, $b \leq 0$, the search performance stays approximately the same. These results were similar in the other collections investigated. Therefore, in the following we used a risk-neutral $b = 0$ attitude for PRFUBE as it provided the best performance.

Table 2. Considered ranking functions (Rank Func.) for shot retrieval (c' binary detector $(P(C|o) > 0.5 \rightarrow c' = 1)$, $p = P(C|R)$, $q = P(C|R) \sim P(C)$)

Rank Func.	Description	Definition
CombMNZ	Multiply non-zero	$\prod_i P(C_i\|o_i)$ with $P(C_i\|o_i) > 0$
CombSUM	Unweighted sum of scores	$\sum_i P(C_i\|o_i)$
PMIWS	Pointwise mutual information weighting scheme	$\sum_i \log\left(\frac{P(C_i\|R)}{P(C_i)}\right) P(C_i\|o_i)$
Borda	Rank based	$\sum_i rank(P(C_i\|o_i))$
BIM	Binary independence model	$\sum_i c'_i \log\left(\frac{p(1-q)}{q(1-p)}\right)$
ELM	Expected concept occurrence language model ($\lambda = 0.1$)	$\prod_i [\lambda P(C_i\|o_i) + (1 - \lambda) P(C_i\|\mathcal{D})]$

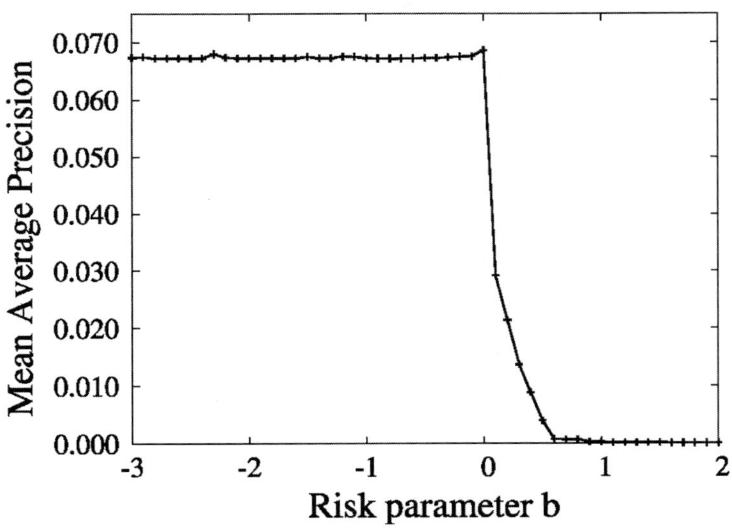

Figure 5. Risk parameter b for the ranking function $RSV(d) = E[d.S|\mathbf{o}] - b\sqrt{\text{var}[d.S|\mathbf{o}]}$

6.2.2 Performance comparison

Table 3 summarizes the retrieval performance of the seven considered ranking functions over five collections with automatically selected concepts using the ADCS method. For each ranking function, the table reports three numbers. First, the optimal performance, in mean average precision (MAP), the method achieved, second, the cut-off value *m*, and finally, the number of concepts *n* used to achieve this performance. On the right, the average rank of the method over the six runs is reported. The PRFUBE is, on average, the best ranking function. In three out of six runs, PRFUBE was the best performing ranking function. In the remaining runs, its performance was the second best and not significantly worse than the best run. When taking the queries of all collections together, the MAP of the PRFUBE was significantly better than the one of the *ELM* method and the PMIWS method.

Table 3. Mean average precision of the ranking functions described in Table 2

Collection Rank Func.	tv05t MM101	tv06t Vireo	tv07t Vireo	tv08t Vireo	tv08t MM09	tv09t MM09	Avg. rank
CombMNZ	0.064	0.033†	0.028	0.024†	0.042†	0.045†	4.7
	10/8	700/30	100/20	10/15	100/30	100/10	
PMIWS	0.054	0.039	0.021	**0.041**	**0.058**	0.067	2.7
	100/8	200/30	200/15	50/4	50/4	50/2	
Borda	0.050†	0.012†	0.020†	0.030	0.045†	0.058	5.5
	10/15	100/10	50/20	10/15	10/2	10/8	
BIM	0.044†	0.024†	0.026	0.037	0.050	0.063	4.8
	10/8	100/2	100/8	100/4	50/2	50/2	
ELM	**0.071**	0.040	0.031	0.040	0.050	0.064	2.3
	10/8	600/30	50/10	100/4	10/2	50/2	
PRFUBE	0.069	**0.043**	**0.039**	0.041	0.056	**0.068**	1.5
	150/10	600/30	100/45	100/4	100/4	50/2	

For each ranking function in each collection, three values are shown: first, the search performance in MAP, second, the number of document considered by the ADCS method (m), and finally the number of considered concepts (n). The † symbol indicates that the method is significantly *worse* than the best method for this collection, according to a two-sided, paired Wilcoxon signed rank test with a significance level of 0.05

6.3 Segment retrieval

We now describe the experiments we undertook to evaluate the performance of the UCLM ranking function from Sect. 5 for segment retrieval. Because of the novelty of the segment retrieval task there is no standard set of queries. Therefore we decided on using the official queries for the tv05t and tv06t collections, replacing the common prefix "*Find shots of*\ldots" with "*Find news items about*\ldots" . Furthermore, we assumed that a news item is relevant to a given query if it contains at least one relevant shot, which we determined from the relevance judgments for the respective shot retrieval task. We propose that for most queries this is realistic since the user could be searching for the news item as a whole, rather than for shots within the news item.5

To the best of our knowledge, no comparable ranking functions exist for the segment retrieval task. Therefore, we compared the UCLM ranking function against extensions of the shot ranking functions from Table 2 and a ranking function which is similar to the one from spoken document retrieval. To use the shot ranking functions for segment retrieval, we used the average probability of concept occurrence in the shots of a segment as the normalized confidence score of the segment6:

$$P(d.C|o_d) = \frac{\sum_j P(d.s_j.C|o_d)}{dl}$$

where $P(d.C|o_d)$ is the normalized average occurrence probability of concept C. Furthermore, using similar analogies of concept occurrences and term utterances as in Sect. 5, we investigated two variants of the language modeling framework. First, we used for every concept its most likely binary state (assuming a concept occurs if $P(d.C|o_d) > 0.5$) and determined the concept frequencies through counting. Segments were then ranked using the language modeling framework with Dirichlet smoothing (Zhai and Lafferty 2004):

$$\text{Best-1}(\mathbf{cf}) = \prod_i^n \frac{cf_i + \mu\, P(C_i|\mathcal{D})}{dl + \mu} \tag{23}$$

where cf_i is the concept frequency of concept C_i. We refer to this ranking function as the Best-1 function. Second, we transferred the ranking function from Chia et al. (2008), which was originally proposed for spoken document retrieval, to a concept-based ranking function, referred to as the expected concept frequency language model ECFLM. The ECFLM method is based on representations of expected concept frequencies, where the expected concept frequency of a single concept is defined as:

$$E[d.CF_i|\mathbf{o}] = \sum_{j=1}^{dl} P(d.s_j.C_i|o_i(d.s_j)) \tag{24}$$

where $E[d.CF_i|\mathbf{o}]$ is the expected concept frequency and $P(d.s_j.C_i|o_i(d.s_j))$ is the occurrence probability of concept C_i in shot $d.s_j$. Similar to the Best-1 ranking function, the ECFLM ranks segments using the language model ranking function in Eq. (23) replacing the concept frequency cf_i with the expected concept frequency in Eq. (24).

To rule out random effects when generating samples for the UCLM method, see Sect. 5, we repeated each run ten times and reported the average.

6.3.1 Risk parameter study

Figure 6 shows a parameter study of the UCLM ranking function on the tv05t collection. The horizontal line represents the search performance of the ECFLM ranking function which is independent of the considered risk. With a risk parameter larger than $b > -1$, the search performance of the UCLM ranking function deteriorated. For values of $b \geq -1$ the method improved over the ECFLM method, and reached its maximum at $b = -2$. We performed similar parameters studies for the Dirichlet parameter μ and the required number of samples NS, see 5. In both cases, the UCLM ranking function was robust against parameter changes. We used $NS = 200$ samples, a Dirichlet parameter of $\mu = 60$, and a risk factor $b = -2$ for the following experiments.

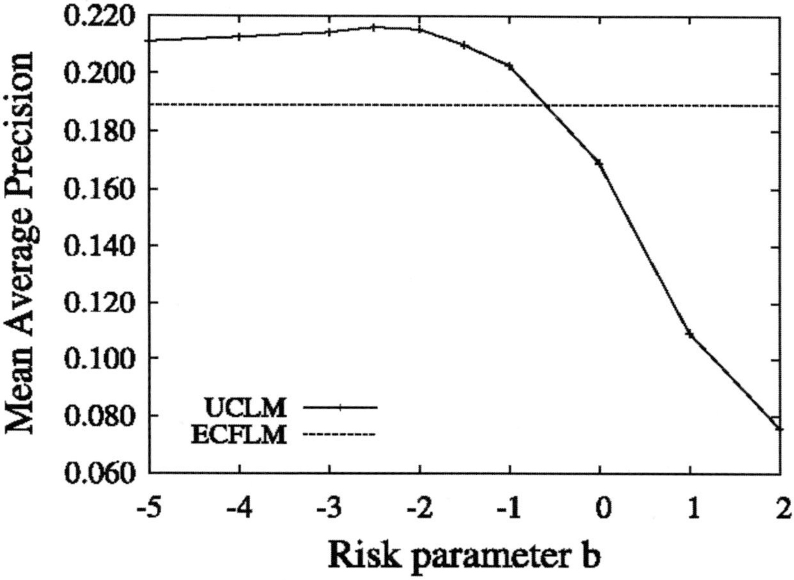

Figure 6. Risk parameter *b* for the ranking function $RSV(d) = E[d.S|\mathbf{o}] - b\sqrt{\mathrm{var}[d.S|\mathbf{o}]}$

6.3.2 Performance comparison

Table 4 shows the comparison results of the described ranking function with the proposed UCLM ranking function. The first column for each collection indicates the number of concepts under which each ranking function performed the best. We see that the ranking functions CombMNZ, CombSUM, PMIWS, Borda, and Best-1 perform worse than the two ranking functions ECFLM and UCLM. The search performance of the UCLM ranking function is 0.214 MAP for the tv05t and 0.135 for the tv06t collection respectively. The improvement of the UCLM ranking function against all other ranking functions was significant according to a two-sided, paired Wilcoxon signed rank test with a significance level of 0.05.

Table 4. Results of comparing the proposed UCLM framework against four other methods described in related work

Ranking function	tv05t			tv06t		
	Concepts *n*	MAP	P10	Concepts *n*	MAP	P10
CombMNZ	10	0.105	0.045	8	0.034	0.040
PMIWS	6	0.102	0.080	2	0.050	0.065
Borda	1	0.090	0.000	2	0.052	0.061
Best-1	5	0.094	0.245	6	0.073	0.083
ECFLM	10	0.192	0.287	32	0.101	0.143
UCLM	10	0.214*	0.291	18	0.135*	0.151

The * symbol indicates that the improvement of the UCLM framework compared to this ranking function were significant according to a two-sided, paired Wilcoxon signed rank test with a significance level of 0.05 against all other methods

6.4 Simulated concept detectors

In this section we describe the results we obtained by simulating the outputs of concept detectors. The simulation procedure required a collection with known concept occurrences, for which we used the *tv*05*d* collection. To make the concept selection realistic, we divided the collection into a test and development set (mm.dev and mm.test respectively) according to Snoek et al. (2006)7. Figure 7shows the results of improved detector performance on improved search performance for the mm.dev collection with realistically set weights estimated by ADCS8. The x-axis shows the increase in detector performance in terms of MAP which resulted from the increase of the mean confidence scores of the shots in which the concept occurs. The y-axis shows the resulting expected search performance in terms of MAP. Figure 7a shows that the PRFUBE method consistently performs better than the other ranking functions at all levels of concept detector performance. With high detector performance, the search performance of the PRUFBE ranking function and the BIM ranking function converges, as both rankings are similar under perfect detection.

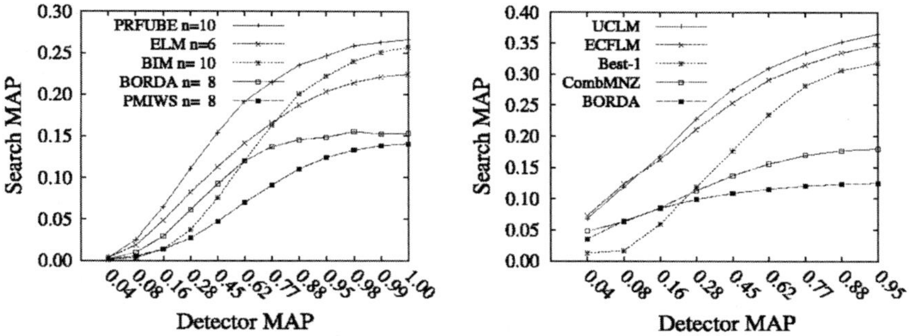

(a) Shot Retrieval (b) Segment Retrieval

Figure 7. Results from simulated concept detectors changing the mean of the positive class μ_1 using realistically set parameters

Figure 7b shows the simulation results for the segment retrieval task. At low detector performance, the UCLM ranking function performs practically identical to the ECFLM ranking function. With a higher detector performance, the UCLM ranking function wins in performance. The Best-1 ranking function increases performance only with much higher detector performance.

6.5 Influence of the scores' standard deviation

For the PRFUBE, the consideration of the scores' standard deviation did not improve performance, see Figure 5, while it did for the UCLM method, see Figure 6. Therefore, we investigated whether the reason for this lies in the relationship between the expected scores and the scores' standard deviation of the respective function. Note that for a risk-loving attitude ($b > 0$), if the standard deviation $\sqrt{\mathrm{var}[d.S]}$ increases monotonically with the expected score $E[d.S]$, it does not affect the ranking compared to only using the expected score. Figure 8 plots the expected score $E[d.S]$ (x-axis) against the standard deviation $\sqrt{\mathrm{var}[d.S]}$ (y-axis) for the 200 highest ranked documents of the given queries in the tv05t collection. For PRFUBE, the standard deviation is roughly monotonically increasing with the expected score, while for UCLM there is much more variability. The results for other queries and collections were similar.

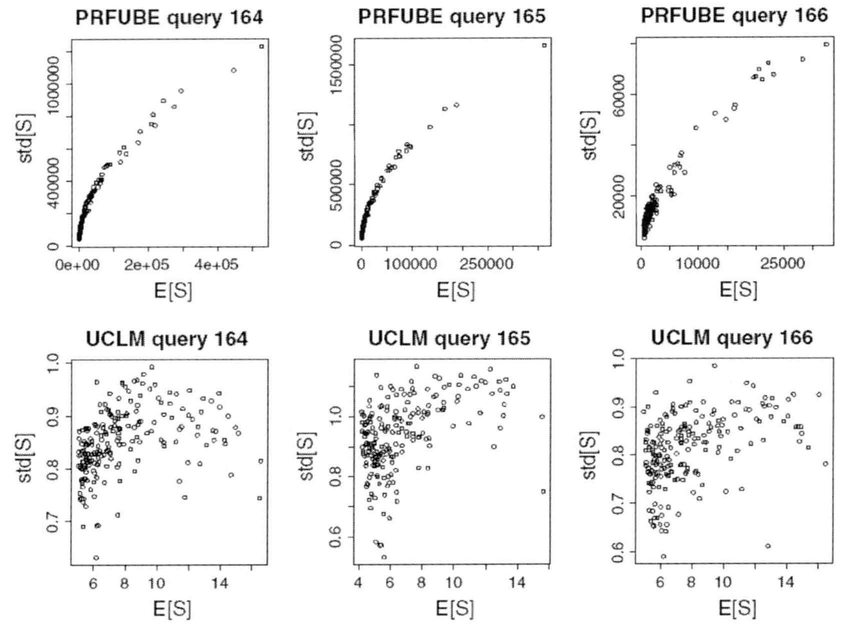

Figure 8. The relationship between expected score and standard deviation of the PRFUBE method and the UCLM method on the tv05t collection

7 DISCUSSION

We now discuss the experimental results obtained in the previous section.

7.1 Effectiveness

Both derivations of the URR framework, PRFUBE and UCLM, showed significant improvement over most other retrieval methods from other uncertainty classes, as shown in Tables 3 and 4. Furthermore, according to the simulations presented in Figure 7, both methods will also continue having a strong performance compared to other methods as concept detector performance improves.

7.2 Robustness

Given the relative low overall performance numbers, strong performance in some collections could be caused by particular "lucky" detections in relevant shots. Therefore, a robust retrieval method is not only effective (has good performance in many collections) but also stable (performs similar across collections). Table 3shows that the PRFUBE is robust in six different collections. Similarly, the UCLM method performed stably for two collections. Furthermore, the detector simulation experiments in Figure 7 suggest that the performance improvements are robust against changes of detectors.

7.3 Risk-attitude

In both instances of the URR framework, a risk-neutral or risk-loving attitude helped performance. For the PRFUBE, the risk-loving attitude did not increase performance. We propose that the almost monotonic relationship between expected score and standard deviation in Figure 8 is the reason why the standard deviation does not improve the ranking for PRFUBE. We expect that the practically monotonic relationship of expected score and standard deviation of the PRFUBE originates from the independence assumptions made in Eq. (11)–(13), which are known not to match the data (Cooper 1995), and propose further investigations for future work. For the UCLM, there was much higher variability in the standard deviation compared to the expected scores, giving the standard deviation the possibility to improve the ranking. Here, a risk-loving attitude improved performance significantly over the strongest baseline.

8 CONCLUSIONS

In summary, we proposed the URR framework that meets the challenge to define*effective* and *robust* ranking functions in concept-based video retrieval under detector uncertainty. While the framework is independent of the retrieval task, we adapted it to the tasks of retrieving *shots* and *(long) segments*. For shot retrieval, our framework improved over five baselines on six collections, and for segment retrieval, it improved significantly over four baselines on two collections. Furthermore, when simulating improved concept detectors these improvements prevailed. We now discuss our conclusions in more detail.

The URR framework considers basic ranking functions adapted from text retrieval based on representations of known concept occurrences. The uncertainty of detectors is handled separately: the framework takes into account multiple concept-based representations per document. It uses the confidence scores of detectors to assign each representation a probability of being the correct representation. The application of the considered basic ranking function to the multiple representations results in multiple scores for each document. Inspired by the mean-variance analysis framework by Wang (2009), the URR framework ranks documents by the expected score plus a weighted expression of the scores' standard deviation, which represents the chance that scores are actually higher than the expected score. We demonstrated the ability of the general framework to produce effective and robust ranking functions by applying it to two retrieval tasks: shot retrieval and segment retrieval.

For shot retrieval, the framework used the probability of relevance given concept occurrences as a ranking function, which was derived from the probability of relevance ranking function originally proposed in text retrieval (Robertson et al.1981). In terms of mean average precision, this ranking function improved over six baselines, representing other approaches to detector uncertainty, on three out of six collections. For the collections where it showed poorer performance than others, those were not significant. When considering all queries of the six collections together, the improvements over all baselines were significant. For segment retrieval, we proposed that ranking functions should include the *within-segment importance* when retrieving long segments. We used the concept frequency to represent the within-segment importance. We calculated the expected score and scores' standard deviation by Monte Carlo Sampling to reduce prohibitively large number of possible representations, using 200 samples. Based on the representation of concept frequencies we used the concept language model as a ranking function, which was originally proposed in Aly et al. (2010) and derived from language models in text retrieval, see Hiemstra (2001). We showed through simulation experiments that the search performance improves with improved detectors. Based on these results, we conclude that the application of the URR framework results in effective ranking functions.

For ranking functions to be *robust*, the URR framework explicitly modeled the risk-neutral choice and the risk of choosing this score by the expected score and the scores' standard deviation respectively. We found that a risk-averse attitude resulted in poor performance for both retrieval tasks. For shot retrieval, the consideration of the scores' standard deviation did not improve over the condition in which only the expected score was used. 9 We found that the scores' standard deviation often increased monotonically with the expected score, which prevents the standard deviation to influence the ranking. We attributed this behavior to the common independence assumptions made in IR, which are also made in the shot ranking function but often do not match the data (Cooper 1995). For the segment retrieval task, the use of the scores' standard deviation significantly improved the search performance compared to the condition of exclusively using the expected score. For both retrieval tasks, the ranking functions derived from the URR framework performed between the best two systems over all considered collections and detectors. Based on these findings we conclude that the ranking functions derived from the URR framework also perform robust.

The URR framework makes few assumptions about the uncertain representation, which was done for the specific shot retrieval task and the segment retrieval task. As future work we therefore aim to apply the URR framework to other uncertain representations, for example the uncertain variants of spoken text generated by probabilistic automatic speech recognition, or the uncertain references to known entities in text retrieval. Finally, the URR framework does not consider the overall performance of concept detectors which recently received research interest (Yang and Hauptmann 2008). Therefore, we propose to extend the URR framework by measures which incorporate the overall detector performance.

FOOTNOTES

[1] We use the terms document and video shot or a longer video segment interchangeably as both refer to retrievable units of information.

[2] We use similar notation to the unusual notation $d_j.Win$ throughout this paper to prevent an excessive amount of subscripts.

[3]The URR framework was originally proposed in the PhD thesis of the first author (Aly 2010).

[4] Note that the distribution of $d.\mathbf{C}$ is discrete, although the score might be real-valued. The reason is that the arguments to *score*, $d.\mathbf{C}$, are discrete.

[5] A similar assumption is made during the creation of relevance judgments for the text retrieval workshop TREC, where a document is relevant if a part of it is relevant.

[6] We also investigated the use of the minimum or maximum confidence score but did not find any improvements.

[7] Note that we used the development collection from Snoek et al. (2006) as a test collection since it contained more shots; making the simulation results more realistic.

[8] For shot retrieval, we left out the CombMNZ ranking function since it has similar results to the PMIWS method. For segment retrieval, we left out the PMIWS since it performed similar to CombMNZ.

[9] Note that the expected score is equivalent to ranking a marginalization approach which we originally proposed in Aly et al. (2008).

ACKNOWLEDGMENTS

We would like to thank the researchers of the MediaMill project and the Vireo project for the contribution of their concept detector output. We also would thank the anonymous reviewers for their productive feedback. Part of the work reported here was funded by the EU Project AXES (FP7-269980). Author DH was funded under grant 639.022.809 of the Netherlands Organization for Scientific Research, NWO. Author AD and AS were funded by Science Foundation Ireland under grant 07/CE/I1147. Author AD is also supported by the Irish Health Research Board under grant MCPD/2010/12.

REFERENCES

1. Aji, S. M., & McEliece, R. J. (2000). The generalized distributive law. *IEEE Transactions on Information Theory, 46*(2), 325–343.

2. Aly, R. (2010). *Modeling representation uncertainty in concept-based multimedia retrieval*, PhD thesis. University of Twente, Enschede.

3. Aly, R., Hiemstra, D., de Vries, A. P., & de Jong, F. (2008). A probabilistic ranking framework using unobservable binary events for video search. In *CIVR '08: Proceedings of the international conference on content-based image and video retrieval 2008* (pp. 349–358). New York: ACM.

4. Aly, R., Hiemstra, D., & de Vries, A. P. (2009). Reusing annotation labor for concept selection. In *CIVR '09: Proceedings of the international conference on content-based image and video retrieval*. New York: ACM.

5. Aly, R., Doherty, A., Hiemstra, D., & Smeaton, A. (2010). Beyond shot retrieval: Searching for broadcast news items using language models of concepts. In *ECIR '10: Proceedings of the 32th European conference on IR research on advances in information retrieval* (pp. 241–252). Berlin, Heidelberg: Springer. Lecture Notes in Computer Science, Vol. 5993.

6. Aly, R., Hiemstra, D., de Jong, F., & Apers, P. (2012). Simulating the future of concept-based video retrieval under improved detector performance. *Multimedia Tools and Applications, 60*(1), 203–231.

7. Benjelloun, O., Sarma, A. D., Halevy, A., & Widom, J. (2006). Uldbs: Databases with uncertainty and lineage. In*Proceedings of the 32nd international conference on very large data bases, VLDB Endowment, VLDB '06* (pp. 953–964).

8. Chia, T. K., Sim, K. C., Li, H., & Ng, H. T. (2008). A lattice-based approach to query-by-example spoken document retrieval. In *SIGIR '08: Proceedings of the 31st annual international ACM SIGIR conference on research and development in information retrieval* (pp. 363–370). New York, NY, USA: ACM.

9. Cooper, W. S. (1995). Some inconsistencies and misidentified modeling assumptions in probabilistic information retrieval. *ACM Transactions on Information Systems, 13*(1), 100–111.

10. Croft, W. B. (1981). Document representations in probabilistic models of information retrieval. *Journal of the American Society of Information Science, 32*(6), 451–457.

11. Ding, Z., & Peng, Y. (2004). A probabilistic extension to ontology language owl. In *System Sciences, 2004. Proceedings of the 37th Annual Hawaii international conference on*, p. 10.

12. Fuhr, N. (1989). Models for retrieval with probabilistic indexing. *Information Processing and Management, 25*(1), 55–72.

13. Hauptmann, A. G., Yan, R., Lin, W. H., Christel, M., & Wactlar, H. (2007). Can high-level concepts fill the semantic gap in video retrieval? A case study with broadcast news. In *IEEE Transactions on Multimedia, Vol. 9–5*, pp. 958–966.

14. Hiemstra, D. (2001). *Using language models for information retrieval*, PhD thesis. University of Twente, Enschede.

15. Hiemstra, D., Rode, H., van Os, T. R., & Flokstra, J. (2006). Pftijah: Text search in an xml database system. In*Proceedings*

of the 2nd international workshop on open source information retrieval (OSIR) (pp. 12–17). Seattle, WA, USA: Ecole Nationale Supérieure des Mines de Saint-Etienne.

16. Hsu, W. H., Kennedy, L. S., & Chang, S.-F. (2006). Video search reranking via information bottleneck principle. In*MULTIMEDIA '06: Proceedings of the 14th annual ACM international conference on multimedia* (pp. 35–44). New York, NY, USA: ACM.

17. Huurnink, B., Hofmann, K., & de Rijke, M. (2008). Assessing concept selection for video retrieval. In *Proceedings of the first MIR conference'08*.

18. Jiang, Y. G., Yang, J., Ngo, C. W., & Hauptmann, A. (2010). Representations of keypoint-based semantic concept detection: A comprehensive study. *IEEE Transactions on Multimedia, 12*(1), 42–53.

19. Kennedy, L., Chang, S.-F., & Natsev, A. (2008). Query-adaptive fusion for multimodal search. *Proceedings of the IEEE, 96*(4), 567–588.

20. Li, X., Wang, D., Li, J., & Zhang, B. (2007). Video search in concept subspace: A text-like paradigm. In *CIVR '07: Proceedings of the 6th ACM international conference on image and video retrieval* (pp. 603–610). New York, NY, USA: ACM.

21. Liu, J. S. (2002). *Monte Carlo strategies in scientific computing*. New York: Springer.

22. Markowitz, H. (1952). Portfolio selection. *The Journal of Finance, 7*(1), 77–91.

23. McDonald, K., & Smeaton, A. F. (2005). A comparison of score, rank and probability-based fusion methods for video shot retrieval. In *Image and video retrieval*. (Vol. 3568/2005, pp. 61–70). Berlin/Heidelberg: Springer.

24. Naphade, M., Smith, J., Tesic, J., Chang, S.-F., Hsu, W., Kennedy, L., Hauptmann, A. G., & Curtis, J. (2006). Large-scale concept ontology for multimedia. *IEEE MultiMedia, 13*(3), 86–91.

25. Papoulis, A. (1984). *Probability, random variables, and stochastic processes*. Singapore: Mc-Graw Hill.

26. Platt, J. (2000). Advances in large margin classifiers. Cambridge, MA: MIT Press, chap probabilistic outputs for support vector machines and comparison to regularized likelihood methods (pp. 61–74).

27. Robertson, S. E., van Rijsbergen, C. J., & Porter, M. F. (1981). Probabilistic models of indexing and searching. In*SIGIR '80: Proceedings of the 3rd annual ACM conference on research and development in information retrieval*(pp. 35–56). Kent, UK: Butterworth & Co.

28. Smeaton, A. F., Over, P., & Kraaij, W. (2006). Evaluation campaigns and trecvid. In *MIR '06: Proceedings of the 8th ACM international workshop on multimedia information retrieval* (pp. 321–330). New York, NY, USA: ACM Press.

29. Snoek, C. G. M., & Worring, M. (2009). Concept-based video retrieval. *Foundations and Trends in Information Retrieval, 4*(2), 215–322.

30. Snoek, C. G. M., Worring, M., van Gemert, J. C., Geusebroek, J. M., & Smeulders, A. W. M. (2006). The challenge problem for automated detection of 101 semantic concepts in multimedia. In *MULTIMEDIA '06: Proceedings of the 14th annual ACM international conference on multimedia* (pp. 421–430). New York, NY, USA: ACM Press.

31. Snoek, C. G. M., Huurnink, B., Hollink, L., de Rijke, M., Schreiber, G., & Worring, M. (2007). Adding semantics to detectors for video retrieval. *IEEE Transactions on Multimedia, 9*(5), 975–986.

32. Snoek, C. G. M., van de Sande, K., de Rooij, O., Huurnink, B., van Gemert, J., Uijlings, J., He, J., Li, X., Everts, I., Nedovic, V., van Liempt, M., van Balen, R., de Rijke, M., Geusebroek, J., Gevers, T., Worring, M., Smeulders, A., Koelma, D., Yan, F., Tahir, M., Mikolajczyk, K., & Kittler, J. (2008). The MediaMill TRECVid 2008 semantic video search engine. In *Proceedings of the 8th TRECVid workshop*, Gaithersburg, USA.

33. Toharia, P., Robles, O. D., Smeaton, A. F., & Rodríguez, A. (2009). Measuring the influence of concept detection on video retrieval. In *CAIP 2009—13th international conference on computer analysis of images and patterns*. Berlin: Springer.

34. Voorhees, E. M., & Harman, D. (2000). Overview of the ninth text retrieval conference (trec-9). In *Proceedings of the ninth text REtrieval conference (TREC-9)*, pp. 1–14.

35. de Vries, A. P., Kazai, G., & Lalmas, M. (2004). Tolerance to irrelevance: A user-effort oriented evaluation of retrieval systems without predefined retrieval unit. In *RIAO 2004 conference proceedings* (pp. 463–473). France: Avignon.

36. Wang, J. (2009). Mean-variance analysis: A new document ranking theory in information retrieval. In *ECIR '09: Proceedings of the 31th European conference on IR research on advances in information retrieval* (pp. 4–16). Berlin, Heidelberg: Springer.

37. Wang, J., & Zhu, J. (2009). Portfolio theory of information retrieval. In *SIGIR '09: Proceedings of the 32nd international ACM SIGIR conference on research and development in information retrieval* (pp. 115–122). New York, NY, USA: ACM.

38. Yan, R. (2006). *Probabilistic models for combining diverse knowledge sources in multimedia retrieval*, PhD thesis. Carnegie Mellon University.

39. Yang, J., & Hauptmann, A. G. (2006). Exploring temporal consistency for video analysis and retrieval. In *MIR '06: Proceedings of the 8th ACM international workshop on multimedia information retrieval* (pp. 33–42). New York, NY, USA: ACM.

40. Yang, J., & Hauptmann, A. G. (2008). (un)reliability of video concept detection. In *CIVR '08: Proceedings of the 2008 international conference on content-based image and video retrieval* (pp. 85–94). New York, NY, USA: ACM.

41. Zhai, C., & Lafferty, J. (2004). A study of smoothing methods for language models applied to information retrieval.*ACM Transactions on Information Systems, 22*(2), 179–214.

42. Zheng, W., Li, J., Si, Z., Lin, F., & Zhang, B. (2006). Using high-level semantic features in video retrieval. In*Image and video retrieval* (Vol. 4071/2006, pp. 370–379). Berlin/Heidelberg: Springer.

8
CHAPTER

The Strange Case of Reproducibility Versus Representativeness in Contextual Suggestion Test Collections

Thaer Samar[1], Alejandro Bellogín[3], Arjen P. de Vries[1,2]

[1]Centrum Wiskunde & Informatica, Amsterdam, The Netherlands

[2]Delft University of Technology, Delft, The Netherlands

[3]Universidad Auto´noma de Madrid, Madrid, Spain

ABSTRACT

The most common approach to measuring the effectiveness of Information Retrieval systems is by using test collections. The Contextual Suggestion (CS) TREC track provides an evaluation framework for systems that recommend items to users given their geographical context. The specific nature of this track allows the participating teams to identify candidate documents either from the Open Web or from the ClueWeb12 collection, a static version of the web. In the judging pool, the documents from the Open Web and ClueWeb12 collection are distinguished. Hence, each system submission should be based only on one resource, either Open Web (identified by URLs) or ClueWeb12 (identified by ids). To achieve reproducibility, ranking web pages from ClueWeb12 should be the preferred method for scientific evaluation of CS systems, but it has been found that the systems that build their suggestion algorithms on top of input taken from the Open Web achieve consistently a higher effectiveness. Because most of the systems take a rather similar approach to making CSs, this raises the question whether systems built by researchers on top of ClueWeb12 are still representative of those that would work directly on industry-strength web search engines. Do we need to sacrifice reproducibility for the sake of representativeness? We study the difference in effectiveness between Open Web systems and ClueWeb12 systems through analyzing the relevance assessments of documents identified from both the Open Web and ClueWeb12. Then, we identify documents that overlap between the relevance assessments of the Open Web and ClueWeb12, observing a dependency between relevance assessments and the source of the document being taken from the Open Web or from ClueWeb12. After that, we identify documents from the relevance assessments of the Open Web which exist in the ClueWeb12 collection but do not exist in the ClueWeb12 relevance assessments. We use these documents to expand the ClueWeb12 relevance assessments. Our main findings are twofold. First, our empirical analysis of the relevance assessments of 2 years of CS track shows that Open Web documents receive better ratings than ClueWeb12 documents, especially if we look at the documents in the overlap. Second, our approach for selecting candidate documents from ClueWeb12 collection based on information obtained from the Open Web makes an improvement step towards partially bridging the gap in effectiveness between Open Web and ClueWeb12 systems, while at the same time we achieve reproducible results on well-known representative sample of the web.

Keywords: Reproducibility; Contextual suggestion; Open vs archived web; Test collections evaluation; Filtering and recommendation; Web IR and social media search

1 INTRODUCTION

Recommender systems aim to help people find items of interest from a large pool of potentially interesting items. The users' preferences may change depending on their current context, such as the time of the day, the device they use, or their location. Hence, those recommendations or suggestions should be tailored to the context of the user. Typically, recommender systems suggest a list of items based on users' preferences. However, awareness of the importance of context as a third dimension beyond users and items has increased, for recommendation (Adomavicius and Tuzhilin 2011) and search (Melucci 2012) alike. The goal is to anticipate users' context without asking them, as stated in The Second Strategic Workshop on Information Retrieval (SWIRL 2012) (Allan et al.2012): "Future information retrieval systems must anticipate user needs and respond with information appropriate to the current context without the user having to enter a query". This problem is known as contextual suggestion in Information Retrieval (IR) and *context-aware recommendation* in the Recommender Systems (RS) community.

The TREC Contextual Suggestion (CS) track introduced in 2012 provides a common evaluation framework for investigating this task (Dean-Hall et al. 2012). The aim of the CS task is to provide a list of ranked suggestions, given a location as the (current) user context and past preferences as the user profile. The public Open Web was the only source for collecting candidate documents in 2012. Using APIs based on the Open Web (either for search or recommendation) has the disadvantage that the end-to-end contextual suggestion process cannot be examined in all detail, and that reproducibility of results is at risk (Hawking et al.2001, 1999). To address this problem, starting from 2013 participating teams were allowed to collect candidate documents either from Open Web or from the ClueWeb12 collection.

In the 2013 and 2014 editions of CS track, there were more submissions based on the Open Web compared to those based on the ClueWeb12 collection. However, to achieve reproducibility, ranking web pages from ClueWeb12 should be the preferred method for scientific evaluation of contextual suggestion systems. It has been found that the systems that build their suggestion algorithms on top of input taken from the Open Web achieve consistently a higher effectiveness than systems based on the ClueWeb12 collection. Most of the existing works have relied on public tourist APIs to address the contextual suggestion problem. These tourist sites (such as Yelp and Foursquare) are specialized in providing tourist suggestions, hence those works are focused on re-ranking the resulting candidate suggestions based on user preferences. Gathering suggestions (potential venues) from the ClueWeb12 collection has indeed proven a challenging task. First, suggestions have to be selected from a very large collection. Second, these documents should be geographically relevant (the attraction should be located as close as possible to the target context), and they should be of interest for the user.

The finding that Open Web results achieve higher effectiveness raises the question whether research systems built on top of the ClueWeb12 collection are still representative of those that would work directly on industry-strength web search engines. In this paper, we focus on analyzing reproducibility and representativeness of the Open Web and ClueWeb12 systems. We study the gap in effectiveness between Open Web and ClueWeb12 systems through analyzing the relevance assessments of documents returned by them. After that, we identify documents that overlap between Open Web and ClueWeb12 results. We define two different sets of overlap: First, the overlap in the relevance assessments of documents returned by Open Web and ClueWeb12 systems, to investigate how these documents were judged according to the relevance assessments gathered when they were considered by Open Web or ClueWeb12 systems. The second type of overlap is defined by the documents in the relevance assessments of the Open Web systems which are in ClueWeb12 collection but not in the relevance assessments of ClueWeb12 systems. The purpose is to use the judgments of these documents (mapped from Open Web on ClueWeb12 collection) to expand the relevance assessments of ClueWeb12 systems resulting on having a new test collection. Figure 1 illustrates these different test collections, the details given in Sect. 3.3. Then, we focus on how many of the documents returned by Open Web systems can be found in the ClueWeb12 collection, an analysis to assess the reproducibility point of view. Finally, we apply the knowledge about the tourist information available in the Open Web for selecting documents from ClueWeb12 to find a representative sample from the ClueWeb12 collection. Specifically, we address the following research questions:

RQ1

Do relevance assessments of Open Web URLs differ (significantly) from relevance assessments of ClueWeb12 documents?

RQ2

Can we identify an overlap between Open Web systems and ClueWeb12 systems in terms of documents suggested by both?, how are those documents in the overlap judged?

RQ3

How many of the documents returned by Open Web systems can be found in the ClueWeb12 collection as a whole?

RQ4

Can we identify a representative sample from the ClueWeb12 collection for the CS track by applying the tourist domain knowledge obtained from the Open Web?

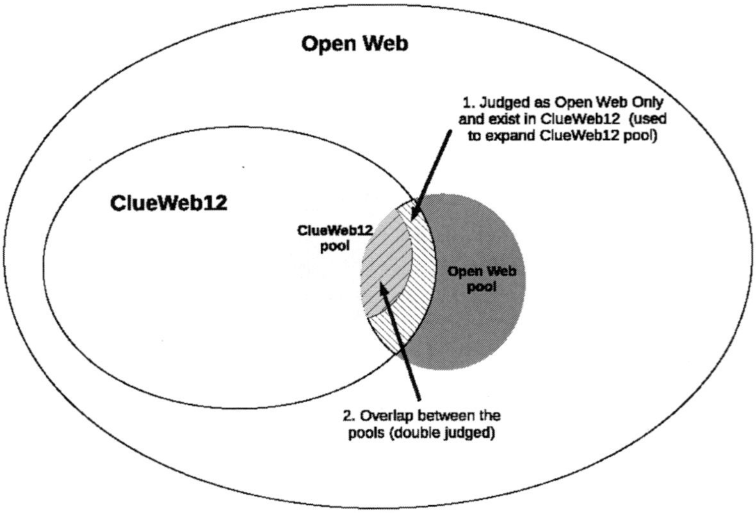

Figure 1. Illustration of the relation between pools and the source of the documents. *Subset 1* represents the documents in the Open Web pool and were found in ClueWeb12 collection but do not exist in the ClueWeb12 pool (this subset is used to expand the ClueWeb12 pool). *Subset 2* represents the overlap between the Open Web pool and ClueWeb12 pool, documents in this subset were double judged (we use this subset to show the bias between Open Web and ClueWeb12 results)

The remainder of the paper is organized as follows: first we discuss related work (Sect. 2), followed by a description of the experimental setup (Sect. 3). After that we present an analysis to compare Open Web and ClueWeb12 relevance assessments (Sect. 4). Then we discuss how much of the Open Web systems can be reproduced from the ClueWeb12 collection, and we evaluate them on the ClueWeb12 test collection (Sect. 5). After that we discuss how to apply tourist domain knowledge available on the public Open Web to annotate documents from the ClueWeb12 collection. Finally, we discuss conclusions drawn from our findings (Sect. 7).

2 RELATED WORK

In the Recommender Systems area, recommendation algorithms for several types of content have been studied (movies, tourist attractions, news, friends, etc.). These types of algorithms are typically categorized according to the information they exploit: collaborative filtering (based on the preferences of like-minded users Resnick et al. 1994) and content-based filtering (based on similar items to those liked by the user Lops et al. 2011). In the Information Retrieval area, approaches to *contextual suggestion* usually follow a content-based recommendation approach. The majority of related work results from the corresponding TREC track, focusing on the specific problem of how to provide tourist attractions given a location as context, where many participants have relied on APIs of location-based services on the Open Web. Candidate suggestions based on location are then ranked based on their similarity with the known user interests. In this case, the key challenge is to model user interests.

Given the description of a set of examples (suggestions) judged by the user, existing studies exploit the descriptions of the suggestions to build her profile, usually represented as the textual information contained in the description of the suggestions. Sappelli et al. (2013) build two user profiles: a positive profile represents terms from those suggestions liked by the user before, whereas a negative profile is based on descriptions of suggestions disliked by the user. In Hubert et al. (2013); Yang and Fang 2012) both the descriptions and the categories of the suggestions are used to build the user profiles. In Yang and Fang (2013), the authors proposed an opinion-based approach to model user profiles by leveraging similar user opinions of suggestions on public tourist APIs. If the user rated a suggestion as relevant, then the positive profile represents all positive reviews of that suggestion. The negative profile represents all negative reviews of the suggestion rated as irrelevant to the user. The aforementioned approaches consider different ranking features based on the similarity between candidate suggestions and positive and negative profiles. On the other hand, a learning to rank model exploiting 64 features using information obtained from Foursquare is presented by Deveaud et al. (2014). They used four groups of features: (a) city-dependent features which describe the context (city) such as total number of venues in the city and total number of likes, (b) category-dependent features that consist of the count of the 10 highest level categories obtained from Foursquare, (c) venue-dependent features which describe the popularity of the venue in the city, and (d) user-dependent features describing the similarity between user profiles and the suggestions. The most effective features were the venue-dependent features, that is, those indicating venue importance.

Besides recommendation, a critical part of our work is how to build test collections and create sub-collections from them. Because of this, we now introduce the topic and survey some of the most relevant works on that area. Creating a test collection is the most common approach for evaluating different Information Retrieval systems. Any test collection consists of a set of topics, a set of relevance assessments, and a set of retrievable documents. Since the beginning of IR evaluation by means of test collections, many researchers have looked at test collections from different angles. For example, what is the optimal number of topics to obtain reliable evaluations? In Voorhees and Buckley (2002) the authors find that to have a reliable order of the systems, at least 50 topics have to be used in the evaluation stage. More recently, in Dean-Hall and Clarke (2015) the authors use data from the CS track to give insights about the required number of assessors. The problem of analyzing the impact of different sub-collections (as a set of test collections) is also studied in the literature. In Scholer et al. (2011), the authors split TREC ad-hoc collections into two sub-collections and compared the effectiveness ranking of retrieval systems on each of them. They obtained a low correlation between the two rank runs, each run based on one of the two sub-collections. Later, in Sanderson et al. (2012) a more exhaustive analysis is presented. The authors studied the impact of different sub-collections on the retrieval effectiveness by analyzing the effect over many test collections divided using different splitting approaches. Their study was based on runs submitted to two different TREC tracks, the ad hoc track from 2002 to 2008 and theterabyte one from 2004 to 2008. The authors found that the effect of these sub-collections is substantial, even affecting the relative performance of retrieval systems. In Santos et al. (2011), the authors analyze the impact of the first-tier documents from ClueWeb09 collection in the effectiveness. The analysis was carried out on the TREC 2009 Web track, where participating teams were encouraged to submit runs based on Category A, and Category B. These categories were extracted from ClueWeb09 collection. Category A consists of 500 million English documents, Category B is a subset from Category A, it consists of 50 million documents of high quality seed documents and Wikipedia documents (they represent the first-tier documents). By analyzing the number of documents per subset and the relevance assessment, the authors found a bias towards Category B documents, in terms of assessed documents and those judged as relevant. In order to investigate this bias, they analyze the effect of first-tier documents on the effectiveness of runs based on Category A. First, they found that there is a high correlation between effectiveness and number of documents retrieved from the first-tier subset. Second, by removing all documents not from the first-tier subset, the effectiveness of almost all runs based on Category A was improved.

In the context of the CS track these questions arise again, since in this track participants share the same topics (profile, context) but they have to return a ranked list of documents for each topic, where these candidate documents can be selected from either the Open Web or ClueWeb12 collection. Considering the potential impact that different collections may have on the retrieval effectiveness, one of our main interests in the rest of the paper is to study the gap in effectiveness between Open Web systems and ClueWeb12 systems in order to achieve reproducible results on a representative sample of the Web from ClueWeb12 collection.

3 EXPERIMENTAL SETUP

3.1 Dataset

Our analyses are based on data collected from the TREC 2013 and 2014 Contextual Suggestion tracks (CS 2013, CS 2014). The CS track provides a set of profiles and a set of geographical contexts (cities in the United States) and the task is to provide a ranked list of suggestions (up to 50) for each topic (profile, context) pair. Each profile represents a single assessor past preferences for a given suggestion. Each user profile consists of two ratings per suggestion, on a 5-point scale; one rating for a suggestion's description as shown in the result list (i.e., a snippet), and another rating for its actual content (i.e., a web page). There are some differences between 2013 and 2014: First, the 50 target contexts used each year are not the same. Second, seeds cities from which the example suggestions were collected: in 2013 examples were collected from Philadelphia, PA, whereas in 2014 examples were collected from Chicago, IL and Santa Fe, NM. Third, the number of assessors also changed in these editions of the track. More details about the CS track can be found in the track's overview papers (Dean-Hall et al.2013, 2014), for 2013 and 2014, respectively.

The evaluation is performed as follows. For each topic—(profile, context) pairs—the top-5 documents of every submission are judged by the actual users whose profile is given (resulting in three ratings: description, actual document content, and geographical relevance assessments) and by NIST assessors (an additional rating for the geographical relevance assessment). Judgments are graded: subjective judgments range from 0 (strongly uninterested) to 4 (strongly interested) whereas objective judgments go from 0 (not geographically appropriate) to 2 (geographically appropriate). In both cases, a value of −−2 indicates that the document could not be assessed (for example, the URL did not load in the judge's Web browser interface).

Documents are identified by their URLs (if they are submitted by runs based on Open Web) or by their ClueWeb12 ids (if they are submitted by runs based on ClueWeb12). In our study, we use ClueWeb12-qrels to refer to relevance assessments of ClueWeb12 documents, and OpenWeb-qrels to refer to relevance assessments of Open Web URLs, both sets of assessments built from the three relevance assessments files provided by the organizers: desc-doc-qrels, geo-user-qrels, and geo-nist-qrels.

The following metrics are used to evaluate the performance of the participating teams: Precision at 5 (P@5), Mean Reciprocal Rank (MRR), and a modified Time-Biased Gain (TBG) (Dean-Hall et al. 2013). These metrics consider geographical and profile relevance (both in terms of document and description judgments), taking as thresholds a value of 1 and 3 (inclusive), respectively.

3.2 URL normalization

A recurring pre-processing step to produce the various results reported in the paper concerns the normalization of URLs. We have normalized URLs consistently by removing their www, http://, https:// prefixes, as well as their trailing "forwarding slash" character /, if any. In the special case of the URL referencing anindex.html Web page, the index.html string is stripped from the URL before the other normalizations are applied.

3.3 Mapping OpenWeb-qrels to ClueWeb12

We identify documents that are included in OpenWeb-qrels and exist in ClueWeb12 collection (these documents are subsets 1 and 2 in Figure 1). We achieve this by obtaining the URLs from the OpenWeb-qrels, then, we search for these URLs in the ClueWeb12 collection. To check the matching between qrels URLs and ClueWeb12 document URLs, both were normalized as described in Sect. 3.2. We shared this subset with the CS track community.1 In Table 1 we summarize the statistics derived from the Open Web and ClueWeb12 relevance assessments in 2013 and 2014. We observe that the qrels do contain duplicates, that are not necessarily assessed the same. The differences can be explained by the CS track evaluation setup, where the top-5 suggestions per topic provided by each submitted run were judged individually (Dean-Hall et al. 2013, 2014).

We have separated these documents into two subsets: subsets 1 and 2 from Figure 1. First, the subset 1 represents documents that were judged as Open Web documents and that have a matching ClueWeb12 document, however they do not exist in ClueWeb12 relevance assessments; we refer to this subset as (OpenWeb-qrels-urls-in-ClueWeb12). We consider these documents as additional judgments that can be used to expand the ClueWeb12 relevance assessments. The second subset consists of documents that overlap between Open Web and ClueWeb12 relevance assessments – that is, they were judged twice –, we refer to this subset as ClueWeb12-qrels (qrels-overlap).

Table 1. Summary of judged documents form the Open Web and the ClueWeb12 collection

	2014			2013		
	total	Unique	In ClueWeb12	Total	Unique	In ClueWeb12
Open Web runs	35,697	8,442	1,892	28,849	10,349	2,894
ClueWeb12 runs	8909	2674	All	7329	3098	All

The `total` column shows the total number of judged documents, while the `unique` presents the number of unique documents

3.4 Expanding ClueWeb12-qrels

We expand the ClueWeb12 relevance assessments by modifying the provided qrels files mentioned in Sect. 3.1. We achieve this by replacing in the qrels the URLs with their ClueWeb12 ids (if they exist) based on the subset identified in Sect. 3.3.

3.5 Mapping URLs from Open Web runs to the ClueWeb12 documents URLs

In this section, we describe how we map all URLs found by Open Web systems (in the submitted runs) to their ClueWeb12 ids. We need this mapping to evaluate Open Web systems on ClueWeb12 collection. In order to achieve this, we obtain the URLs from the Open Web runs. Then, we search for these URLs in ClueWeb12 collection by matching the normalized URLs against documents normalized URLs in ClueWeb12 collection. The result of this process is a mapping between URLs in the Open Web runs and their corresponding ClueWeb12 ids (OpenWeb-runs-urls-in-ClueWeb12). Table 2 presents a summary about the Open Web URLs and the number of URLs found in ClueWeb12 collection. As we see in the table, for CS 2013 around 25.6 % of URLs have a matching document in ClueWeb12, while for CS 2014 only 13.2 % exist in ClueWeb12 collection.

Table 2. URLs obtained from Open Web runs

	2014	2013
Total number of URls	15,339,209	35,949,067
Unique number of URLs	75,719	102,649
Found in ClueWeb12	10,014	26,248

4 COMPARING OPEN WEB AND CLOSED WEB RELEVANCE ASSESSMENTS

In this section we present an analysis to compare Open Web and ClueWeb12 relevance assessments. In Bellogín et al. (2014), we already showed that Open Web runs tend to receive better judgments than ClueWeb12 results, based on analyzing the CS 2013 results. We repeat here the same experiment in order to investigate whether such tendency is still present in the 2014 test collection. We first compare Open Web and ClueWeb12 in general (the distribution of relevance assessments of documents returned by Open Web systems versus those documents returned by ClueWeb12 systems). Next, we focus on the documents in the overlap of the relevance assessments between Open Web systems and ClueWeb12 systems.

4.1 Fair comparison of test collections

In this section, we study RQ1: Do relevance assessments of Open Web URLs differ (significantly) from relevance assessments of ClueWeb12 documents? We analyze the distribution of profile judgments of documents returned by Open Web and ClueWeb12 runs. In our analysis, we leave out the user, context, and system variables, and compare the judgments given to documents from the Open Web against those from ClueWeb12. In Figure 2, we observe that the Open Web histogram is slightly skewed towards the positive, relevant judgments. Even though we are not interested in comparing the actual frequencies. This would not be fair, mainly because there were many more Open Web submissions than ClueWeb12 ones. Specifically, in TREC CS 2013, 27 runs submitted

URLs from the Open Web, and only 7 runs used ClueWeb12 documents. However, it is still relevant to see the relative frequency of −−2's or −−1's (document could not load at assessing time), used in CS 2013 and CS 2014, respectively. 4's (strongly interested) in each dataset: this is an important difference which will impact the performance of the systems using ClueWeb12 documents.

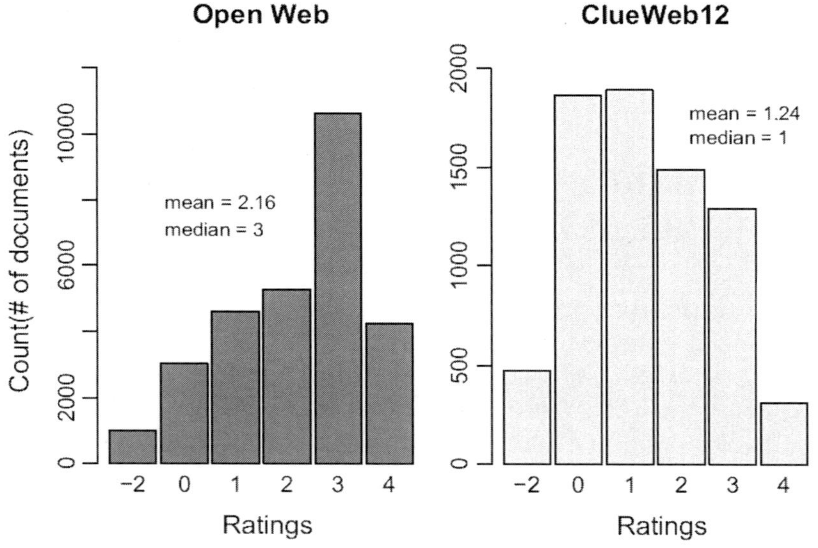

Figure 2. Judgments (document relevance) histogram of documents from Open Web (*left*) and from ClueWeb12 (*right*) **CS 2013**

Figure 3 shows the same analyses based on 2014 test collection. In that year of the track, 25 runs submitted URLs from the Open Web, and only 6 runs used ClueWeb12 documents. We find that the judgments of documents from Open Web are skewed towards the positive (relevant) side, while judgments of documents from ClueWeb12 are—again—skewed towards the negative (not relevant) part of the rating scale, similar to the findings on the 2013 test collection.

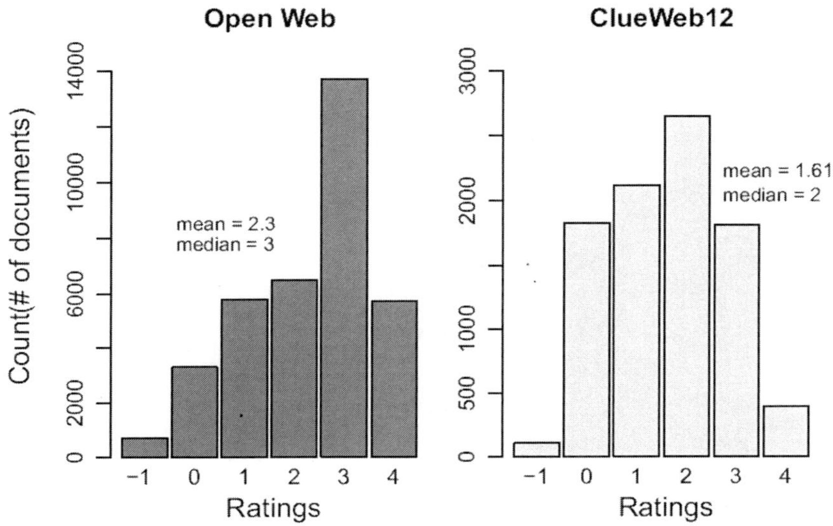

Figure 3. Judgments (document relevance) histogram of documents from Open Web runs (*left*) and ClueWeb12 runs (*right*) **CS 2014**

4.2 Difference in evaluation of identical documents from Open Web and ClueWeb12

In Sect. 3.3, we identified two subsets of overlap between Open Web and ClueWeb12 results: first, OpenWeb-qrels-urls-in-ClueWeb12 that maps URLs from OpenWeb-qrels to ClueWeb12 collection, and qrels-overlap that contains documents that exist in both OpenWeb-qrels and ClueWeb12-qrels. Based on these datasets, we investigate RQ2: Can we identify an overlap between Open Web systems and ClueWeb12 systems in terms of documents suggested by both?, how are those documents in the overlap judged?

Figure 4 shows the distribution of relevance assessments of documents inOpenWeb-qrels-urls-in-ClueWeb12 for both CS 2013 and CS 2014. We observe that the distribution of judgments of these documents have a similar behavior as the whole Open Web judged documents. More precisely, we observe that the distribution is skewed towards the positive ratings when we look at 3 and 4 ratings for 2013 and 2014 datasets.

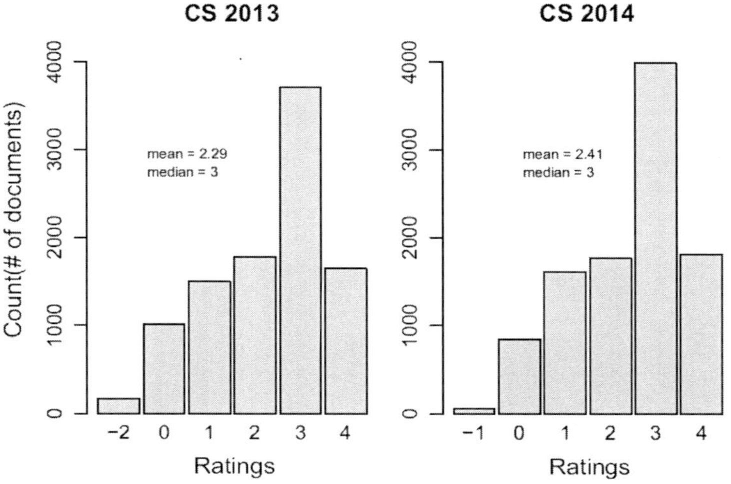

Figure 4. Judgments histogram of documents from Open Web qrels which exist in ClueWeb12 collection for CS 2013 (*left*) and CS 2014 (*right*)

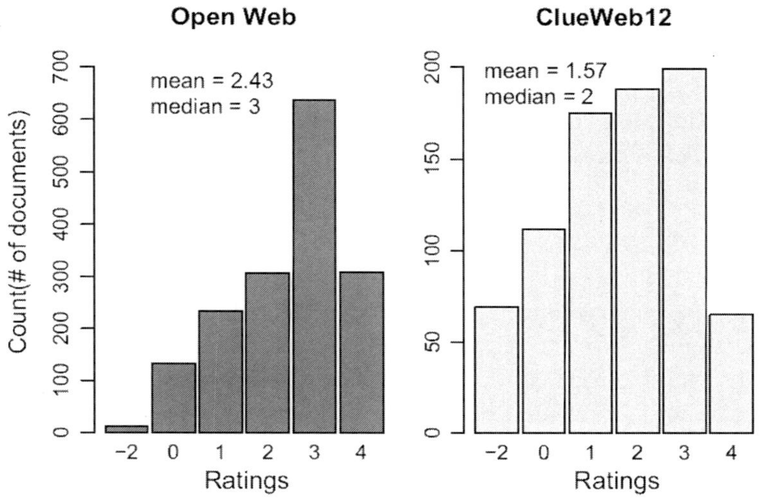

Figure 5. Judgments histogram of documents that exist in both Open Web qrels and ClueWeb12 qrels. Figure on the (*left*) shows how these documents were judged as Open Web URLs, while the figure on the (*right*) shows how the same documents were judged as ClueWeb12 documents **CS 2013**

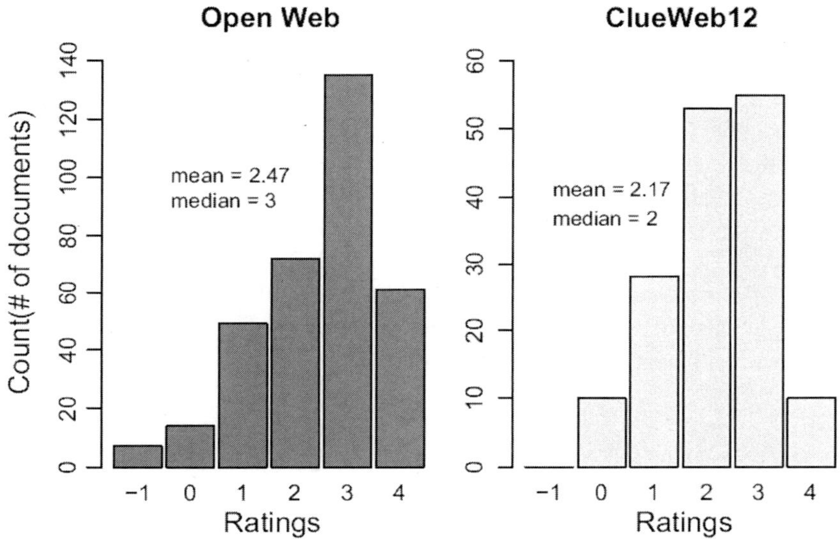

Figure 6. Judgments histogram of documents that exist in both Open Web qrels and ClueWeb12 qrels. Figure on the (*left*) shows how these documents were judged as Open Web URLs, while the figure on the (*right*) shows how the same documents were judged as ClueWeb12 documents **CS 2014**

Now we focus on the qrels-overlap subset which contains documents shared by both OpenWeb-qrels and ClueWeb12-qrels. Our aim here is to detect any bias towards any of the document collections (the Open Web vs. ClueWeb12) based on the available sample of the judgments. In principle, the relevance judgments should be the same for the two sources, since in each situation the same document was retrieved by different systems for exactly the same user and context, the only difference being how the document was identified (as a URL or as a ClueWeb12 id). Figures 5 and 6 show how documents in the qrels-overlap were judged as Open Web URLs and as ClueWeb12 documents in CS 2013 and CS 2014 test collections, respectively. We find that the documents in the overlap were judged differently. The judgments distributions of the documents shared by both OpenWeb-qrels and ClueWeb12-qrels suggest that there is a bias towards OpenWeb-qrels and this bias is consistent in 2013 and 2014 data. For CS 2013, part of the differences in judgments was attributed to a different rendering of the document for each source.2 Assessors are influenced by several conditions, one of them is the visual aspect of the interface, but also the response time, the order of examination, the familiarity with the interface, etc. (Kelly 2009). Therefore, it is important that these details are kept as stable as possible when different datasets are evaluated at the same time. It is also interesting to note that the number of ClueWeb12 documents that could not load is higher in CS 2013 (−2−2) compared to CS 2014 (−1−1), probably due to the efforts of the organizers in the latter edition of running a fairer evaluation (Dean-Hall and Clarke 2015).

5 REPRODUCIBILITY OF OPEN WEB SYSTEMS

In this section, we investigate RQ3: How many of the documents returned by Open Web systems can be found in the ClueWeb12 collection as a whole? The goal of this analysis is to show how many of the results obtained by Open Web systems can be reproduced based on ClueWeb12 collection. In Sect. 3.5, we presented the number of URLs found by Open Web systems and have a matching documents in ClueWeb12 collection. Precisely in Table 2, we showed that for CS 2013 26,248 out of 102,649 URLs have a matching with ClueWeb12 documents (25.6 %), while for CS 2014 10,014 out of the 75,719 URLs (13.2 %) have ClueWeb12 documents match. In this section, we evaluate Open Web systems on ClueWeb12 data. Analyzing the impact of ClueWeb12 documents on the effectiveness of Open Web systems requires the following. First, we need to modify the Open Web runs using the OpenWeb-runs-urls-in-ClueWeb12 dataset which has the mapping between Open Web URLs to ClueWeb12 ids. Second—for evaluation completeness—we use the expanded ClueWeb12-qrels which was generated based on the OpenWeb-qrels URLs found in the ClueWeb12 collection (OpenWeb-qrels-urls-in-ClueWeb12 subset described in Sect. 3.4).

While modifying the Open Web runs, if the suggested URL has a matching in ClueWeb12, we replace the URL with its corresponding ClueWeb12 id. If the URL has no match, then we skip the line containing that URL. We hence change the ranking after skipping those URLs. We present the effectiveness of original Open Web runs and the effectiveness of modified runs (replacing URLs with ClueWeb12 ids), and we show the percentage of relative improvement in effectiveness of Open Web systems (on Open Web data vs ClueWeb12). Nonetheless, replacing the URLs with their matching ClueWeb12 ids and pushing up their ranks by removing the URLs which have no ClueWeb12 match will overestimate the performance and not show the corresponding impact on performance of those ClueWeb12 documents if the ranking was preserved. To give an insight about the importance of ClueWeb12 documents compared to the Open Web URLs that have no ClueWeb12 match, we also include the percentage of ClueWeb12 documents occurring in the top-5. To achieve this, when modifying the Open Web run, we replace the URLs with their match ClueWeb12 ids, and keep the URLs as they are if they do not have a match. Then, for each topic, we compute the percentage of ClueWeb12 documents in the top-5. The score for each run is the mean across all topics.

For CS 2013 systems (see Table 3) and for CS 2014 systems (see Table 4), we report the effectiveness of Open Web systems using their original run files as submitted to the track based on the original qrels (column named original). We report their effectiveness using the modified run files based on the expanded qrels as described above. Finally, we report the percentage of ClueWeb12 documents in the top-5 as described above (how many ClueWeb12 documents remain in the top-5 while preserving the URLs with no match).

In both tables, we observe the following: First, for some Open Web systems we were not able to reproduce their results based on ClueWeb12 data, mainly because some systems have no matching at all with ClueWeb12 collection. For systems that rely on the Yelp API to obtain candidate documents, we could not find any document whose host is Yelp in ClueWeb12 collection, this is due to very strict indexing rules.3 Second, we observe that the performance of Open Web systems decreases. However, this reduction in performance varies between systems, suggesting that pushing ClueWeb12 documents up in the submitted rankings by removing URLs with no ClueWeb12 id match has a different effect on each Open Web system. Third, some of top performing Open Web systems are performing very well when constrained to the ClueWeb12 collection. For example, in the CS 2014 edition, UDInfoCS2014_2, BJUTa, and BJUTb systems even perform better than ClueWeb12 systems (underlined systems in the table). Fourth, in terms of how representative ClueWeb12 documents in the top-5, the percentage of ClueWeb12 documents in the top-5 ranges from 1 to 46 % (19 % the mean across all Open Web systems, median = 22 %) for CS 2014 systems. For CS 2013, it ranges from 1 to 51 % (22 % the mean across all Open Web systems, median = 25 %).

Table 3. Performance of Open Web systems on Open Web data vs. their performance on ClueWeb12 data

	P@5			% ClueWeb12	MRR			TBG		
	Original	Replaced	%	In top-5	Original	Replaced	%	Original	Replaced	%
UDInfoCS1	0.5094	0.1444	−71.7	3.6	0.6320	0.2375	−62.4	2.4474	0.2273	−90.7
UDInfoCS2	0.4969	0.1379	−72.2	6.6	0.6300	0.2448	−61.1	2.4310	0.2993	−87.7
SimpleScore	0.4332	0.1063	−75.5	3.1	0.5871	0.1974	−66.4	1.8374	0.1970	−89.3
ComplexScore	0.4152	0.1000	−75.9	3.5	0.5777	0.1500	−74.0	1.8226	0.1900	−89.6
DuTH_B	0.4090	0.1509	−63.1	24.9	0.5955	0.2999	−49.6	1.8508	0.4280	−76.9
1	0.3857	0.1688	−56.2	35.2	0.5588	0.3371	−39.7	1.5329	0.5450	−64.4
2	0.3731	0.1696	−54.5	32.6	0.5785	0.3144	−45.7	1.5843	0.5290	−66.6
udel_run_D	0.3659	0.1898	−48.1	39.8	0.5544	0.4182	−24.6	1.5243	0.7448	−51.1
isirun	0.3650	0.1568	−57.0	38.0	0.5165	0.2862	−44.6	1.6278	0.4265	−73.8
udel_run_SD	0.3354	0.1238	−63.1	25.4	0.5061	0.3131	−38.1	1.2882	0.4463	−65.4
york13cr2	0.3309	0.1198	−63.8	36.9	0.4637	0.2633	−43.2	1.3483	0.3762	−72.1
DuTH_A	0.3283	0.0991	−69.8	15.2	0.4836	0.2009	−58.5	1.3109	0.2287	−82.6
york13cr1	0.3274	0.1159	−64.6	36.9	0.4743	0.2667	−43.8	1.2970	0.3943	−69.6
UAmsTF30WU	0.3121	0.1182	−62.1	22.0	0.4803	0.2459	−48.8	1.1905	0.3626	−69.5
IRIT.OpenWeb	0.3112	0.1149	−63.1	25.0	0.4915	0.2492	−49.3	1.4638	0.4248	−71.0
CIRG_IRDISCOA	0.3013	0.1006	−66.6	23.0	0.4567	0.2010	−56.0	1.1681	0.2303	−80.3
CIRG_IRDISCOB	0.2906	0.1074	−63.0	24.3	0.4212	0.2042	−51.5	1.1183	0.2550	−77.2
uncsils_param	0.2780	No match	NaN	No match	0.4271	No match	NaN	1.3115	No match	NaN
uogTrCFP	0.2753	0.1000	−63.7	1.0	0.4327	0.3700	−14.5	1.3568	0.3784	−72.1
ming_1	0.2601	No match	NaN	No match	0.3816	No match	NaN	1.0495	No match	NaN
uncsils_base	0.2565	No match	NaN	No match	0.4136	No match	NaN	1.1374	No match	NaN
ming_2	0.2493	No match	NaN	No match	0.3473	No match	NaN	0.9673	No match	NaN
uogTrCFX	0.2332	0.0500	−78.6	0.8	0.4022	0.1562	−61.2	1.0894	0.1542	−85.8
run01	0.1650	0.1722	4.4	100.0	0.2994	0.3194	6.7	0.7359	0.7735	5.1
BaselineB	0.1417	n/a	n/a	100.0	0.2452	n/a	n/a	0.4797	n/a	n/a
BaselineA	0.1372	0.0841	−38.7	50.7	0.2316	0.1450	−37.4	0.5234	0.3001	−42.7
BOW_V17	0.1022	n/a	n/a	100.0	0.1877	n/a	n/a	0.3389	n/a	n/a
BOW_V18	0.1004	n/a	n/a	100.0	0.1971	n/a	n/a	0.3514	n/a	n/a
IRIT.ClueWeb	0.0798	n/a	n/a	100.0	0.1346	n/a	n/a	0.3279	n/a	n/a
RUN1	0.0628	n/a	n/a	100.0	0.1265	n/a	n/a	0.2069	n/a	n/a
csui02	0.0565	No match	NaN	No match	0.1200	No match	NaN	0.1785	No match	NaN
csui01	0.0565	No match	NaN	No match	0.1016	No match	NaN	0.1765	No match	NaN
RUN2	0.0565	n/a	n/a	100.0	0.1223	n/a	n/a	0.2020	n/a	n/a
IBCosTop1	0.0448	n/a	n/a	100.0	0.0569	n/a	n/a	0.1029	n/a	n/a

Under each metric we present three values: original, replaced, and the relative improvement in effectiveness. The column named `original` presents the performance of submitted runs using the original qrels as provided by the organizers, whereas the column `replaced` shows the performance of modified runs (replacing URLs with their match ClueWeb12 id and removing URLs with no match) using the expanded qrels. The % of ClueWeb12 documents in top-5 column presents the percentage of ClueWeb12 documents in the top-5 after replacing the URLs with their match ClueWeb12 ids while preserving the ranks. The ClueWeb12 systems (underlined) are included to show how they perform in comparison with Open Web systems evaluated on ClueWeb12 data. For ClueWeb12 systems no replacement has been applied, denoted by *n/a* under `replaced` and % of improvement **CS 2013 systems**

Table 4. Performance of Open Web systems on Open Web data versus their performance on ClueWeb12 data

	P@5			% ClueWeb12	MRR			TBG		
	Original	Replaced	%	In top-5	Original	Replaced	%	Original	Replaced	%
UDInfoCS2014_2	0.5585	0.2275	−59.3	22.0	0.7482	0.5506	−26.4	2.7021	0.8604	−68.2
RAMARUN2	0.5017	no match	NaN	no match	0.6846	no match	NaN	2.3718	no match	NaN
BJUTa	0.5010	0.1781	−64.5	28.3	0.6677	0.3290	−50.7	2.2209	0.4752	−78.6
BJUTb	0.4983	0.1805	−63.8	29.5	0.6626	0.3319	−49.9	2.1949	0.4955	−77.4
uogTrBunSumF	0.4943	0.0769	−84.4	0.9	0.6704	0.1628	−75.7	2.1526	0.1690	−92.1
RUN1	0.4930	no match	NaN	no match	0.6646	no match	NaN	2.2866	no match	NaN
webis_1	0.4823	0.1768	−63.3	25.8	0.6479	0.3600	−44.4	2.1700	0.6195	−71.5
simpleScoreImp	0.4602	0.1283	−72.1	4.2	0.6408	0.2632	−58.9	1.9795	0.2595	−86.9
webis_2	0.4569	0.1768	−61.3	25.8	0.5980	0.3600	−39.8	2.1008	0.6195	−70.5
simpleScore	0.4538	0.1147	−74.7	5.4	0.6394	0.2368	−63.0	1.9804	0.2477	−87.5
run_FDwD	0.4348	0.1581	−63.6	30.6	0.5916	0.3390	−42.7	1.7684	0.5429	−69.3
waterlooB	0.4308	0.0932	−78.4	11.0	0.6244	0.2263	−63.8	1.8379	0.2686	−85.4
waterlooA	0.4167	0.0951	−77.2	12.0	0.6021	0.2280	−62.1	1.7364	0.2587	−85.1
UDInfoCS2014_1	0.4080	0.1278	−68.7	17.7	0.5559	0.2629	−52.7	1.6435	0.3185	−80.6
dixltiemu	0.3980	0.1735	−56.4	29.0	0.5366	0.3210	−40.2	1.5110	0.5240	−65.3
uogTrCsLtrF	0.3906	0.0667	−82.9	0.9	0.5185	0.0903	−82.6	1.9164	0.1285	−93.3
run_DwD	0.3177	0.1177	−63.0	25.8	0.3766	0.1718	−54.4	0.9684	0.1721	−82.2
tueNet	0.2261	0.0258	−88.6	2.6	0.3820	0.0452	−88.2	0.9224	0.0825	−91.1
choqrun	0.2254	0.1145	−49.2	33.2	0.3412	0.2223	−34.8	0.7372	0.3314	−55.0
tueRforest	0.2227	0.0258	−88.4	2.6	0.3604	0.0452	−87.5	0.9293	0.0825	−91.1
cat	0.2087	0.0954	−54.3	46.4	0.3496	0.1807	−48.3	0.6120	0.2544	−58.4
BUPT_PRIS_01	0.1452	0.1000	−31.1	16.2	0.4475	0.2982	−33.4	0.7453	0.3564	−52.2
CWI_CW12.MapWeb	0.1445	n/a	n/a	100.0	0.2307	n/a	n/a	0.6078	n/a	n/a
BUPT_PRIS_02	0.1425	0.0966	−32.2	17.4	0.3467	0.2080	−40.0	0.6601	0.2479	−62.4
gw1	0.1024	0.0386	−62.3	24.4	0.1694	0.0800	−52.8	0.3646	0.1150	−68.5
Model1	0.0903	n/a	n/a	100.0	0.1979	n/a	n/a	0.3411	n/a	n/a
lda	0.0843	0.0457	−45.8	30.4	0.1564	0.0928	−40.7	0.2461	0.1159	−52.9
Model0	0.0582	n/a	n/a	100.0	0.1023	n/a	n/a	0.1994	n/a	n/a
runA	0.0482	n/a	n/a	100.0	0.0856	n/a	n/a	0.1647	n/a	n/a
CWI_CW12_Full	0.0468	n/a	n/a	100.0	0.0767	n/a	n/a	0.1256	n/a	n/a
runB	0.0254	n/a	n/a	100.0	0.0552	n/a	n/a	0.0614	n/a	n/a

Notation as in Table 3 CS 2014 systems

6 SELECTION METHOD FOR IDENTIFYING A REPRESENTATIVE SAMPLE OF THE OPEN WEB FROM CLUEWEB12

In this section we study RQ4: Can we identify a representative sample from the ClueWeb12 collection for the CS track by applying the tourist domain knowledge obtained from the Open Web? We use the tourist domain knowledge available on the Open Web to annotate documents in ClueWeb12 collection. The aim is not only to obtain reproducible results based on ClueWeb12 collection, but also to obtain a representative sample of the Open Web.

6.1 Selection methods of candidate documents from ClueWeb12

We formulate the problem of candidate selection from ClueWeb12 as follows. We have a set of contexts (locations) C—which correspond to US cities—provided by the organizers of the CS track. For each context c∈Cc∈C, we generate a set of suggestions ScSc from the ClueWeb12 collection, which are expected to be located in that context.

We define four filters for selecting documents from ClueWeb12 collection, each of them will generate a sub-collection. The first filter is a straightforward filter based on the content of the document. The remaining three filters use knowledge derived from the Open Web about sites existing in ClueWeb12 that provide touristic information. We will show empirically that the additional information acquired from tourist APIs provides the evidence needed to generate high quality contextual suggestions. While our results still depend upon information that is external to the collection, we only need to annotate ClueWeb12 with the tourist domain knowledge identified to achieve reproducible research results. We describe the filters in more detail in the following sections.

6.1.1 Geographically filtered sub-collection

Our main hypothesis in this approach is that a good suggestion (a venue) will contain its location correctly mentioned in its textual content. Therefore, we implemented a content-based geographical filter geo_filter that selects documents mentioning a specific context with the format (City, ST), ignoring those mentioning the city with different states or those matching multiple contexts. With this selection method we aim to ensure that the specific target context is mentioned in the filtered documents (hence, being geographically relevant documents). We will still miss relevant documents, for example due to misspellings or because they mention more than one city at the same web page.

In the simplest instantiation of our model, the probability of any document in ClueWeb12 to be included in the **Geographic Filtered** sub-collection is assigned to 0 or 1 depending on whether it passes the geo_filter:

$$P(s) = \begin{cases} 1, & \text{if(s) passesgeo\_filter} \\ 0, & \text{otherwise} \end{cases} \quad (1)$$

Approximately 9 million documents (8,883,068) from the ClueWeb12 collection pass the geo_filter. The resulting set of candidates forms the first sub-collection, referred to as **GeographicFiltered**.

6.1.2 Domain-oriented filter

The first type of domain knowledge depends on a list of hosts that are well-known to provide tourist information, and are publicly available (and have been crawled during the construction of ClueWeb12). We manually selected the set of hosts H:= {yelp, xpedia, tripadvisor, wikitravel, zagat, orbitz, and travel.yahoo}, some of these host APIs were used by the Open Web systems. We consider these hosts as a domain filter to select suggestions from ClueWeb12 collection. Again, the probability of a document in ClueWeb12 to be a candidate suggestion is either 0 or 1 depending only on its host. We define the probability *P*(*s*) as:

$$P(s) = \begin{cases} 1, & \text{if host(s)} \in \mathcal{H} \\ 0, & \text{otherwise} \end{cases} \quad (2)$$

We refer to the set of documents that pass the domain filter defined in Eq. (2) as TouristSites.

We assume pages about tourist information also have links to other interesting related pages, acknowledging the fact that pages on the same topic are connected to each other (Davison 2000). In order to maximize the extracted number of documents from the tourist domain we also consider the outlinks of documents from touristic sites. For each suggestion s∈s∈ TouristSites, we extract its outlinks outlinks(s) and combine all of them together in a set OO; including links between documents from two different hosts (external links) as well as links between pages from the same host (internal links). Notice that some of the outlinks may also be part of the TouristSites set, in particular whenever they satisfy Eq. (2). Next, we extract any document from ClueWeb12 whose normalized URL matches one of the outlinks in OO. The probability of document *s*to be selected in this case is defined as:

$$P(s) = \begin{cases} 1, & \text{if URL}(s) \in \mathcal{O} \\ 0, & \text{otherwise} \end{cases} \tag{3}$$

The set of candidate suggestions that pass this filter is called Tourist Sites Outlinks.

6.1.3 Attraction-oriented filter

The previously described selection method relies on a manually selected list of sites to generate the set of candidate suggestions. We will now consider a different type of domain knowledge, by leveraging the information available on the Foursquare API.4 For each context *c*, we obtain a set of URLs by querying Foursquare API. If the document's URL is not returned by Foursquare (we are not interested in the page describing that venue inside Foursquare, but its corresponding webpage), we use the combination of document name and context to issue a query to the Google search API e.g., "Gannon University Erie, PA" for name Gannon University and context Erie, PA. Extracting the hosts of the URLs obtained results in a set of 1, 454 unique hosts. We then select all web pages in ClueWeb12 from these hosts as the candidate suggestions, with its probability defined in the same way as in Eq. 2.

The set of documents that pass the host filter is referred to by Attractions.

Together, the three subsets of candidate suggestions TouristSites, TouristSites Outlinks and Attractions form our second ClueWeb12 sub-collection that we refer to as **Tourist Filtered**.

$$\textbf{TouristFiltered} := \texttt{TouristSites} \cup \texttt{TouristSitesOutlinks} \cup \texttt{Attractions}$$

Table 5 shows the number of documents found by each filter.

Table 5. Number of documents passing each filter. Documents that pass the first three filters represent the**Tourist Filtered** sub-collection, whereas the **Geographic Filtered** sub-collection is composed by those documents passing the geo_filter

Part	Number of documents
`TouristSites`	175,260
`TouristSitesOutlinks`	46,801
`Attractions`	102,313
TouristFiltered sub-collection	324,374
GeographicFiltered	8,775,711

6.2 Impact of domain knowledge filters

Our contribution to the CS track included the following two runs: a first one based on the **Geographic Filtered** sub-collection, and a second one based on the **Tourist Filtered** sub-collection. We have found that the run based on**Tourist Filtered** sub-collection is significantly better than the one based on **Geographic Filtered** sub-collection in every evaluation metric (see Table 6). However, a more discriminative analysis should be done to properly estimate the impact of the tourist domain knowledge filters used to generate the **Tourist Filtered** sub-collection, for this, we shall evaluate the performance of the different sub-collections generated by each of the domain knowledge filters.

Recall that assessments are made considering geographical and profile relevance independently from each other. The latter one is further assessed as relevant based on the document or on the description provided by the method. Considering this information, we recomputed the evaluation metrics for each topic while taking into account the geographical relevance provided by the assessors, as well as the description and document judgments, both separately and combined (that is, a document that is relevant both based on the description and when the assessor visited its URL). We present in Table 7 the contribution to the relevance dimensions of each of the **Tourist Filtered** sub-collection subsets, where each subset was selected based on different domain knowledge filter. The run based on **Tourist Filtered** sub-collection contains documents from the three subsets. We modified the run based on **Tourist Filtered** sub-collection by start computing effectiveness based only on suggestions from TouristSites subset (second column), then we add to them suggestions from TouristSitesOutlinks, and finally suggestions from Attractions. The main conclusion from this table is that the larger improvement in performance happens after adding the candidates from Attractions subset. It is interesting to note that the performance of this part alone (last column) is comparable to that of the whole sub-collection.

Table 6. Performance of the run based on **GeographicFiltered** sub-collection and the run based on**TouristFiltered** sub-collection

Metric	GeographicFiltered	TouristFiltered
P@5	0.0431	0.1374
MRR	0.0763	0.2305
TBG	0.1234	0.5953

Table 7. Effect of each part of the **Tourist Filtered** sub-collection on performance

P@5_all	0.0392	0.0518	32.1 %	0.1374	165.3 %	0.1057
P@5_desc-doc	0.0758	0.1004	32.5 %	0.2222	121.3 %	0.1562
P@5_desc	0.0917	0.1200	30.9 %	0.2788	132.3 %	0.1973
P@5_doc	0.1008	0.1310	30.0 %	0.2949	125.1 %	0.2101
P@5_geo	0.2067	0.2659	28.6 %	0.4808	80.8 %	0.4667
MRR_all	0.1378	0.1715	24.5 %	0.2305	34.4 %	0.1834
MRR_desc-doc	0.2213	0.2738	23.7 %	0.3630	32.6 %	0.2860
MRR_desc	0.2616	0.3133	19.8 %	0.4395	40.3 %	0.3674
MRR_doc	0.2817	0.3463	22.9 %	0.4718	36.2 %	0.3776
MRR_geo	0.5342	0.5865	9.8 %	0.6627	13.0 %	0.6132
TBG	0.2180	0.2705	24.1 %	0.5953	120.1 %	0.5138
TBG_doc	0.2305	0.2860	24.1 %	0.6379	123.0 %	0.5503

Union symbol (UU) represents adding suggestions from the sub-collection or filter presented in the previous column. The percentage shows the relative improvement in effectiveness due to filter

6.3 Discussion

Because systems based on Open Web can still be competitive when the candidate documents are constrained to the ClueWeb12 collection, we have shown that there exist documents in ClueWeb12 that are relevant for the Contextual Suggestion task we address in this paper. However, the candidate selection process is challenging, and the use of external, manually curated tourist services make this task easier, by promoting those relevant documents at the cost of reducing the reproducibility of the whole process.

In this section we aim to understand the candidate selection process and to provide recommendations in order to improve it. With this goal in mind, we study the **Geographic Filtered** and Attractions sub-collections by comparing the actual documents that pass the corresponding filters, so that we can analyze these sub-collections from the user perspective (what will the user receive?) instead of from the system perspective (what is the performance of the system?), as we have presented previously in the paper.

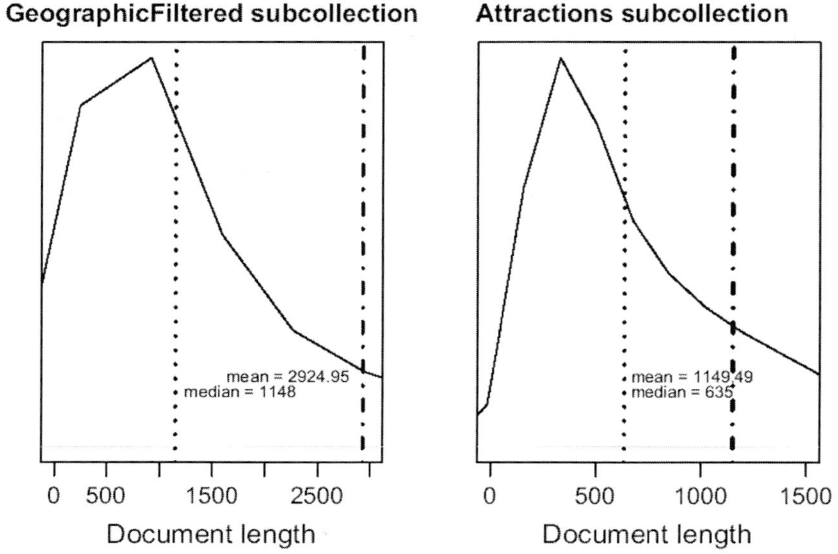

Figure 7. Distribution of the document length in words for the **GeographicFiltered** (*left*) and Attractions (*right*) sub-collections. Note the different range in the X axis

A first aspect we consider is the document length (in terms of words included in the processed HTML code), which gives an insight about how much information is contained (and shown to the user) in each sub-collection. We observe from Figure 7that documents from the **Geographic Filtered** sub-collection are much larger than those from Attractions: their average length is twice as large as those from the other filter. This may suggest that relevant documents in the tourist domain should be short or, at least, they should not present too much information to the user. If this was true, it would be more interesting to retrieve—in the contextual suggestion scenario—home pages such as the main page of a museum or a restaurant, instead of their corresponding Contact or How to access sub-pages. Because of this, in the future we aim to take information about the URL depth into account when selecting the candidates, since it has been observed in (Kraaij et al. 2002) that the probability of being a home page is inversely related to its URL depth.

Figure 8. Screenshots of a document retrieved by the **GeographicFiltered** sub-collection (*left*) and by theAttractions sub-collection (*right*). The document in the left (clueweb12-0202wb-00-19744) was rated in average with a value of 1.9, whereas the one in the right (clueweb12-0200tw-67-19011) with a 3

Related to the aforementioned aspect, we now want to check manually the content of some pages from each sub-collection. For this analysis we aggregate the judgments received to the documents submitted in each sub-collection, and then focus on documents with very bad or very good ratings in any of them. Specifically, we have found two candidate documents (presented in Figure 8) that clearly illustrate the main difference between these two sub-collections, and further corroborates the previous assumption: the **Geographic Filtered** subcollection requires pages where the target city and state are present, which in turn favors pages containing listings of places located in that city, resulting in documents not very informative for an average tourist. On the other hand, the Attractions sub-collection tend to retrieve the home page of significant tourist places.

Finally, we have run an automatic classifier on the documents of each sub-collection to gain some insights about whether the content of the pages are actually different. We have used decision trees J48 (Quinlan 1993) as implemented in the Weka library5) and tried with different combinations of parameters (stemming, stopwords, confidence value for pruning, number of words to consider, etc.). For the sake of presentation, we have used a very restrictive setting, so that a limited number of leafs are generated. In Figure 9 we show the branch of the decision tree where *states* appears at least once in the documents; hence, we find that states is the most discriminative term in this situation, and in decreasing order the terms: *internist* and *america*. The classifier represented in this way was trained using a vector representation using the TF-IDF values of the terms in each document, considering only top-20 words with the highest frequency and discarding stopwords and numbers. Additionally, the classifier was parameterized with a confidence threshold of 0.5 and a minimum number of instances per leaf of 500. We conclude from the figure that the Attractions sub-collection uses a different vocabulary than the **Geographic Filtered** sub-collection, where terms such as *md*, *st*, or *america* tend to appear with much less frequency. In the future we want to exploit this information to improve the candidate selection process and the corresponding filters.

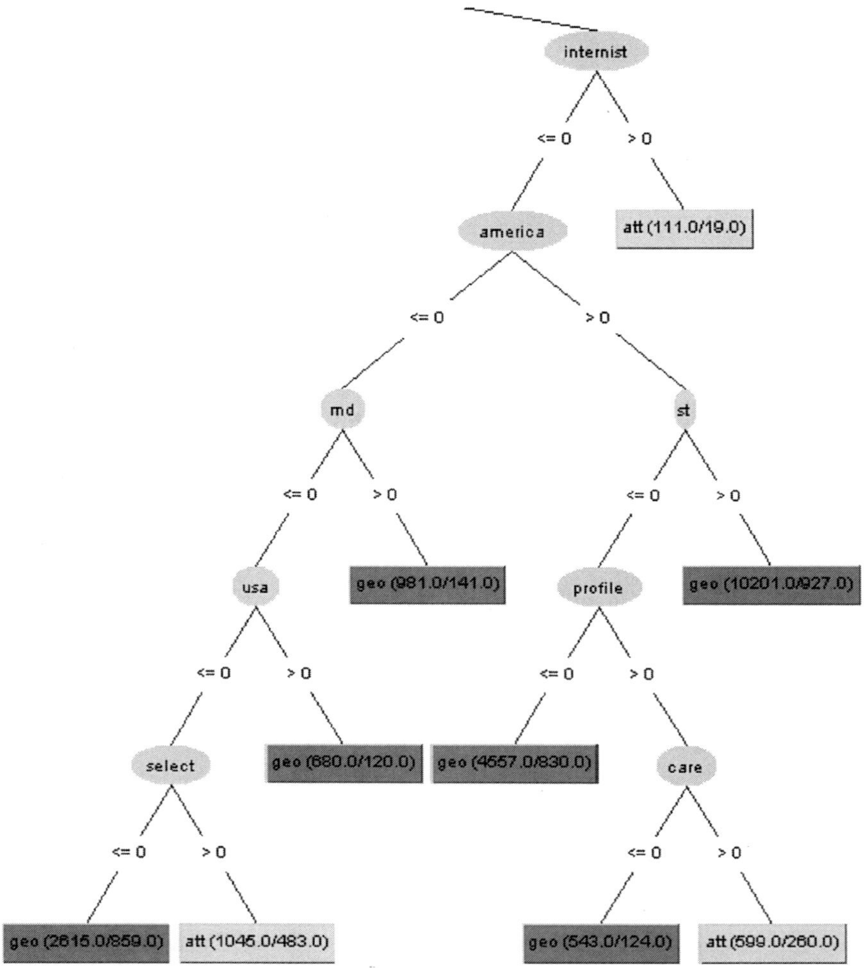

Figure 9. Visualization of a branch of the J48 decision tree trained using documents from the Attractions (att) and **GeographicFiltered** (geo) sub-collections. This branch corresponds to the case where the term *states* appears at least once. In every leaf, the label of the classified instances appears together with the total number of instances reaching that leaf (*first number*) and the number of missclassified instances (hence, the lower this number the better)

7 CONCLUSIONS

In this paper we have analyzed and discussed the balance between reproducibility and representativeness when building test collections. We have focused our analysis on the Contextual Suggestion TREC track, where in 2013 and 2014 it was possible to submit runs based on Open Web or based on ClueWeb12, a static version of the web. In both editions of the track, there were more runs based on Open Web compared to those based on ClueWeb12 collection, which seems to go against any reproducibility criteria we may expect from such a competition. The main reason, as we have shown in this paper, for that behavior is that systems based on Open Web perform better than systems based on ClueWeb12 collection in terms of returning more relevant documents.

We have studied such difference in effectiveness from various perspectives. First, the analysis of relevance assessments of 2 years of the Contextual Suggestion track shows that documents returned by Open Web systems receive better ratings than documents returned by ClueWeb12 systems. More specifically, we have found differences in judgment when looking at identical documents that were returned by both Open Web and ClueWeb12 systems. Second, based on an expanded version of the relevance assessments—considering documents in the overlap of Open Web and ClueWeb12 systems—and on generating ClueWeb12-based runs from Open Web runs, we have investigated the representativeness of ClueWeb12 collection. Although the performance of Open Web systems decreases, we find a representative sample of ClueWeb12 collection in Open Web runs. Third, we proposed an approach for selecting candidate documents from ClueWeb12 collection using the information available on the Open Web. Our results are promising, and evidence that there is still room for improvement by using different and more information available on the Open Web.

For future work, we plan to collect candidate documents from different crawls of the web besides ClueWeb12 collection, such as the Common Crawl. 6 Both crawls will complement each other and help to find more representative samples of the web; in this way we could evaluate them by participating in future editions of the Contextual Suggestion track. Another aspect we would like to explore in the future is that of improving the candidate selection filters. We have learnt some features that seem to be frequent in the sub-collection generated from the Open Web. We would like to incorporate that information into our geographical filters, so that better candidate documents are found, and—in principle—lead to better contextual recommendations.

FOOTNOTES

[1]https://sites.google.com/site/treccontext/trec-2014/open-web-to-clueweb12-mapping.

[2]Confirmed via email with the organisers for 2013 dataset.

[3]See http://yelp.com/robots.txt.

[4]https://developer.foursquare.com/docs/venues/search.

[5] http://www.cs.waikato.ac.nz/ml/weka/.

[6]https://commoncrawl.org/.

ACKNOWLEDGMENTS

This research was supported by the Netherlands Organization for Scientific Research (WebART Project, NWO CATCH #640.005.001). Part of this work was supported by the Spanish Ministry of Science and Innovation (TIN2013-47090-C3-2). This work was carried out on the Dutch national e-infrastructure with the support of SURF Foundation.

REFERENCES

1. Adomavicius, G., & Tuzhilin, A. (2011). Context-aware recommender systems. In F. Ricci, L. Rokach, B. Shapira, F. Ricci, L. Rokach, B. Shapira, P. B. Kantor, & P. B. Kantor (Eds.), *Recommender systems handbook* (pp. 217–253). Boston, MA: Springer.

2. Allan, J., Croft, W. B., Moffat, A., & Sanderson, M. (2012). Frontiers, challenges, and opportunities for information retrieval: Report from SWIRL 2012 the second strategic workshop on information retrieval in lorne. *SIGIR Forum*,*46*(1), 2–32.

3. Bellogín, A., Samar, T., de Vries, A. P., & Said, A. (2014). Challenges on combining open web and dataset evaluation results: The case of the contextual suggestion track. In M. de Rijke, T. Kenter, A. P. de Vries, C. Zhai, F. de Jong, K. Radinsky, & K. Hofmann (Eds.), *Advances in information retrieval-36th European conference on IR research, proceedings, Springer, Lecture Notes in Computer Science* (Vol. 8416, pp. 430–436). Amsterdam, The Netherlands: ECIR 2014.

4. Davison, B. D. (2000). Topical locality in the web. In *Proceedings of the 23rd annual international conference on research and development in information retrieval (SIGIR 2000)* (pp. 272–279). ACM Press.

5. Dean-Hall, A., & Clarke, C. L. A. (2015). The power of contextual suggestion. In A. Hanbury, G. Kazai, A. Rauber, N. Fuhr (Eds.), *Advances in information retrieval-37th European conference on IR research, ECIR 2015, proceedings, Lecture Notes in Computer Science* (Vol. 9022, pp. 352–357), Vienna, Austria, March 29–April 2, 2015.

6. Dean-Hall, A., Clarke, C. L. A., Kamps, J., Thomas, P., & Voorhees, E. M. (2012). Overview of the TREC 2012 contextual suggestion track. In E. M. Voorhees, L. P. Buckland (Eds.), *Proceedings of the twenty-first text retrieval conference, TREC 2012*, National Institute of Standards and Technology (NIST), Vol Special Publication 500-298, Gaithersburg, Maryland, USA, November 6–9, 2012. http://trec.nist.gov/pubs/trec21/papers/CONTEXTUAL12.overview.pdf.

7. Dean-Hall, A., Clarke, C. L. A., Kamps, J., & Thomas, P. (2013). Evaluating contextual suggestion. In*Proceedings of the fifth international workshop on evaluating information access (EVIA 2013)*.

8. Dean-Hall, A., Clarke, C. L. A., Simone, N., Kamps, J., Thomas, P., & Voorhees, E. M. (2013). Overview of the TREC 2013 contextual suggestion track. In E. M. Voorhees (Ed.), *Proceedings of the twenty-second text retrieval conference, TREC 2013*, National Institute of Standards and Technology (NIST), Vol Special Publication 500-302, Gaithersburg, Maryland, USA, November 19–22, 2013. http://trec.nist.gov/pubs/trec22/papers/CONTEXT.OVERVIEW.pdf.

9. Dean-Hall, A., Clarke, C. L. A., Kamps, J., Thomas, P., Voorhees, E. M. (2014). Overview of the TREC 2014 contextual suggestion track. In E. M. Voorhees, A. Ellis, (Eds.), *Proceedings of the twenty-third text retrieval conference, TREC 2014*, National Institute of Standards and Technology (NIST), vol Special Publication 500-308, Gaithersburg, Maryland, USA, November 19–21, 2014. http://trec.nist.gov/pubs/trec23/papers/overview-context.pdf

10. Deveaud, R., Albakour, M. D., Macdonald, C., & Ounis, I. (2014). On the importance of venue-dependent features for learning to rank contextual suggestions. In *Proceedings of the 23rd ACM international conference on conference on information and knowledge management, CIKM '14* (pp. 1827–1830). New York, NY, USA: ACM.

11. Hawking, D., Craswell, N., Thistlewaite, P. B., & Harman, D. (1999). Results and challenges in web search evaluation. *Computer Networks, 31*(11–16), 1321–1330.

12. Hawking, D., Craswell, N., Bailey, P., & Griffiths, K. (2001). Measuring search engine quality. *Information Retrieval, 4*(1), 33–59.

13. Hubert, G., Cabanac, G., Pinel-Sauvagnat, K., Palacio, D., & Sallaberry, C. (2013). IRIT, GeoComp, and LIUPPA at the TREC 2013 contextual suggestion track. In *Proceedings of TREC.*

14. Kelly, D. (2009). Methods for evaluating interactive information retrieval systems with users. *Foundations and Trends in Information Retrieval, 3*(1–2), 1–224.

15. Kraaij, W., Westerveld, T., & Hiemstra, D. (2002). The importance of prior probabilities for entry page search. In*SIGIR 2002: Proceedings of the 25th annual international ACM SIGIR conference on research and development in information retrieval* (pp. 27–34). Tampere, Finland: ACM, August 11–15, 2002.

16. Lops, P., de Gemmis, M., & Semeraro, G. (2011). Content-based recommender systems: State of the art and trends. In F. Ricci, L. Rokach, B. Shapira, F. Ricci, L. Rokach, B. Shapira, P. B. Kantor, & P. B. Kantor (Eds.),*Recommender systems handbook* (pp. 73–105). Boston, MA: Springer.

17. Melucci, M. (2012). Contextual search: A computational framework. *Foundations and Trends in Information Retrieval, 6*(4–5), 257–405.

18. Quinlan, R. (1993). *C4.5: Programs for machine learning*. San Mateo, CA: Morgan Kaufmann Publishers.

19. Resnick, P., Iacovou, N., Suchak, M., Bergstrom, P., Riedl, J. (1994). Grouplens: An open architecture for collaborative filtering of netnews. In *CSCW* (pp. 175–186).

20. Sanderson, M., Turpin, A., Zhang, Y., & Scholer, F. (2012). Differences in effectiveness across sub-collections. In: X. Chen, G. Lebanon, H. Wang, & M. J. Zaki (Eds.), *21st ACM international conference on information and knowledge management, CIKM'12* (pp. 1965–1969) Maui, HI, USA: ACM, October 29–November 02, 2012.

21. Santos, R. L. T., Macdonald, C., & Ounis, I. (2011). Effectiveness beyond the first crawl tier. In C. Macdonald, I. Ounis I. Ruthven (Eds.), *Proceedings of the 20th ACM conference on information and knowledge management, CIKM 2011* (pp. 1937–1940). Glasgow, United Kingdom: ACM, October 24–28, 2011.

22. Sappelli, M., Verberne, S., & Kraaij, W. (2013). Recommending personalized touristic sights using google places. In: *Proceedings of the 36th international ACM SIGIR conference on research and development in information retrieval, SIGIR '13* (pp. 781–784). New York, NY, USA: ACM.

23. Scholer, F., Turpin, A., & Sanderson, M. (2011). Quantifying test collection quality based on the consistency of relevance judgements. In: W. Ma, J. Nie, R. A. Baeza-Yates, T. Chua, W. B. Croft (Eds.), *Proceeding of the 34th international ACM SIGIR conference on research and development in information retrieval, SIGIR 2011* (pp. 1063–1072) Beijing, China: ACM, July 25–29, 2011.

24. Voorhees, E. M., & Buckley, C. (2002). The effect of topic set size on retrieval experiment error. In *Proceedings of the 25th annual international ACM SIGIR conference on research and development in information retrieval, SIGIR '02* (pp. 316–323). New York, NY, USA: ACM.

25. Yang, P., & Fang, H. (2012). An Exploration of ranking-based strategy for contextual suggestions. In *Proceedings of TREC.*

26. Yang, P., & Fang, H. (2013). Opinion-based user profile modeling for contextual suggestions. In *Proceedings of the 2013 conference on the theory of information retrieval ICTIR '13* (pp. 18:80–18:83). New York, NY, USA: ACM.

Index